Blackthorn : Whitethorn

BLACKTHORN WHITETHORN
Ways of Witchery

By

Nigel G. Pearson

First printing in paperback
September 2023

ISBN 978-1-909602-61-8

Published by Troy Books
www.troybooks.co.uk

Troy Books Publishing
BM Box 8003
London WC1N 3XX

Cover art & design Nigel G. Pearson

Dedication.

For Anthony.
With Love. All Ways.

Acknowledgements.

I would first like to thank Jane Marriott who, all unknowingly, suggested the title for this book to me some 20-odd years ago. All else is my fault and nothing to do with her!

Big thanks must also go to Stuart Inman for writing the insightful and informative Preface to this book, his kind consideration of my work, his support and permission to quote from his unpublished manuscript in Chapter One. His help and advice over the years has been much appreciated and instrumental in my own understanding and learning of many associated concepts.

To Nigel Pennick, long-standing practitioner and scholar of the East Anglian Nameless Art and Cunning Crafts, I would like to express my gratitude. Not only for permission to quote from his work in this book, but for the immense amount of research and information he has made available through his own publications over the years.

My thanks also go to those unnamed Witches and Magical practitioners, both living and dead, who have taught, guided, inspired and informed me throughout my own years of learning.

And last, but by no means least, the Spirits and Powers who stood at my shoulder throughout and made this book possible by their constant support, input, encouragement and not a little nagging – it's not what I intended to write, but its what they wanted!

Contents

Photoplates
between pages 162 - 163

All photos by the author except photo no 1. (C) Ticky Wright)

PREFACE
A View From An Entangled Thicket

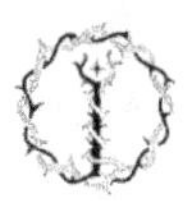

A while ago I received a message from Nigel Pearson, asking me what I understood by 'the entangled thicket'. Nigel and I have been in irregular, but reasonably frequent, correspondence for quite some years, although at the time of writing we have never met. This message was quite out of the blue, an apparently random question. But as I am the Magister of The Clan of the Entangled Thicket and it is this title and the name of my clan that led Nigel to pose his question you will see a context for his question. Our correspondence had begun some years earlier with my critical appreciation of Nigel's first book *Treading the Mill* which had recently been published by the sadly now defunct Capall Bann. I thought it a good introductory book on that curious entity 'traditional witchcraft' but not a perfect one and, when I gave my opinion, Nigel responded in very good humour. I don't think I was the only person to criticise the book, and Nigel's own attitude was sufficiently critical to revise it and the much improved second edition was published by Troy Books. His second book, *Walking the Tides*, could not elicit any such criticisms. I was an immediate admirer of this work, and although that too has now been revised, it was from the beginning an excellent and very original work. It looks at the seasons and the land as a focus for our spirituality and our magic. Although it does so from the viewpoint of the English landscape and climate, I think it provides a template for anybody to develop their own system of seasonal correspondences for wherever they may be. While, even in this age of climate change, Britain still has four, admittedly somewhat uneven seasons, somebody the other side of the world might have to think differently. I remember an American correspondent in Louisiana saying that they had two seasons, hot and dry and hot and wet. Inevitably this must lead to a different setup, and there would be different crops, different trees and plants and different animals, but the principles of *Walking the Tides* can be adapted by anybody willing to do the work. (Being willing can, of course, be the problem…) The essential point here is that he gives a set of principles and examples that can be interpreted quite fluidly rather than a rigid schema to be followed.

In the following years I was able to help Nigel with some information on the Toad Bone Rite for his book *The Devil's Plantation*, a fascinating book, full of lore and learning and two I must admit to not having read yet, *Wortcunning* and *A Ring Around the Moon.* I'll get there, but my 'books to be read' pile grows and grows and never seems to shrink, despite my best efforts. You should understand from the above that I regard a book by Nigel Pearson to be one worth reading, a source of learning as well as interest, and, sooner or later, I will read these books!

Returning to that message, it became apparent that Nigel was asking me about my understanding of the entangled thicket for more than mere curiosity. He had written a book that explored this theme. I explained briefly what I understood by this term and sent him the draft chapter of my, as yet still unfinished, book on the 1734 Tradition that dealt with such matters. (Inman, Stuart: *Hidden In Plain Sight: A Primer of 1734 Traditional Witchcraft.* (unpublished).

Nigel was subsequently good enough to send me the first chapter of his book and to include a long quotation from my text. I was sufficiently enthused to offer to write a preface for his book, not, I swear, because he had quoted me, and Nigel had the good grace to say that he'd planned to ask me if I'd do so, a happy tale that I hope has an equally happy ending, avoids back-slapping mutual admiration and achieves a sharper, clearer appreciation of each other's understanding.

That said, what is my understanding of the Entangled Thicket and why might this be of importance to the 'traditional witch'? It was, along with the concept of the Three Guardians, Lapwing, Dog and Roebuck, my way in to an understanding of what 1734 is. If you are unfamiliar with it, the very short version is that 1734 is a system of Craft devised by my teacher, Joe Wilson, an American pioneer of modern Craft, based on the teachings of his own first teacher, who he called 'Sean', the teachings of Ruth Wynn Owen, matriarch of Y Plant Bran, and, most famously, his correspondence with Roy Bowers, also known as Robert Cochrane. Bowers had used Robert Graves' The White Goddess as a way of teaching Joe, not so much specific lore (The White Goddess is notoriously unreliable in its scholarship) as a way of poetic thinking that can allow access to a very different vision of the world. For me, these beasts, emerging from Welsh Bardic legend, made a connection with something very culturally different, the animals representing the Three Poisons in Buddhism. Where in Buddhism the cockerel represents pride and desire, the snake hatred-aversion and the pig ignorance, I saw the Lapwing as desire-glamour, the Dog as fear and the Roebuck, hiding in the Entangled Thicket was a fundamental ignorance, "Not being able to see the wood for the trees". All of them in different ways therefore represented at this level, duality of vision. While chasing the lapwing we are consumed with the glamour of our quest, we might think we are being terribly spiritual, but it is a world of glitter wands and fantasy. When we see how shallow it is, we might be put off, subject to fear and disillusionment, the spiritual path is just a big scary black dog. If, by courage or cunning, we get past the Dog, we find the Entangled Thicket, but the Roebuck is hiding and all we see are endless tangled branches. By coming to terms with these dualisms and learning the lessons of the Guardians, from the Lapwing we learn the first lesson necessary for all esoteric work, discrimination, from the Dog we learn courage and from the Roebuck we learn true understanding .

The Roebuck is hidden for two linked reasons, both called 'duality'. The first one is the most obvious one of seeing things as intrinsically different, the other is a sort of blurring of our vision, so in short, we have to achieve non-duality in order to find the Roebuck. I think it is very important to understand that non-dual vision is something quite sharp and precise, not a cosy mush of "Oh, we are all the same thing really". Well, in one sense we are, but we have to understand the modalities of this a bit. Essentially, dualistic vision tends to see the world as comprised of things, non-duality as process and relationship. This not only applies the actual world around us (and of course ourselves) but to all things, including questions of good and evil. I would hope that you would not have espoused a too rigid system of morality and would rather consider a more fluid, but firmly principled ethics as your guide to behaviour. The idea that what seems fair might be foul and vice versa isn't some slogan allowing for bad behaviour, but the start of a questioning of all our values. If we don't see the values handed down to us as inadequate – at least until severely questioned – we have probably never thought much about life, or the world around us at all, and I'd suggest that, not only do we need to ask questions of those values, but never cease asking. It's easy to assume that atrocity emerges out of evil, but usually those who commit genocide, for instance, think they are doing the right thing, they believe they are good people. This, of course, is one of the greatest horrors that we have to deal with in this world, however grim straightforward evil may be, it is less than moral self-justification of atrocity.

Much of what we regard as moral or ethical doesn't present itself in black and white terms, but as endless shades of grey, and to reintroduce a key image, a confusing tangle, of right and wrong, each apparently growing from the other's roots. Much that is traditionally thought of as evil is nothing of the sort (most witches for instance) and much of magic occupies an ethical neutral ground that can be directed for good or ill. Clearly what is important is the nature of the witch, magician, sorcerer, the magic is like a knife that can be used to cut bread, a branch or a person equally.

Nigel's book addresses two questions, the first, implicitly, how to find this wonderful non-dual state, and the second, explicitly, how to navigate with increased awareness and knowledge, a world full of apparent dualisms. The "way of witchery" is a twisting path betwixt and between contradictions and oppositions, noting both extremes, but never assuming the sad, soggy proposition that 'the truth probably lies somewhere in the middle'. If, without going further into the matter here, we just say that the truth is exactly where the truth is, in any matter we examine, a way of witchery does not presuppose that we already know the truth any more than we'd assume that truth is unknowable, it may be difficult to discover and learn and we may be using the wrong tools to discover it, but that surely means we change tools, change direction and seek differently. If the strange, ambiguous entity we call witchcraft is indeed a system of wisdom, as some like to call it, a 'wise craft', truth must matter, however obscure it may seem, and our voyage must navigate without prejudice or ideological fixation through the fudged and dodgy areas of life.

The key images in this book, that give its title and theme are the blackthorn and the whitethorn. The names present a nice simple polar opposition, black and white. Blackthorn sometimes has a sinister reputation, blackthorn wands are used for blasting and ill-wishing, toads were traditionally impaled on their thorns as a gruesome preamble to the toad-bone rite, but as Nigel quickly shows, the Whitethorn has its own ambiguous lore, both are path-markers and gateways to the realm of Faerie. Both trees have fierce thorns and both produce more or less edible fruits, most people know sloe gin, many fewer know the delicious Basque liqueur Patxaran, a sloe-flavoured anise. The hawthorn's berries can be made into an intriguing jelly, good with cheese and meats. The key idea is, I think, ambiguity and that leads us to the other main themes of this book.

In his discussion of the whitethorn Nigel Pearson offers a method for introducing yourself to the Queen of Elphame. Later on, he picks up the theme again while discussing the ancestors. My teacher, Joe Wilson, spoke frequently of the importance of the ancestors in traditional modes of thinking. At the psychological level we all carry what we might call ancestral scars because, for instance, our grandparents may have been mistreated by our great grandparents and passed on something of that trauma to our parents and perhaps we also suffer and resent them for that. All the same, the majority of parents, however inadequately, wish the best for us and do what they believe to be the best. A connection to the ancestors is an essential aspect of most traditional cultures, but is something, not exactly lost, but shoved into the background and watered down in ours. So, a forging of new connections with our ancestral dead is an important task for traditional witches. Joe talked of there being three kinds of ancestors. The first are our literal, biological ancestors, our parents, grandparents and other relations who have died. The second are the ancestors of our spiritual lineage. If you belong to a long-established tradition, the founders and every generation that has passed on become our spiritual ancestors. In may traditions – for instance the Vajrayana Buddhist – there are elaborate lineage trees and a homage to those ancestors is an essential part of the practice. Finally, the cultural ancestors are those people we find perpetually inspiring, but to whom we have no connection through family or lineage. The most obvious example for the traditional witch might be Robert Cochrane. You can't claim lineage from Cochrane unless you are a member of the Clan of Tubal Cain, but many of us consider him with the greatest respect, so make of him a cultural ancestor in this way, which never claims too much, doesn't infringe upon the lineage of Tubal Cain but reflects our debt to that remarkable man.

We can consider another aspect of the ancestors that Nigel discusses, their connection or identity with the Good Folk, the Faerie. While conventional Christian belief consigns the dead to heaven or hell, older beliefs, still embedded in folk tradition see the afterlife rather differently and Elphame is the destination of at least the unshriven souls, and possibly a more fun destination too. It could be germane to mention that in our clan's compass winter's Dark Mound of the Dead sits opposite to summer's Green and Hollow Hills of the Fae and they should be understood as reflections of each other and, ultimately, one and the same.

If you didn't already know it, you learn that Lilith's Lantern is a name for the moon and obviously signifies an identity with Lilith, Adam's first wife, sometime daemoness, occasionally a goddess, and initiator of Cain, the First Horseman. Lilith usually gets a bad rap, but here, as we tease out these ambiguities, perhaps we can see something more akin to the fierce or wrathful dakinis of Tantra? Her apparent ferocity is a form of compassionate wisdom.

Similarly, I'd suggest we need to see the last figure in this book, the Devil, not as the traditional embodiment of evil, but as many things, a creature of quicksilver, initiator, assisting spirit, god, divine rebel, opposer, trickster. I remember a rather strange online discussion when the Devil was mentioned and a Wiccan lady of quite conventional views stated that, quite simply, the Devil did not exist. But he is an important figure in Traditional Craft – doesn't matter, he doesn't exist! I suggested that before we say a being doesn't exist we need to define what that being is – doesn't matter, he doesn't exist! Eventually I suggested that he might be understood in terms of the Jungian Shadow, and oddly enough, this was acceptable. Actually, it isn't a bad place to start, if the Devil is everything that is repressed in our culture, whether psychologically, because we were told "Thou shalt not..." or whatever is deemed unacceptable, not respectable or civilised, foreign and strange. At the time of writing the status of transgender people seems to be the obsession of many people I'd have thought too intelligent to go for a biological fundamentalism in terms of gender and it would seem to be the Devil's party here who has most sympathy for those whose gender or sexuality is ambiguous. I'm really glad that Nigel has dealt with this issue in a way that is sensible, sympathetic and open-minded.

The Devil can be a title for the great fallen angel Lucifer, whose name means Light-bringer (but you already knew this) it can also refer to the somewhat mischievious and tricksterish folk devils who, despite their cunning, can be outwitted by simple peasants. I remember a story about an old couple in Sussex who had grown too old to easily plough their field. The Devil appeared and offered to plough it for them, but if he could plough the whole field before cock-crow, their souls would be forfeit. They agreed, sure that he couldn't plough the field in such a short time, but the devil started ploughing with such speed they feared for their souls. They got hold of a sieve and a lamp and shone the lamp through the sieve, thus waking their rooster who, tricked into thinking it was sunrise, started to crow. The Devil was thus tricked out of his prize. The Crossroads contract with the Devil is well known, especially through the story of the great Blues singer and guitarist Robert Johnson, reputed to have sold his soul in order to learn guitar. There's a couple of problems with the story, the Johnson who really was supposed to have made this deal wasn't Robert and, according to Hoodoo lore, the spirit is not the Devil. He is rather a useful spirit whose help may be gained by a pact that requires rather less than one's soul as payment. (Although some souls may be so threadbare that they'd be refused in payment anyway.) I think we can ask when is the Devil not a devil, given that all spirits may be regarded by orthodoxy as devilish. Remember also that Robert Cochrane described himself as "the devil of a small clan" – the very human leader of his group, but as Magister the representative of the god, the devil and sacrificial roebuck.

A theme that is discussed at about midpoint in the book is 'Witchwalking', but I would say it is implicit throughout. What I mean here is that Nigel constantly suggests a way of moving, and being in the world, fearless but cautious, respectful of creatures and forces that one may encounter whether it be a fox or deer or fey or phantom. You will notice that along with suggested rituals, there's a number of guided meditation exercises, pathworkings, but while some of them could be performed from an armchair he's not advocating armchair magic, but actually getting outside and getting a bit of mud on your boots. Similarly, the rituals are designed for the outdoors rather than comfortable living room temples. From my own experience I have found that dealing with a world of real places and objects can help make the imagined landscapes more real and concrete. The two are woven together to make the Mythic Landscape. This is not a term used here by Nigel Pearson, nor one that I invented, I think I first saw it used by Griffin ap Ked of House Ked, but in some form or other it runs through many strains of traditional craft. It is, if you like, the way in which the imaginal realm becomes embodied in the physical. When I first started to develop an area for working in many years back, it wasn't just the actual compass area, but various points throughout the woods we were using, a bridge, a crossroad, this or that tree, one especially that had been partly hollowed out, creating a natural offerings table. Beyond this, we also had spots further away, an Iron age hillfort and an abandoned chapel for instance, that we'd do meditations and workings at. The point here is that they were not just random places, but loci within our mythic landscape that we could visit both physically and mentally, that meshed together internally as one greater landscape one could visit at will. Each point had a resonance with the clan mythos and physical and mental aspects reinforced each other, made both more real, more magical.

As Nigel says "liminality is the name of the game here". As we weave between the mundane and magical, sacred and profane, all becomes illuminated by its apparent opposite and the sense of being separate becomes slowly undone. Everything relates to everything else, the mundane can be magical, the profane far more closely related to the sacred than we ever imagined, and we step through the gaps and thresholds between realms and kingdoms. We can develop a new relationship with this bigger world with its seeming contradictions and its complexities that goes beyond the kitsch and shallow idea of simply being a bit witchy and instead becoming one who truly crosses from world to world, moving from light to shadow and back to light, accepting both as the interplay of forces that make our world.

Weaving and walking a liminal path between opposites requires a map of the territory that you'll be exploring. In the end, the map will be one drawn from your own experience, but it is also compiled from other sources, previous explorers' maps and this book is, among other things, a suggestive map, of use to beginner and seasoned explorer alike, from which you can draw as needed. Assured, but modest in its claims, Nigel Pearson's book is a fine exploration of the liminal realms and the entangled thicket. I hope that in reading it, the thicket will seem less impenetrable, that you'll come to see that not only are you already in it, but are your own Roebuck hidden at its centre.

Stuart Inman
Wiltshire, 12th Night 2023

Introduction

When I was a child, my parents bought a caravan on the Suffolk coast, on a holiday site next to an old manor house, which we enjoyed for many years. The grounds of this manor house were very overgrown and neglected, left to run wild, much like us children at that time. In part of the grounds was an area that we called The Forest of Canes; this was a patch of bamboo that had been left untended for gods know how long and had grown into what appeared to us to be a small jungle. At the heart of this jungle was a clearing and in the centre of this clearing was a tall column, ending in a bust of the Great God Pan. This had obviously at some point in the past been a garden feature, set in a sculpted landscape, now left to the whims of nature. But to us it was a temple, a shrine, a holy place. To us this was a most magical place and just being in the presence of the statue brought up feelings of awe, reverence and not a little fear. We used to bring small offerings to Pan and leave them at the base of the column; flowers, cakes, sweets and all sorts. If we were in the mood, we would then commence our own "rituals" there, joining hands around the column and dancing in a ring, singing and chanting anything that came to mind at the time, until we were exhausted and fell to the ground. We would then eat some of the rest of the cakes and sweets we had brought, gazing up at the face of the Great God in silent reverence. It was a magical time then, of flickering sunlight between the stems of the bamboo, semi-twilight in the shade, no grown-ups, just us and our very own God. Anything was possible; anything could happen; magic was real and we knew it.

As is the way of things, time moves on and, as far as I am aware, all these years later I am the only one who still dances to the tune of the Pipes of Pan and leaves offerings to the God of Wild Things. The manor house has now been converted into a Christian Conference Centre and the grounds are strictly off limits to non-residents (not that we should have been playing there all those years ago anyway!). The statue of Pan has long since been toppled and, unfortunately, defaced and broken, but also rescued by a fellow compatriot of those days and now resides in her garden, still loved and honoured. I still visit the area and stay at the same caravan site for breaks and holidays, now with my own family and dogs. And, although I am unable to perform ritual in the Forest of Canes as in the distant past, I still work my magic and honour the Great Horned God in a location not so very far away, almost within sight of it, that I have used for very many years now. It sits in a small grove of Birch trees, surrounded by a dense thicket of Blackthorn bushes, with Hawthorn screening these at the side of the road. A liminal place, next to the sea, high up on a cliff, yet part of the sandy heathland just back from it. A liminal place, neither completely of one world or another, yet partaking of both. A liminal place, just like the nature of the Witch. You see, something was awakened in that small boy who was me, many years ago, dancing in the half-light, chanting in the shadows, honouring the God of Wild Things, that never went back to sleep again. Witch. And all the Ways that go with it.

This might seem to be a very fanciful introduction to a book of lore and magic on Traditional Witchcraft, but I wish to get across the essential essence of the soul of a Witch. It is fanciful, it is capricious, it is not wholly of one world or another – liminality is the name of the game here and there are many natures to the Witch and, hence, many Ways. The Craft has always been a thing of the shadows, an underground practice for the few, not the many. In whatever culture it occurs, the

Witch has always been seen as the one set apart, different, the one shunned, the one on the edges and margins of society. People both fear and desire their powers and abilities, but are never too willing to do the things involved in learning them. A Witch is useful when all else fails and they are turned to in times of need, but persecuted at other times when things are going well. The path of the Witch is hard, difficult, strenuous, frightening at times, mind-altering and requires a certain type of psyche and person to pursue it. It is not and never has been a path for the many, but a path for the few. It is a path which fits not quite in this world and not totally in the Other. It deals with Spirits, with plants, with elemental powers, in Light and Shadow, with "Good" and "Evil" and all that goes with and in-between. I call this Neither-Neither, which to me sums up and exemplifies the nature of the Witch in a nutshell; not quite one thing or another; not quite of one world or the Other, but partaking of the essence of both. To me, it is the Way both of the Blackthorn and the Whitethorn.

As such, this is exemplified in the nature of the Powers with which we work, no more so than the Great Horned Master Himself.

My views on and understanding of "the Devil" have changed, and continue to change, over time and my period of practice in the Craft. I suppose that they change as my understanding – hopefully – grows and I learn more. My thoughts and feelings are no longer those of a 10 year old boy in a bamboo grove, standing before a statue of Pan, but those of a mature adult in middle age, who has been trained in some of the Ways of Traditional Witchcraft. To me He is my God, my Lord and Master. He is the firstborn from the Darkness of Night, but contains within Himself Night's opposite – the bright and blinding Light. He is therefore a complete duality in Himself, both Dark and Bright, which exemplifies the liminal nature so prominent in the Witch themselves. He is ancient, terrible, awesome, wise and learned. He contains elements of many of the Horned Gods of prehistory, (or should I say that they contain elements of Him?), but is not simply one or a combination of any of them. He is very much the Trickster, the Guiser, lurking in shadow, teasing and misleading to bring about a greater learning in His followers. He is the Opposer, going against the general norms of society and standard religion or belief patterns, forcing His People to look beyond the surface of things and look deeper, to challenge, to consider different realities. He is also very much Lucifer, the Light Bearer, as it is through Him that knowledge and enlightenment are gained and He carries the torch of Illumination between His horns. Again, the horns can be seen as exemplifying both the Light and the Dark, Blackthorn and Whitethorn if you will, both within one individuality. He can be a hard Master, pushing and challenging the Witch to achieve things that they didn't think possible or attainable. He can be kind and supportive, but is never soft or gentle, although He can be forgiving and patient. His face changes with the natural tides and seasons, but he is not a "fertility god", however lusty He can be at times; He far transcends this and His origin is far beyond just this planet, in the realms of the stars and beyond. Ultimately, He is the great Mystery, to be worked with and called upon to open oneself up to greater things than can be readily achieved otherwise.

Traditional Witchcraft then, for me, is the path of following the Master, as described above. It is the use of magic to achieve both mundane and occult ends, with the aim of becoming greater than you are and achieving inner illumination. It is the use of the tides and energies of the changing year to learn and to grow to achieve these aims and to grow in knowledge of the world around us and the Spirits and other Beings that inhabit it. It is working with these Spirits and Beings, for mutual benefit and to further the knowledge and wisdom of the Witch. It is using the resources of the natural world – trees, herbs, plants, animals, stones, etc. - to work the magic that will gain the greatest knowledge and experience, to further one's ends. It is the path of knowledge, of power, of wisdom and of understanding and the workings of the Ways to achieve these. Because of this, the nature of the Witch is inherently changeable, ever turning this way and that, to both accommodate new experiences in this and Other worlds and to embrace the information that these bring.

In this book, I wish to show some of the Ways that these experiences can be achieved and how this knowledge may be gained, through some of the many paths of the working Witch, both Dark and Bright and those that fall in between. It will be seen that I use as exemplars of these Ways the images of the Blackthorn and the Whitethorn (Hawthorn); one "Dark" and one "Bright", yet both containing elements of the other and of many things in between. I will look at the many ways in which they, their lore and magic deriving directly, or indirectly, from them may be utilised to bring about these experiences and knowledge. Although I may draw from a wide range of references, my main sources of information and inspiration will be those derived from my home region, that of the lore and magic of the Witchcraft of East Anglia and of those magic-workers who have gone before, their Ways, practices and examples. Much of the information given here will be based on the teachings I have received during my time both training and practising as an old-style Witch and may differ quite widely from others' training and experience. I make no excuse or apology for this, as one can only discuss and pass on what is most meaningful to the individual and what one knows best. It is my hope that the reader will learn things that they have not come across before in their own studies or, at least, to view their own lore and knowledge from a different angle. This is a work of Light and Shade, of Opposites and Conjunctions, of Mixings and Meldings and of the results obtained therefrom. Ultimately it is intended as a work of integration and wholeness. I hope it is a journey that the reader will find both interesting, Illuminating and useful.

Nigel G. Pearson
Suffolk,
East Anglia.
Yuletide 2022.

The Entangled Thicket

"In that eldritch realm we shall doubtless encounter many strange things but if we let the scales of illusion fall from our eyes we may discern a rare wisdom."
Nigel Aldcroft Jackson - "Call of the Horned Piper".

The Land is the greatest book of magic one may ever have the privilege to read and the growing things that arise from the Land are the words that comprise the oldest spells and speak of the deepest Mysteries. There are complete Ways of Witchery available to those who are tree-knowing and wort-knowing, those who view the growing things of the wild as the Witching Powers that they are, but also as the expressions of the presence of sentient Beings and Spirits that they are. The woods are as much our natural home as anything that dwells there - though modern man thinks of towns and cities first as "home". Therefore, in using the images of the Blackthorn and the Whitethorn as the prime exemplars in this work, I must first give some knowledge of their botany, lore, magic and also practical uses, the better for the reader to understand how I perceive them and am using them. Aspects of this knowledge may be known to anyone who has studied these plants themselves, but I hope to show that they may also have some additional or different attributes and uses to those normally associated with them and, hence, as to why I am using them as the prime images of Ways in this book.

Blackthorn

Possibly the tree that is most associated with Old-style, British witchcraft, the Blackthorn (*Prunus spinosa*), is actually more of a shrub than a tree and was categorised as such in the old Irish Brehon Laws of the 7th Century. It is native to Britain, Europe, North-West Africa, Western Asia and has become naturalised in parts of the Eastern USA, Tasmania and New Zealand, due to imported specimens escaping into the wild. It is a deciduous plant, rarely attaining a height of much over 20 feet, which needs plenty of sunlight to thrive and, whilst it can be found in dense woodland, is much more likely to be found at the edges of woods, in hedgerows, on commons, grassy tracks and embankments. Left to its own devices it will grow into thick, impenetrable tangles, which offer excellent protection to nesting birds and their young and to smaller types of mammals, who make the interior their home. Part of the reason it is so protective, is that it is covered in very long, thin twigs, which change into hard and sharp thorns which can deal a deathly wound, but more of that anon. The bark is usually a very beautiful dark brown to black – hence the name – which is quite tough and can grow into a rugged, stony finish on very old specimens. Contrasting with this, the Blackthorn flowers very early in the year, producing masses of pure white blossom as early as February or March, before it puts out its leaves and usually prior to any other tree stirring into life. The blossoms can sometimes cover the whole tree, with tiny, five-petalled, star-shaped flowers, totally obscuring the black and sinister bark underneath. A later flowering – which can often coincide with a return to bitterly cold weather – is known as a "Blackthorn Winter" and is greatly feared by country-folk, due to the damage the cold can do to earlier sprouting crops. The scent of the blossoms is quite musky, heady, very strong and potently erotic. This is a deliberate lure to early-awakening insects, so that the plant may be pollinated ahead of anything else and ensure a continued production of fruit and, hence, seed. The flowers were/are considered to be an omen of ill-luck or misfortune by some and should be banned from being brought into the house, it is thought. They were associated with death, possibly because of their nature of blooming on bare, dark branches at Winter's end, at a time of want and starvation.

After the flowers have fallen, the plant begins to unfurl its leaves, usually around late April to early May. The leaves are small, neat oval shapes and turn a mid to dark, matt green colour when fully open. These, too, tend to completely cover the tree, again hiding the wickedly sharp points beneath. As the year progresses, the fruits begin to become noticeable, starting off as tiny points of hard, dark greenness, gradually swelling throughout the summer. These change colour, until they become small, purplish-black, plum-shaped spheres, covered in a dusty, silvery-blue bloom. These fruits are known as Sloes, which is a word deriving from a Germanic origin meaning "plum" and which gives the plant its alternative name of Sloe tree. It is thought that the Blackthorn may be the wild ancestor of later cultivated Plums, Damsons and Greengages, sharing a common origin with them and the lesser known Mirabelle plum. Certainly it is a close cousin of the Bullace, a fruiting tree similar to the Greengage which grows wild in many parts of East Anglia and from which a sweet and heady wine can be made. All are members of the Family *Rosaceae*.

The wood of the Blackthorn is hard, tough and durable, the grain forming beautifully intricate whorls of colour, especially when polished to a high sheen with a beeswax or linseed oil. Because of its durability it has been used for centuries for practical objects, such as cloak pins, spoons, handles for tools and for walking sticks and staffs. The fearsome Irish fighting club – which may be quite small, like a large cosh, or as large as an actual staff – known as the *Shillelagh*, is made from the hard wood of the Blackthorn. A piece of the thicker, central stem is cut for this, then traditionally polished with either pigs fat or butter. It is then put up the chimney to dry out and harden further, becoming coated with soot which, when rubbed into the wood, enhances the blackened effect of the bark. Older examples of these have become collectors items and can fetch quite high prices. (Interestingly, Robert Graves in his poetic work, *The White Goddess*, claims that the original shillelaghs were made from Oak, another tough and durable wood, but gives no supporting material for this).

The fruit of the Blackthorn, the Sloe, is well known for producing that popular liqueur, Sloe Gin, although it can equally well be made with other high proof spirits, such as Vodka or Whiskey and is just as potably enjoyable. It makes an excellent offering, not only for just the Blackthorn, but for workings of all kinds. It is also a good intoxicant for spirit-contact of all kinds, not just with Blackthorn, when used with knowledge and care. However, the sloe has been used in many other ways over the years, mainly for medicinal purposes. Whilst the flowers have been used as a tonic and mild laxative, the leaves as a mouthwash, gargle and to stimulate the appetite and the bark to reduce fevers, the fruit has been used for kidney, bladder and digestive disorders; according to mediaeval herbalists, the sloe was the regulator of the stomach. The bitter fruit was held to bind loose bowels and due to its marked astringent properties, was made into wines, syrups, jellies, jams and syrups. It was also used to make a particularly acidic liquor known as *verjuice* and was a chief ingredient in fruit cheeses, used to cleanse the bowels. Alternatively, the leaves, dried and chopped may be used as a tangy substitute for black tea and, if more finely chopped or powdered, can be mixed in with normal tobacco to make it go further, or simply used as a tobacco substitute itself.

In folk and magical-lore, Blackthorn traditionally has a grim reputation and is considered a most sinister tree. Many of its uses are seen to be to do with maleficia or ill wishing, but this need not necessarily be the case, as I shall hope to show anon. Worked with on a different level, the tree can act as a most useful ally and friend to the adaptable and knowledgeable Witch. The plant itself is said to be the home of the Spirit variously known as the Lunantishee, Black Tom, Black Jack, or simply Black or Dark Faerie. These Spirits are fiercely protective of their woody homes and woe betide anyone who attempts to take a branch, fruit, thorns or blossom without their permission, particularly at the beginning and ending of Winter and Summer, by the old calendar, namely 11th May and 11th November (Roodmas and Hallowmas in old reckoning). They can inflict dire retribution on any who do not ask permission and leave an offering for items taken, which can result in a run of severe bad luck, accidents or even death in extreme cases. However, approached with respect and honour, these Spirits may be encouraged to give of their knowledge and energy, to the great benefit of the patient Witch. They may even be willing to help with approaches to and the conjuring/summoning of other types of spirit, if approached in the right manner and with the right attitude. To find a tree that would be willing to work with you, it is first necessary to approach it in a certain way. I have described a technique that I call Wight Tracking in a previous book (*Treading the Mill: Workings in Traditional Witchcraft* – see Bibliography) and this is essentially the technique needed to be used in this instance. I will here describe it, adapted for this current use, but see the previous work for a fuller explanation.

First, decide on a location where you know that there are a fair number of Blackthorn trees that you may approach for their aid and assistance. The idea of this practice is to introduce the individual into the environment of the Blackthorn Spirits, in a way that may endear him or her to them and encourage the Spirits to appear or acknowledge the individual's presence or existence in some way. Best performed at dawn or dusk, when the Moon is still visible in the sky. The phase of the Moon is also relevant here, in that the Waning phase is traditionally considered the best time for spirit contact of all types. This may or may not be true for the individual Witch however, so attempts at different times may need to be made for the best results.

The attitude that you must bear in mind is that of a hunter; you will be stalking your "prey" in the wild, just as our ancestors did, but with a different intent. You wish to *encounter* and engage with, not capture and kill your "prey". This will be more difficult than killing, as your "prey" is wily, skilled and at one with its environment, so you must be likewise.

Begin your tracking by taking a path into your chosen landscape. Step lightly on the earth, but do not tiptoe or crouch down; a gentle walk will do. It is the attitude that counts here. You must be as aware as you possibly can of everything that is happening around you, use all your senses to experience your journey. Smell the wind, taste the breeze, hear all the sounds around you, touch the earth/trees/bushes as you walk and take everything in with your eyes. You must be totally aware. At the same time, you must still all "dialogue" in your head; cease to think of anything at all (as far as possible), and just experience. You may begin by inducing a light trance, but this "wide open" approach will encourage one anyway. Walk at a slow but steady pace, making as little impact on your surroundings as you can. As you progress – and this may take some time, so be prepared – your senses may gradually become overloaded and "shut down", until only one or two are left. You may feel that your hearing is tuning out and that you can no longer smell anything, but that your sight is becoming more and more acute in your surroundings. Or perhaps your sight and hearing are beginning to fade and your sense of smell is sharpened to extraordinary levels. Just go with whatever happens and "follow your nose" so to speak. Walk into your chosen environment, keeping the thought in mind that you wish to encounter and make contact with one of the Blackthorn Spirits. If you are lucky, it is at this point that you may become aware of one, or more, of the Spirits of your location. They may present themselves to you in many different ways, but do not be alarmed; accept the appearance/feel/sensation for what it is. When you are aware of a presence, stop your tracking and either sit down or stand still. Let whatever happens happen, but do not try to analyse it. You should by this point be in a mild trance state anyway and not wholly in the everyday world, so normal rules may not apply. Do not approach the Spirit; let it approach you if it chooses to. Communication may occur, but is unusual on a first encounter, which is normally quite brief. Experience it for as long as it lasts, until the Spirit draws away or disappears. Make a suitable offering at this point; maybe some Sloe gin, etc. or some fresh bread, milk and/or honey. Then rise, if you are sitting, or turn if you are standing and silently walk back the way you have come, without looking back. As soon as you arrive back at your starting point, or back home, have something to eat and drink (not alcohol), as this will help to "earth" you and bring you entirely back to the realm of everyday life.

You may repeat this exercise over and again, to build up a rapport both with your local Blackthorn Spirits and with the Land itself in your locality. Don't be disappointed if nothing happens the first time – it rarely does – but you will all the time be developing a relationship with your chosen locale, its energies and the other Spirits in the vicinity, which will only stand you in good stead for improved working relationships in general.

Once you have made contact with the Spirit, you may continue to develop it at your own – and its – pace. Never push or rush and always be polite and respectful. Always take and leave an offering and never demand anything; ask politely and wait for a reply, hopefully in the affirmative. If it isn't, it may not be the right time for whatever you have asked for and you can try again later on. Mostly, you will be asking two types of question in my experience. Firstly – "*can I have some of your wood/bark/fruit/leaves/blossom*"? In this case, place your hand gently on the tree and wait until you receive a positive answer/feeling and then proceed to cut/

take what you need, as swiftly as you can, causing as little damage to the tree as possible. If taking wood, (but also see below), cut swiftly with a very sharp tool and immediately cover the wound so as to keep any form of infection out of the tree and preventing it from becoming damaged. You can easily make your own ointment to seal the wound as follows; over a low heat melt a small amount of pure, natural beeswax, about half a dinner candles-worth. When it is gently molten, add a couple of teaspoons of pure, Linseed oil, and a pinch of dried Blackthorn leaves (ground up). Add a couple of drops of Benzoin essential oil and mix all well together. Then pour the whole into a clean, glass jar with a screw-top lid, that you have previously sterilised. The ointment should cool to a soft set, which will enable you to smear a covering over the raw branch end.

The second type of question you may ask is more of an esoteric one, enquiring of the knowledge and wisdom of the Blackthorn Spirit, such as; "*can you give me a spell for X*"? Or, "*what would be the best way to do such-and-such*"? Or,"*is there a method to do XYZ*"? There is a way to go about this, which is both simple and difficult to achieve, which involves combining or merging your vital energy field directly with that of the tree Spirit's. Many people will tell you that all that is necessary to do this is to either touch the tree with your bare flesh (i.e. hand), or to embrace the tree in a hug. Whilst this will bring you close to the tree's energy field, it won't unite the pair of you directly, which is what is needed to pass/share information. To do this, you need to sit down at the base of the tree, as close as you can and place your spine right up against the trunk of the tree, as closely as possible, sitting as straight as you can (you can also do this standing, but sitting is easier and best). Get as much of your spine touching the trunk of the tree as you can. Your spine, esoterically speaking, is the vehicle of your essential energy; it is the column up and down of which pass the vital energies by which you live and have your being. Likewise, the trunk of the tree performs the same function, channelling the vital energies up and own, from the roots to the branches and vice versa. By placing your spine as closely as possible to the trunk of the tree and aligning them, a form of merging and transferral of energies may take place. This also involves entering a light to moderate trance state, the better to appreciate the energies of the Spirit of the tree and enable a form of communication. (Again, I describe techniques for entering trance states in *Treading the Mill*, and I advise the reader to look there if they are not yet proficient in entering these states). Once you are ready and have achieved as close a communion as you can with the tree's Spirit (bearing in mind you should by now be used to communication with the Spirit and each should be used to the other), mentally ask your question and wait for a reply. This may come in many forms, so be open to anything. You may "see" the answer. You may just have a whole concept dumped into your head at once (in which case it may take some working out or "unravelling" at a later date). You may receive a form of words, or maybe just a keyword or two. Alternatively, your answer may not come at this time at all, but you may receive a reply in the form of a dream, or daydream, later on. So just be open to different forms of reply and not expect it in the form that you asked it. Once you have your reply, or it is evident that you won't get one at that time, gently disengage from your joint merging with the tree/Spirit, make your customary offering, give thanks and walk away. (This is also the technique that is needed if you are intending to take some wood for magical purposes, such as a wand, staff or Stang and you wish it to be Live wood, i.e. retaining a piece of the Spirit of the tree in the cut portion. You need to develop a close relationship with the Spirit in this case, which may take some time, but be honest with yourself in the replies that you get and you will generally be well rewarded).

Having established a working relationship with the Spirit of the Blackthorn, you will now be able to work much better with the energies of this tree and make use of them for all the different purposes that they are known. The lore surrounding the Blackthorn is the result of possibly thousands of years of conflicting opinions concerning its "morality", and so you will find that it is used for both maleficia and beneficia, although it is most often known for the first. To many Witches, it may represent the dark side of the Craft. It is a tree sacred to the Dark, or Crone aspect of the Feminine Power, and represents the Waning and Dark Moons. Blackthorn is known as "the increaser and keeper of dark secrets". The tree is linked with warfare, wounding and death, sometimes associated with the Cailleach - the Crone of Death. I would like to show that it can be used equally in the many Ways of Witchery and is of great benefit, however it is used.

A well known use for the Sloes is in the curing, or charming, of warts. Take a plump, juicy fruit and rub the wart with it, smearing it well with the juice. Turn your back to the tree from which you plucked the Sloe and throw it over your shoulder, mentally casting the wart away with it. Walk away without looking back. Alternatively, you may rub the wart with a piece of meat (bacon or beef is considered best), which has been stolen, or otherwise obtained without permission. Go to your familiar Blackthorn and hang the meat on a sharp thorn, piercing the meat thoroughly as you do so. Turn your back and walk away. If chopped finely, slivers of the wood and the flesh from the dried berries can be used in incenses of your own devising and are excellent for rituals of banishment, both of negative energies, illness, ill-wishing and all forms of harm, and also for individuals who are "in the way". Collect a supply of these well in advance and experiment in making up your own incense blends, perhaps asking the Spirit for advice or help as well. Anointing a few twigs with oil and your focussed intent and then burning some at both noon and midnight, on seven consecutive days, will remove even the most persistent negative energies, persons or problems. Having got rid of all your negativity, you can then pluck a leaf or berry and place it in a small charm bag, which you should carry with you at all times, for protection and good fortune. You may also place a fresh leaf or sprig of blossom in your charm bag with a written petition to the Spirit and carry it with you – your request is sure to be granted. Fastening a ribbon or piece of fabric torn from your clothing to the tree with your request is also advised; as you tie the cloth, focus on your wish and hold a visual image of it in your mind for best results. The juice of the Sloe is of great use in any magical working you may wish to undertake, because of its raw, energetic force and power. Stab the point of a pen or quill into a plump, raw fruit and obtain the purply-black juice. Use this as an ink to write your charm or request onto parchment or thin card, cloth or linen and then hang the charm onto a Blackthorn spike, whispering the charm as you do so. Turn around and walk away without looking back.

As we have already seen, the blossoms of the Blackthorn are powerfully erotic and sexual, exuding their heady scent early in the year. The wise Witch would do well to collect as many blossoms as they are able while they are in flower, dry them well and keep them ready. These can later be used either as they are, powdered or added to other ingredients to aid in matters of attraction, fertility, sexual arousal and in wedding blessings. Appropriate methods would be in incenses, charm bags, as powders scattered over a person/ couple, or in infusions to be drunk or used as washes. Use your imagination and ask your Spirit.

Another, major use for the blossoms is in an incense compounded especially to honour and call upon the Horned One, or Devil of the Witches. Whilst some categorise the Blackthorn as a dark sister of the Whitethorn, in traditional Old Craft it has normally been viewed as a manifestation of the power of the Witch's Master, or Devil. I have given this recipe before elsewhere (see *Treading the Mill*), but it seems apposite to repeat it here now.

Incense for the WitchFather.

1 measure Pine needles
1 measure Holly wood
1 measure Basil
1 measure Wormwood
1 measure Pine resin
1/2 measure Blackthorn flowers
2 drops Pine oil
2 drops Clove oil
Small amount of Honey
Few drops of Sloe Gin.

The thorns of the Blackthorn, sometimes called Spikes or Points, are generally known for their use in curse-making and other forms of harm or retribution. Whilst this is certainly true, there is also another side and use for these barbs and I would like to take a look at this aspect first, before considering their use in maleficia. As a point, the thorn is obviously ideal for protective as well as offensive magic and there are various ways in which these can be used. Often stuck into or tied into objects, the thorn can be equally used the other way round; here is a charm from East Anglia that can be adapted for many purposes. Take a reasonable sized Apple that still has its stalk attached and tie a ribbon/cord to it, by which it may hang. Take a handful of fresh Spikes and poke these into the Apple, one at a time, with the pointed end *outwards*, i.e., the thicker end into the Apple. As you do so, intone a charm of your own making, to the intent of the spell. Cover the entire Apple, so that it looks like a Hedgehog, entirely surrounded in protective thorns. This can then be hung wherever it is intended to do its job; in a window to protect the house; over a babe's crib to protect the child; in a car; even over a hospital bed against illness. The possibilities are many and varied. The juice from the Apple will keep the thorns fresh for quite a while but eventually both will dry out. Leave the charm until it is quite dry, then replace it with a fresh one, if needed (although some say that the drier and harder it gets, the better the magic – the choice is yours). A variation on this charm calls for the Apple to be cut in two sideways – hence displaying the magical five-pointed star within – before studding it with thorns. Write out your spell/petition on a piece of paper and place it between the two halves. Reunite the pieces of the Apple and pin them together with Blackthorn spikes, making sure the points go through the petition as well, before studding the Apple as above. Again, using an Apple, stud the fruit all over with thorns, but pointing inwards this time, whilst naming any ills of body or mind that you wish to be rid of; visualise the complaint being pierced as you do so. Take the Apple and bury it to the North of your property, well away from the house and leave it to rot away completely.

Another way to use the spikes in a defensive measure, is to blacken and powder them, usually in combination with the blossoms and leaves. Dry all the ingredients well and place them in an iron pan over a high heat, but watch them well in case they burn. Allow them to just turn in colour until all are darkened/black; if completely dry, this will not take long, so be careful they do not catch light. Grind the ingredients well together, until they are finely powdered and keep safely in a wooden box in a dry place. When needed, the powder can be sprinkled around an object, person or place that you wish to protect and keep safe from harm, or may be placed in a charm bag – perhaps with other protective herbs or ingredients – and worn around the neck. This powder is also ideal for workings of banishment, when it can be used as an incense, or cast to the winds in the direction of the person/thing you wish to be rid of, with suitable charms and visualisations.

Blackthorn spikes have long been used in image magic, for both offensive and defensive magic, as well as healing and blessing. It is traditional to make an image of the person (or thing), you wish to work on and then insert the thorns into corresponding parts of the image, whilst intoning either curses, blessings or healing charms. If cursing, it is traditional to end the charm with the words: "*I'll smite thee, I'll smite thee, I'll smite thee.*" Or, if the Witch is from Suffolk, "*I'll tudd (toad), ee.*", referring to the famed power of the Toad Bone Rite, used as a maleficium. If used in this manner as a cursing tool, particularly if tipped with a poisonous substance, the spike was known as "the pin of slumber". Depending on the material that the image has been made from, it is then buried, wrapped and kept safe somewhere, dried out – in the case of clay – and/or roasted, put up the chimney or, in the case of wax, melted with further imprecations or blessings. The import of this sort of magic, is that it is the inherent power or force in the Blackthorns themselves that are being utilised, irrespective of the desired end result. It can thus be seen that, far from an entirely malefic force, the Blackthorn is a multi-faceted being, just like the Witch themselves.

Following on from this, it was said that Old Hornie Himself pricked his followers with a Blackthorn spike on the finger at their initiation, giving them the "Devil's mark" and making them His own. It is true that some paths of Old Craft mark their members in this fashion, usually on a given finger on the left hand, depending on the Tradition. This is usually put down to the fact that Blackthorn spikes are notoriously wickedly sharp and will easily pierce human flesh, the wound often turning septic, or leaving a nasty scar if unattended. A wound made in this manner could readily become permanent, but easily hidden if made in a surreptitious place on the hand, if a compound of herbs mixed with a colourant like soot or woad were to be rubbed in immediately the mark were made. Thus marking the bearer as one of the Devil's own. The point about this marking is that it could just as easily be done with a pin or the point of a knife, but that it is the Blackthorn that is used. It is the power and force of the Blackthorn, as representative of the dual-faced Master of Witches that is the essential point here – the Witch is marked with the essence of the Devil

Himself, with the power to bless or curse, to heal or to harm and all that lies between.

Having said this, the Blackthorn is notoriously used for its powerful energy as a blasting or cursing agent. Indeed, a wand made from the wood of this tree is very often known as a Blasting Rod in itself. Sometimes it is simply a length of Blackthorn wood, traditionally a cubit in length and cut according to the prescribed methods of the Old Craft, or it can equally be shaped and/or carved, with Blackthorn spikes being inserted into the end. Sometimes the rune Thurisaz/Thorn is marked on it in some manner, to enhance the inherent energies. Each Witch would have their own rod and would use it only in dire circumstances, sometimes possessing one for years without utilising it. A lot of time, energy and effort goes into making these items and they are not used lightly, not the least as it costs the Witch a lot of their own being to perform the magic itself. In some cases the rod is lost entirely during the operation, being burnt to ashes as part of the magic, the ashes then being cast as needed. In the past it is said that the pyres lit to burn Witches on the European continent were made of Blackthorn and that their wands were cast into the flames as a final insult. Many Old Craft Witches today have a personal wand made of Blackthorn, as do I, not necessarily just to curse with, but because this wood, although primarily standing for the Devil Himself, may also represent the powers of the Witch Mother, those of the Dark Moon and the deep, primordial forces of the womb-like Underworld, from which we all come. Another example that, like all magic, the power is neutral and the responsibility for its use lies with the Witch that utilises it.

Perhaps the most important use for the Blackthorn, is as the wood used in making the Stang for a Magister of an Old Craft coven. The only ceremonial use for this is in the rarely performed formal rite of cursing, when the coven itself, or one of its members, is under attack and the coven needs to defend itself. In this instance, the Blackthorn embodies the sheer force and power of the energies of the Traditional Craft of the Witch and stands in for the Horned Master Himself. In this case, a special fire will be ritually created and lit with full ceremony in the presence of the whole coven. The Magister will then strike the fire with the Blackthorn Stang, whilst reciting a curse during the Dark of the Moon and then direct it towards the enemy. This is an act not performed without dire provocation and only as a last resort, as the results cannot be predicted beforehand and cannot be undone or recalled, once unleashed.

Blackthorn is a notoriously difficult energy to control and handle, but is not sinister or malefic in and of itself per se. It can be seen that, whilst a strong and powerful tree, its power may be used in many different ways and is entirely up to the individual Witch and their own craft as to how it is done.

Whitethorn

Known also as Hawthorn, Hagthorn, (the) May or simply Thorn, the Whitethorn rivals the Blackthorn as a tree of lore and magic, though with a less sinister – but nonetheless powerful - reputation. There are several hundred species of *Crataegus* in the genus, native to temperate regions in Europe, North America, Asia and North Africa, but the two indigenous to the British Isles are *Crataegus monogyna* (Common) and *C. laevigata*,(English or Midland). Like the Blackthorn, all species belong to the *Rosaceae* family. The first variety is widespread throughout the whole of the territory, except Scotland, the latter growing mostly in the East Midlands, the East and South of England. They can be distinguished by the fact that the Common has leaves with distinct lobes and indentations, often reaching to the main rib, with the tips of the lobes serrated; its blossoms are pure white and grow massively, sometimes covering the entire tree. The leaves of the English Thorn tend to be more rounded with smaller lobes and indentations; the blossoms are pink/red or white with pink tips and do not tend to cover the whole tree as much. For the purposes of traditional lore, both species are treated identically.

Similar to the Blackthorn, the Whitethorn is a smallish tree or shrub, growing to a maximum of 30 feet but is usually much smaller and, very often, wider than it is tall. It grows well on most soils, liking open habitats such as commons, heathland, hillsides, pastures and the edge of woodlands. It has long been used as a hedging plant – the Anglo-Saxon word *Haegthorn* meaning hedge-tree giving us one of its common names – but also notably grows individually if left to its own devices. The use of the tree for hedging goes back thousands of years, both to protect fields and pastures and also for more defensive measures. Signs of Whitethorn hedges have been excavated around the edges of exposed Roman forts in Britain and it was a major tool for implementing the Enclosure Laws centuries later. When expertly layered into a living hedge, it grows densely, with intertwining branches, fiercely-armed with short, but exceptionally sharp, spines or thorns. These form practically impenetrable barriers to both livestock and humans and a properly maintained hedge can last for centuries. The tree itself can live to over 400 years, but 100 to 300 is more usual, having the capacity to flower twice a year, depending on suitable weather conditions. Whitethorn grows rapidly, sending out plenty of side shoots and branches, which make excellent barriers when used in hedging. It, too, has plenty of wickedly sharp thorns – hence the name – but these tends to be much smaller than in the Blackthorn and are actually stunted side-shoots. Unlike Blackthorn it does not send out suckers to spread its growth and does not have a large root system; this means it does not take up a lot of the local soil's nutrients and hence much other plant life grows in its environment. It is an ancient tree, pollen remains showing that it was widespread in the British Isles prior to 6,000 B.C.E. and plentiful remains have been found in megalithic tomb mounds.

After its Winter dormancy, the leaves begin to appear on the Whitethorn generally during March or April, sometimes as early as the Vernal Equinox. The bright green of the upper surface gradually fades during the Summer, giving way to brilliant oranges, reds and yellows in the Common variety, the English form mostly just fading before they drop in early Winter. The leaves give this tree one of its other common folk-names, that being "*Bread & Cheese*". Much loved by cattle and horses, the leaves were often picked by travellers in the past – and by children up until very recently – to stave off the pangs of hunger on long journeys when food was either scarce or not to be had for many hours yet. The taste is nothing like its namesake, being somewhat nutty in flavour, but acts in its stead to convince the stomach it is not quite that empty.

Flowering just after the leaves appear, Whitethorn also takes on the name of "May" and is well known for its profusion of flowers which herald the beginning of Summer. Although traditionally held to appear at the beginning of the May month, signifying the timing of the Traditional Witch festival of Roodmas, the blossoms can actually unfold over a much longer period of time. Due both to previous, historical calendar changes and to global warming in more modern times, the Whitethorn rarely flowers exactly at the beginning of May any more and so it is up to the individual Witch as to how they deal with this. However, the blossom has long been seen as one of the main features of the tree and contains a wealth of historical lore surrounding it. The blossoms contain both male and female parts and are fertilised by the insects that crawl over them, of which there are many, the Whitethorn hosting some fifty species. Like the Blackthorn, the blossoms of the May exude a strangely disturbing scent, but perhaps even more so. Modern science has now isolated the chemicals released by the flowers, which include the same chemicals given off both by rotting meat and also – separately – by the sexual secretions of human females. The blooms have traditionally been considered both as a sign of imminent bad luck, if not death, and also of rampant sexuality. It was taboo to bring the flowers indoors for any reason, or dire circumstances would result. The only exception to this was the tradition in my native Suffolk, that the first serving maiden to bring a branch of blossoming Whitethorn into the house on May morn would receive a dish of fresh cream from the Mistress of the house – a rare treat in times gone by. The May blossom has a strong tradition of betokening human sexuality, reproduction and fertility, which was noted by the poet Chaucer in his verse;

> *"Mark the fair blooming of the Hawthorn Tree,*
> *Who, finely clothed in a robe of white,*
> *Fills full the wanton eye with May's delight."*

It was perfectly acceptable, however, to gather flowering boughs of May to decorate the house, and other buildings, *outside* and these would be hung above doorways, windows and over barns and horse/cattle sheds, both as a blessing and as apotropaic devices to protect against hexing by malefic witches. Garlands of May blossom were used as decorations for weddings and wreaths to decorate the brides' hair were very popular, all with the added frisson of the sexual undercurrent involved.

After they have been fertilised, the blooms drop their petals and the tiny fruits – known as Haws – begin to grow. Starting out as small, green orbs, these gradually swell and darken until, by Autumn, they become the well known clusters of shiny, red fruit, standing out in bright profusion against the lighter green background. The Haws are much loved by birds and provide a good source of food for them in the latter part of the year. They return the favour by distributing the seeds in their droppings, hence helping to propagate the tree widely. Not only birds enjoy this bounty, but humans, too, have used these tiny fruits for centuries in many ways. They have been used in jellies, jams, cordials, fruit cheeses, wines and meads; they are also high in pectin content and hence make a good setting agent for other fruit preparations as well.

Medicinally speaking, Whitethorn is an exceptionally valuable plant and rivals many modern medicines in effectiveness, without unpleasant side effects. It contains chemical components which are sedative to the nervous system, anti-spasmodic, anti-hypertensive, diuretic and a cholesterol and mineral solvent. All parts are used in the treatment of angina, both high and low blood pressure and raised cholesterol levels. Whitethorn helps to increase blood flow through the heart, whilst strengthening the heart muscle, without increasing the beat or raising the blood pressure. However, being a haemostatic, it can both lower and raise blood pressure, depending on the needs of the particular body. The fruits are generally taken in the form of a tincture, but the leaves and flowers may also be taken thusly, in teas or infusions. Adding dried leaves to make your morning cup of tea – using equal quantities of tea and leaves - is also an excellent way to keep the heart in good condition. However, care must be observed in prescribing and taking any form of heart medicine and professional, medical help should always be sought before undertaking any course of treatment. Having said that, folklore maintains that a wash of the flowers can heal facial blemishes and acne;

> *"The fair Maid who, the first of May,*
> *Goes to the field at the break of day,*
> *And washes in dew from the Hawthorn Tree,*
> *Will ever after handsome be."*
> *(ANON).*

As the Whitethorn is only a small tree, it doesn't provide large pieces of wood for physical projects, but it does have excellent uses nonetheless. The wood is tough and hard-wearing and makes excellent handles for all types of tools, particularly for knives and daggers, as it was considered a protective wood, but more of that anon. Because of its beautifully fine grain, the root wood has been used historically for small boxes and ladies combs and as inlays in marquetry. The bark was used as a dye in Scotland to colour wool black and twigs and small branches make excellent charcoal; this burns exceedingly hot and so was much used in ancient smelting techniques. Being tough, the wood is also good for making walking sticks and staffs, as well as wands and Stangs which will last more than a lifetime, if you can find pieces large enough.

In folk and magical-lore, if the Blackthorn is generally considered to have a sinister reputation and be a tree of ill-luck, cursing and blasting, then the Whitethorn is, generally, considered to be its opposite. It is usually looked upon as a protective, blessing and healing tree, but with otherworldly associations that I will come onto later. It was traditional in many areas of the British Isles to begin the New Year by making a Whitethorn Ball, to protect the house and its inhabitants for the coming year. On New Years Day, using wood cut on the Eve, the women of the house would make a sphere, by twisting and plaiting together the long, thin branches, until they had a smooth ball. This would be dried over the hearth/in the oven, but must be ever-so slightly singed to be effective, thus protecting against fire and other forms of harm. This would then be hung up in the home for the rest of the year. Whilst this was being done, the men of the household would take out the previous years ball into the fields and set light to it (if the new ball can be singed in the old one's fire, then so much the better). It must then be carried around the fields, such that burning whisps of ash fell into the furrows, bringing life and fertility to the crops. This may be adapted today for home protection, the ash from the previous year's ball being sprinkled around your garden/property for good fortune. The canny Witch might also like to make an addition to the ball as well. Take a hagstone suspended on a red cord and leave it hanging in a Whitethorn, either for the three nights of the Full Moon previously, or the three nights prior to New Year; whilst making your ball, suspend this within the sphere for added protection for you and yours.

If using the wood of the Whitethorn, the exact same procedures for taking anything from it as described above for Blackthorn must be observed, particularly if wanting to use Live Wood. The animating Spirit of the Whitethorn is no less fierce than that of the Blackthorn, if after a different type but, again, more of that anon. Make sure you have the permission of the Spirit of the tree if taking anything from it – particularly for magical purposes – or you may regret it! Having said that, folklore and Witch-tradition give many uses for the blossoms, leaves and other parts of the tree.

Pluck a sprig of flowering Whitethorn and hang it over a child's bed to place it under the protection of the guardian Spirit. Alternatively, make up a pouch of the blossoms and leaves and sew this directly into the child's pillow. The taboo on bringing the flowers into the house does not seem to apply to children. Also, an infusion or wash can be made of the flowers and leaves, which may be sprinkled around the house to repel evil spirits, ill-wishing and other, negative, energies. An incense made of the dried wood, berries and leaves may be used as a form of purificatory smoke and to attract more beneficial influences. Soak the berries, dried or fresh, in pure, spring water and use this as a cleansing agent, particularly for magical tools. Wash the windows of the house with this, or dab it around the window and door sills to attract protective energies. The blossoms, if gathered and dried, are good to add to any form of love magic, be that as an incense, powdered, or in a charm bag. Be careful on the amount, as love is NOT the same thing as lust! Whitethorn trees may be planted around the home to keep out evil or negative energies and to protect from lightning strikes, for as the old saw goes;

"Beware the Oak – it courts the stroke.
Beware the Ash – it courts the flash.
Creep under the Thorn – it will save you from harm."

A more magical and less well-known practice, is that of "Thorning the Ground". Stout Whitethorn twigs must be taken, respectfully, from the tree at the Dark of the Moon, by a person other than the operator of the spell. These must then be ritually "planted" around the property (or ritual area) – forming a circle of protection (a miniature hedge, actually), whilst calling on the Spirit of the tree for their aid. This is useful for many reasons of protection and sorcery, not the least of which creates a secure, magical enclosure in which to safely work one's witchery. But the twigs must be gathered by another person for their potency to be good.

The berries of the Whitethorn are excellent for use as natural "beads", which may be used for many purposes by the adaptable Witch. For this use, the berries must be obtained fresh, strung onto cord or thread and left to dry, which may take some time, so plan well in advance. They dry very hard, so are quite durable and last a long time, so are good for both long-term magics and for constant use. The forms of this type of magic are manifold and only limited by the magical imagination of the operator. Strings of these beads may be used as "rosaries", the number being determined by the end-use and wishes of the Witch. An odd number of beads is usual for these, in multiples of 3, 7 or 9, but the choice is individual. The intent must be kept in mind whilst threading the berries on the cord, with perhaps a whispered charm as well. These can be used to keep count of repetitions in a spell, for trance working by continuous chanting whilst "telling the beads", or any other form of counting. They are good for tying in spells between the beads, for instance in healing magic; these can then be wrapped/tied around the afflicted limb or part of the body of the patient. The string of knots known as the Witch's Ladder may be adapted here, with spells more used to the attributes of the Whitethorn and other objects tied in-between the beads; again, the use of the Witch's magical mind is paramount.

I have already spoken above of the use of Blackthorn spines in Witch magics and the same principles may be applied here, but after a different manner. The Whitethorn tends to be more protective in nature, so defensive magics are more to the fore. Being shorter and, perhaps, less unwieldy, the thorns of this tree may be of more use in candle magic, or for inserting into poppets for the use of rites other than cursing or blasting. Healing is the first thing that comes to mind here, but also charms of blessing and hallowing, either for a person or place may be beneficially practised using Whitethorn spines. A pouch containing multiples of three, seven or nine thorns, bound with red thread, may be given as a gift for a wedding couple, to place in a new home, or to guard a shop or place of business. Again, the imagination of the Witch is the only constraint here.

If Blackthorn is known as having its own, fierce, guardian Spirits, the same is also true of the Whitethorn, as this is THE Faerie Tree, par excellence. This is particularly true of single, lone trees that are encountered in fields, on mountainsides, at the side of a well or spring, by the edge of a style or in a hedge on its own without others of its kind around. For long ages, the Whitethorn has been seen as a doorway to the Underworld or, more generally, the Otherworld, where the Bright Ones, the Shining or Lordly ones live. The Whitethorn is their tree and they protect it fiercely. These are places where the veil between worlds is thin. Many shrines still exist, both seen and unseen, where ancient Thorns still stand sentinel and they are still visited by those of the Wise who look to the Whitethorn as intermediary between themselves and the Otherworldly Powers. Such visitors may leave appropriate "wish-rags" and offerings tied to the tree's branches or at the base of the trunk, in order to attract the knowledge, wisdom, power and understanding that they desire. These sites are excellent for performing rites of divination and scrying, as the veil between worlds is notoriously thin here.

William Bottrell, sometime around 1870, collected the report of a traditional sorcerer who used the Thorn to access the "powers below"- the powers of the dead merged with the underworld- to gain magical assistance. He recounted the sorcerer saying:

> *"I went on my knees under a White-thorn tree by the crossroads, and there, for the best part of that night, I called on the powers till they helped me cast the spells that gave old Jemmy and his family plenty of junket and sour milk for a time."*
> ("*Traditions and Hearthside Stories of West Cornwall*").

This is the reason that, although revered for its properties of protection and defence, the spiny Whitethorn hedge is also feared as a passage-way into the realms of these unworldly creatures, that the unwary person may accidentally fall through; they are places of glamour, of illusion and enchantment, where all may not be as it at first seems to be. Not only protecting the field or village that it surrounds, the hedge is also a barrier between worlds and care must be taken in its vicinity. Folklore states that lone trees, especially, are risky places to be alone, particularly at night as, if you fall asleep under a Whitethorn, there is no knowing where you may awaken. Dire consequences will also befall anyone who damages or cuts down a single or lone tree; broken limbs, house fires, blood poisoning and even deaths have been associated with such disrespect and irreverence. Many single trees have their own names in local myth and folklore, such as Old Sally, Old Meg, The Hag and many others. Not only does this denote a reverence for the Spirit that is considered to dwell there, but is also a memory of the rites that may have been carried out there in the past. For the knowing Witch, far from fearing such places, uses their properties and energies for their own purposes. Indeed, many of the indwelling Spirits are considered to be old-time Witches who remain in the tree post mortem, or indeed the Witch themselves shape-shifted. Using such places with knowledge, the Witch may pass through into other worlds and expand their experience of other worlds and other Ways of knowledge.

Perennially associated with May Day, the Whitethorn is known to house the Spirit known as Jack-in-the-Green. He it is who rouses the lusty lads to court the young maidens during the rites and festivities of May Eve and inspires them to feats of love and ardour previously thought unattainable. His leafy-masked face can be seen peering from the canopy of fresh leaves as the revels take place and his leery chuckle heard in the wind as it passes through the branches overhead. Beware his Spirit on the nights of May Eve, as many a poor lad and lass have been led astray by Him – for is He not the Green Lord of the Witches in His summer guise? Perhaps even more associated with the Whitethorn though, especially at May and All Hallows, is the Queen of Faerie, the May Queen and, perhaps to some, the Lady of the Witches Herself. It is She who is the Queen of Enchantment, the embodiment of the Whitethorn in all its magic and might, who will teach the Witch the deeper lore of Faerie and the Greenwood if approached in the right manner. Some say that to encounter Her on one of the above dates was to be whisked away to the Land of Faerie, there to serve Her for seven years. On your return you would be endowed with the gifts of healing and blessing, but would appear to other humans as old, wrinkled and ugly, as many more than seven years in human time would actually have passed. If you actually *were* lucky enough to be taken by Herself, then this would be a small price to pay, but folklore often hides a truth in disguise; to be taught the Mysteries by the Otherworldly Powers, one must be prepared to give up something valuable, as a gift requires a gift and nothing is gained by nothing. Those that work with the Powers know this and are willing to make sacrifices to gain their knowledge and wisdom.

For those that wish to make the attempt to walk with the Queen of Elphame, there is a way to begin to attract Her attention. You will need to have become adept at the "tree-merging" exercise given above for Blackthorn, having performed it many times also with a chosen, lone Whitethorn and been accepted by the tree. It is best to perform this exercise on either May Eve or all Hallows Eve, especially if these times fall on a Full Moon, but any time is actually acceptable. Go to your kin-tree and seat yourself with your back up against the trunk as normal. Perform the merging as usual and spend some time in communion with the Spirit, explaining what it is you desire. If you receive a negative response or feeling, end the contact in the usual manner, give offerings and leave. If the response is positive, continue in this manner. Begin to chant the following charm, over and over, whilst picturing yourself descending down through the trunk of the tree, into the roots. See the roots as hollow and, choosing a Way, follow it on down, into the ground below. Continue the charm all the while you do so:

"Queen of Elphame, I now seek,
Whitethorn's Dame, I do beseech,
That you my hand shall take and lead,
Within the Land that lies beneath."

If you are performing the exercise effectively, your visualisation should be accompanied by both a shift in perception (things take on a life/colour of their own) and a "dropping" sensation in the stomach, a bit like being in a lift that is going down a bit too quickly. When both these things happen, then you can expect results. At some point after this, you may feel a hand take yours in theirs, a hand on your shoulder guiding you, or a strong sense of direction overtake you. Go with whatever happens here and do not question or judge. It is at this point that teachings may be given, knowledge may be imparted, you may receive visions or who can say what else. It is unlikely that you will see the Queen Herself but, if so, consider yourself honoured and blessed and accept it for what it is – a mark of favour.

When your experiences end – and you will know when this is the case – you will most likely find yourself sitting back at the foot of your tree. If this is not the case, retrace your steps or simply will yourself back to where you began. End the working in your normal fashion with thanks to the Spirit of your tree and make your usual offerings of gratitude and respect. Stand up and walk away without looking back.

You may perform this exercise as often as you will, but it is better that you keep it for important issues and/or powerful times of year and those of the Land. Those who dwell within do not take kindly to being continually petitioned and you may find that your contacts become less strong or ignored altogether.

If you have been successful in your experiences with the Spirit of the Whitethorn and/or its Lady, it is at this point that you might consider taking a piece of wood for magical purposes, such as a wand, staff or Stang. It is unusual to find a piece of wood that is suitable for the two latter tools, as the Whitethorn is not generally known for growing branches large enough for this and to take one may actually do great damage to, or even kill, the tree itself. However, it should be quite possible to find a piece large enough for an excellent wand and this may be taken, observing all the etiquette of wood-taking from a living tree. A Whitethorn wand is the embodiment of enchantment, encapsulating as it does the virtue of the Faerie realms and their Queen and therefore is most suitable for use in casting spells of all kinds, although those concerning healing, blessings and Otherworld travel would be most appropriate.

The Entangled Thicket

Having reached this point, I hope it may now be becoming clear as to why I have used the exemplars of Blackthorn and Whitethorn as the main working themes of this book and as guides on the Ways of Witchery. As with the Craft itself, neither is wholly benevolent or malevolent, both contain elements of the uses/lore of each other and both may be readily worked with magically to contact Otherworldly Spirits of knowledge and wisdom, if not the actual Powers of Old Witchcraft Themselves, The Devil and the Dame. They may be seen, in a way, as guides into deeper aspects of the Craft than are normally more readily available or apprehended by initial study and may lead on to deeper understandings of the Ways of Witchery; they may be used as types of initiators if you will. However, here we come to a point of dichotomy - the core of this work - that I wish to address, which is the concept of duality, or seeming duality, both within the Craft and within the Witch's perception in general. I have entitled this chapter and section, The Entangled Thicket for this very reason, in that this phrase holds a key concept in some forms of Traditional Craft, which is apposite here.

The Entangled Thicket is used as a term to denote the seeming contradictions of perception encountered by many on the magical path – that of duality, isolation, confusion and perhaps not a little bit of despair. It is my hope that this book may help to clear some of this for the Seeker and let a little light in. Much of this concept derives from *The White Goddess*, by Robert Graves, previously mentioned and adopted/taken up by some Witch Traditions, but continues a theme already existent within Craft lore. I will here give a précis of the concept described by Graves, so that the reader unfamiliar with it may follow my meaning. However, I shall be using the idea of the Entangled Thicket in a slightly different and maybe more idiosyncratic - albeit related - way, more suited to the theme of this book and my understanding of the Ways of Witchery, so bear with me!

Graves describes three animals, the Lapwing, The Dog/ Hound and the Roebuck, as being Guardians of The Mysteries - the end result of magical practice and training, if you will - after three different manners.

The Lapwing guards by *Disguising* the Mysteries, by throwing seekers off the scent, by illusion, by trickery, by misdirection and deception. The Lapwing bird is well known for protecting its nest by pretending to have a broken wing, or being lame and running off in the opposite direction to the nest site, to deceive the attacker and drawing them away from the eggs/chicks. Thus *disguising* the nest site.

The Dog protects by *Guarding* the Mysteries, by inspiring fear and/or discouragement. Although originally described by Graves as one of the red-eared, white hounds of Annwfn, he is, more typically in British Craft lore, one of the legendary Black Hounds that appear on the path by your side and scares the willies out of you. Black Shuck is a well known example from East Anglia and other regions. Or like Cerebus guarding the gates to Hades (or Fluffy in Harry Potter if you like!). He inspires terror and, hence, *guards* his charge.

The Roebuck guards by *Hiding* the Mysteries; it runs into the forest and it and it's antlers can't be seen amongst the trees – literally you can't see the wood (antlers) for the trees. It literally IS the secret of the Mysteries and *hides* itself in the Entangled Thicket. And here we come to the point I am trying to make; it is the Thicket that we mostly see in our searching/learning, which is the illusion and not the reality of the Mysteries. The Entangled Thicket is the duality, the confusion, the seeming isolation of one thing from another, that often leads to despair in the search for knowledge and wisdom. It is the very thing that hides that which we seek and masks it from us, when all the time it is before us in plain sight, if only we could realise/see it.

Stuart Inman, Magister of the Clan of the Entangled Thicket, within the 1734 Witchcraft Tradition, puts it like this;

> *"While the lapwing represents the mind's ability to delude itself with romantic notions, desires and glamour, the Roebuck represents that more fundamental propensity towards dualistic thinking and resulting confusion."*
>
> *"The Roebuck is, if you like, the aim of the spiritual journey as represented in Arthurian legends by the various white stags or by the Questing Beast. Try to visualise it, you chased after a lapwing, happily and fruitlessly until you realised that it was leading you away from its nest. You turned around and found a huge dog barring your way. You got past the dog, either through*

strength and courage or by cunning, and there, instead of the lapwing's nest is the Thicket. You stare into it, but can't see the Roebuck, or to put it another way, you can't see the wood for the trees. The most obvious way to understand this is to consider the Roebuck hiding in the thicket, only the antlers visible, but they blend in with branches of the trees. Applied to our spiritual state, we are at once caught up in a dualistic experience of reality and at the same time exhibit a subtle confusion that masks that duality."

"I have previously suggested that our Craft can be understood through two fundamental aspects, the poetic understanding of the Mysteries and the entry into the dimension of Silence. The former suggests that we need the "mythic trappings" in order to fully understand our path in all its richness, devoid of reductive formulae, but without the deep insights arising from silent awareness they might well indeed be no more than trappings, just as meditative insight might never find a proper focus in experience without the mythical form. Thus, together, they render the practitioner able both to overcome the duality of experience and the finer discrimination that allows subtle discrimination to arise."

(Excerpts from an, as yet, unpublished manuscript shown to this author. Inman, Stuart: *Hidden In Plain Sight: A Primer of 1734 Traditional Witchcraft.*).

This is the reason that I have chosen to use the Blackthorn and the Whitethorn as the prime images of this work. As such, they exemplify both the illusion of duality – black/white, maleficia/beneficia, male/female, god/goddess – and at the same time the resolution of that duality in themselves, in that both contain the essence of the opposite and are actually neither in themselves. And here we find ourselves returning to the image of the Horned One as described in the Introduction, the Devil-Master of the Witches Himself; the two-horned One who bears the flaming torch between His horns – the ultimate resolution of all dualities in a single image.

This may be somewhat difficult to grasp as a concept, without any practical application and so I would like to offer a journey into the Entangled Thicket itself, as a starting point to both begin to resolve the illusions of all the dualities inherent in Witchery (and there are many) and to help the reader to understand that *they* are the Roebuck, the ultimate Mystery; until this is understood and appreciated then there *is* no resolution.

This working is, very loosely, based on the many different versions of the *Sleeping Beauty* tale, plus the teachings and lore of the Old Craft as I have had them handed on to me. As I have mentioned before, folklore and tales often contain grains of truth that are overlooked and this one is no exception. Within Sleeping Beauty, the Princess is put into an enchanted slumber and surrounded by an impenetrable thicket of thorns, only to be awakened by a Prince who has overcome the barriers placed in his way. It is not usually described what the thicket of thorns is comprised of but, being a thorny barrier, it can be of nothing other than Blackthorn and Whitethorn, the ultimate and original Entangled Thicket.

The journey is intended to at least make the seeker aware of the dualities both within themselves and those we project outwards, and to attempt to begin the resolution of these. The lessons and insights learned from this may be applied to the rest of the working elements in this book, with the continued aims of attaining the knowledge, power, wisdom and understanding inherent within the Ways of Witchery.

Before starting, make an infusion consisting of half Blackthorn and half Whitethorn leaves, taken with full permission from your kin-trees, having explained what it is you wish to do. Drink this about half an hour before beginning this working, to allow time for the essential virtues of the trees to be fully absorbed. Try to perform this working outside, in a safe place, but **not** at the site of either of your kin-trees – you must not favour either in this. If this is not possible, indoors is acceptable, but in this case, please have some greenery, etc. from both trees surrounding you. Seat yourself comfortably, as you may be there some time; compose yourself as for meditation or trance-work and begin. (It will be necessary to have read through this script several times beforehand to familiarise yourself completely with it, so that you may follow it with internal visualisation, without artificial aids).

The Journey into the Entangled Thicket.

Dressed warmly, you take up your Stang and begin your journey. Dusk is gathering as you stand at the end of a very long, straight and narrow country lane, that disappears into the distance. Known as the Roamers Road, or simply Roaming Road it has trees and bushes lining it on either side, which meet and bow over in the middle overhead, like walking down the aisle of a verdant tunnel. As you step forward you notice the trees on either side of you; dark, smooth and sharply thorny Blackthorn to your left and gnarled, scored, dark-silvery-grey, bedecked with red berries, the Whitethorn to your right. The trees rustle together in the light breeze as you walk down the path, carrying the musty scent of both death and sex to you on the wind, which both invigorates and stimulates you and at the same time sends cold shivers through you on your journey.

As you continue on down the road, you perceive what appears to be an optical illusion, in that the foliage on your left gets darker and darker, stretching into the distance, whereas the hedge on your right appears to grow brighter and brighter, almost shimmering in the gathering gloom. Both disappear off into the distance, where they seem to merge and become one. As you walk on, the illusion seems to change every now and then, so that the trees seem to swap over; sometimes the Blackthorn is on your left and the Whitethorn on your right, but then they seem to change over and appear on opposite sides. You grasp your Stang tightly and continue walking, deeper into the encroaching gloom.

At a certain point, the smooth road comes to an end and the metalled surface gives way to sand and gravel, leading on to a fork in the road. To your left the trail disappears into diseased looking trees that seem distinctly unhealthy, so you turn to your right and follow the path along.

The way is now sandy and soft underfoot and, in the rapidly deteriorating light, you can make out that it is bordered highly on either side by a mixture of both Black and White thorn intertwined, interspersed with the occasional Bramble and Fern. You hear the call of night birds, starting out on their own journeys and pull your garments more closely around you. The cry of a Fox rips through the air and startles you; you are not alone on your journey as the night begins to wake around you. Continuing on along the path, the Thorn trees seem to tower up on both sides, not quite blocking out what little light remains and you tightly grasp your Stang as you resolutely walk ahead. The way becomes even more sandy and slightly muddy and you have to watch your step here and there so as not to trip into the occasional shallow depression or ruts left by wheels in wetter weather. The hedging either side seems to be closing in on you, squeezing you into a more and more narrow passage, the thorns beginning to grasp at your clothing as you pass; sharp, dark Blackthorn spines seem to reach out at you, supported by the shorter and stouter Whitethorn spikes, intertwined in an almost impassable tangle. The branches loom even higher and rustle as the night creatures scurry through the undergrowth.

Abruptly, the road makes a sharp turn and you are faced with an almost impenetrable wall of intertwined branches; the dark and light, Blackthorn and Whitethorn, so interwoven as to be impossible to tell where one begins and the other ends. It is almost completely dark now and so you pick your way very carefully along, almost feeling your way with your heightened senses and the small amount of light from the Moon and stars above you that finds its way through the thick, entangled branches. Shortly, to your right, there is a barely discernible gap in the Thorny wall and, to those that know the way, this is the gateway through which you must pass to the glade within. You turn and carefully push your way past the wickedly sharp thorns, using your Stang to gently hold back the branches and to gain you access, sliding carefully and cautiously between the entwined boughs. It is now inky black and you find the way with difficulty, but press on in your desire to reach your goal. Gently testing the way with both feet and Stang, you finally brush past the last few branches and step out into a clear space, completely hidden and surrounded by the encircling Thorn trees.

The space before you is roughly circular, of what appears in this light to be lightly turfed ground and is gentle underfoot, after your long journey. At the very centre of this glade is a large Stang, planted securely in the ground. Between its forked tines is a brightly burning, thick candle, lighting the whole area with a welcome and illuminating glow. The staff initially appears to be made of both Black and White-thorn, intertwined and growing together; in fact the Stang itself now seems to be a living thing,neither one tree nor the other but of a different type entirely, rooted firmly and strongly into the Land. On the ground, directly in front of the Stang, is a wide, shallow pan, made out of what appears to be bronze. It is filled with water and the light from between the horns of the Stang shines brightly on the surface.

There is an air of sanctity and holiness in this place, but at the same time, the air is alive with scents and vibrations and you feel alive with a wild energy that is strangely both sacred and profane.

The choice is now yours; do you step forward into the Glade and gaze within the shining waters?

Take as long a time as you need here and fully immerse yourself in whatever you may find.

Once you have completed your journey, whatever your choice or result, return to normal, waking reality in your usual fashion, if your working has not already brought you there. Take some time to absorb your experiences (and this may well be an ongoing process over some period, so allow for this), and be aware that your perceptions may well have shifted, in however subtle a manner. As a token of this you may wish to create a small "charm" to use in future work, or carry about you, embodying the nature of your experiences and realisations. From each of your kin-trees, both Blackthorn and Whitethorn, take three small twigs (observing all the usual rules of etiquette), which only need to be about a thumbs-length in size. Place these all together, side-by-side. Bind one end of the bundle together with black thread and the other end with white thread. In the middle, tie a thread of the colour that you most associate with your experiences, that sums them up for you and reminds you of their force and virtue. Keep this about you, maybe in a small pouch or suchlike, both when next you embark on the above journey – as you WILL want to do it more than once – and in your magical workings. You will find that it gives you a reminder and a greater focus of the way things can be seen differently and, maybe, a greater power to your magics because of it.

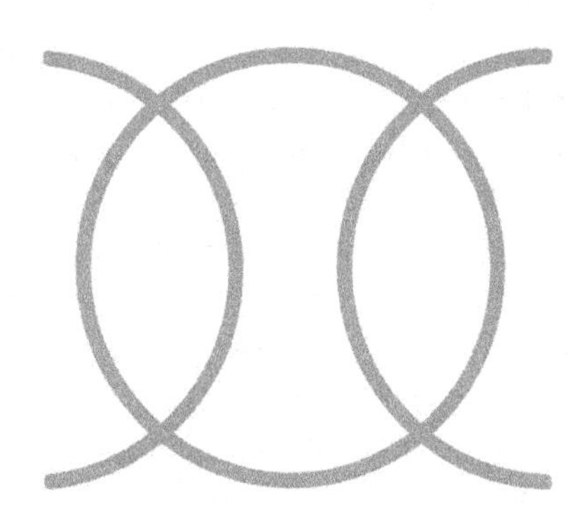

By the Light of Lilith's Lantern

"The ceaseless ebbing and flowing of the tides as Earth, Moon and Sun move in their eternal cosmic dance are the most fundamental rhythms that move and shape our being."
Levannah Morgan - "Mirror, Moon and Tides" in "Hands of Apostasy: Essays on Traditional Witchcraft".

The Moon is a prime image both of shifting duality, of opposites and conjoinings, possessing both light and dark aspects and of those in-between, and also of the many Ways of Witchery, being a prime image in the Craft and its Magic. But why Lilith? She does not originate from these shores and many would see Her as purely a Middle-Eastern deity with no connection to British magic. However, "Lilith's Lantern" is an arcane term in English poetry and folklore for our closest celestial orb and aspects of Her legends and lore have long been adopted and intertwined within the mythology and workings of Old Craft Witches; hence She is more than a fitting image to illuminate the Mysteries of the Moon.

The lore of this Power has come a long way; She originated in ancient Sumeria, daughter of Ninlil, goddess of grain and the wind, who gave birth to the Moon. She was associated both with Owls, jackals and "the dogs of the night", Her powers being greatest at the time of the Waning Moon. She was said to be the leader of the "Lilu", a race of female, vampiric spirits of the air who, manifesting by night during stormy weather, preyed on pregnant women. By stealing the "nocturnal emissions" of sleeping men (or semen spilled by masturbation, or offered up in sacrifice), Lilith conceived a race of demons/elves/faeries, which were said to be the progenitors of the Witches.

Passing through Canaan, She became the first wife of Adam, according to the Hebrews, created before Eve as a sexual plaything for the first Man. Refusing to accept the subordinate position during sex, as She considered Herself at least an equal to Adam, She departed in a frustrated rage. She shape-shifted into the form of an owl and became the succubus ghost in the night, once again causing women to miscarry and stealing men's ejaculate to create demons and elementals. She was given the titles of "harlot vampire", "mother of witches", "beautiful maiden" and "screech owl" amongst others. The actual name "Lilith", comes from the Hebrew "*Layil*", meaning "night" and Sumerian "*Lil*", meaning either "wind" or "death"; quite literally the death that comes on the night wind.

Conversely, Her lore also has another side. To some, it is She who is considered to be the Shekinah, the divine feminine presence that resided in the Ark of the Covenant in the Temple of Solomon in Jerusalem, before it was conquered by the Persians and the Ark carried off to Babylon. The Shekinah – wife to the Old Testament Yahweh – has been seen as Sophia, The Divine Principle of Wisdom, and is said to have been with Yahweh since the beginning of creation. The Gnostics say that, "*Lilith knows the secret of darkness and light, and she unites Heaven and Hell. Her aspect is that of wisdom.*" ("*The Gnostic Gospels*", Dr. E. Pagels – see Bibliography). It is as this essentially feminine spirit that Lilith is linked with the Moon, particularly in its Dark phase; thus giving rise to the tales of depriving pregnant women of their unborn children. We can see here a distinctly patriarchal outlook on the female menstrual cycle, Lilith's refusal to be a subservient sexual partner, refusing to service Men and refusing to simply be a brood-mare for their children. This is a distinctly misogynistic attitude and outlook, one that has no place in Old Craft and, hence - because of Her refusal to accept this attitude - one reason why Lilith is so honoured in Traditional Witch lore.

In addition to her role as the "wife" of the Old Testament Yahweh, Lilith was also linked in lore to the legends of the Watchers. She was considered a partner of the fallen angel Lucifer, a wife of the Angel of Death Samael-Azrael and also the consort of the leader of the "*seirim*" or hairy ones, the goat-god Azazel. It is through their agencies, that Lilith begets the compatriots of the Witches – the races of Elves and Faerie creatures who delight in dancing to the light of the Moon at night.

Travelling westwards into Europe, Lilith became associated with the goddesses Diana, Hecate and Aradia/Herodias, particularly in the magical lore of the Romany travellers, who were highly likely to have introduced much of Her lore into the magical current of British Witchcraft from an early period. In so linking Lilith with these other Lunar Powers, She became even more intricately linked to the Moon and her tides and phases. At some point, she appears to have acquired twelve daughters which, with Herself, comes to a total of thirteen; this has been seen by occultists such as Doreen Valiente and C.G. Leland to link Her even more closely with the Moon, being a possible number of Full Moons in a year (more on that number later). Valiente sees Lilith as "*the personification of the dangerous feminine glamour of the Moon*", equating Her with Hecate (*ABC of Witchcraft*), and Graves in the *White Goddess* connects her with both the Welsh Flower goddess, Blodeuwedd, and also the Black/Blue Hag deity, Annis; he bases this on the Owl image, assumed by all of these Powers in their magical ecstasis. As progenitrix of the Elven and Faerie races, She is seen as a type of "Faerie Godmother" and particularly honoured within some lines of British Traditional Craft, as it is through and by these Folk that much magical lore has been learned. Contact with these non-human races is a vital constituent in the teachings of some of the Ways of Witchery and a method by which valuable esoteric connections have been maintained over the centuries. Within East Anglian Craft, Lilith is particularly honoured by some within the rites practised to acquire the legendary Toad Bone. As sister/lover to the legendary Cain - The Man in the Moon - it is by Her light and under Her auspices that the attempt to snatch the magical bone is made and to Her that prayers are offered for its safe retrieval. Indeed, in some forms, the operation to acquire the famed Toad Bone is actually named, "The Waters of the Moon". She is, therefore, more than a fitting image to exemplify the Mysteries and fluctuations of our Lunar companion, in both their light and dark phases, and all in-between.

Lunar Rhythms and Rounds.

Before I continue with the more particularly esoteric side of Moon lore, I would first like to address the physical side of the revolutions, tides and periods of our nearest neighbour in space. Whilst much of magical working, it's timing, type and style of meaning is governed by the Moon, there seems to be a curious lack of basic knowledge amongst a lot of practitioners as to the actual mechanics of the movements of the Moon, both on the physical level and as to how it specifically influences the energies we work with. Whilst many other forces and factors may need to be considered in any act of magic, be it charm, spell, spirit calling, divination rite or the timing of a festival perhaps, as our nearest and most influential celestial power-house, a thorough working-knowledge of the patterns and cycles of the Moon needs to be first and foremost in the armoury of any Witch worthy of the name. Some practitioners, I have found, dismiss this practical knowledge as unnecessary as, they say, they are not dealing with the physical Moon, but the energies it governs, moves and shapes; but this is to miss the point entirely. It's like saying that you can heal the human body of illness, without having a knowledge of how it functions properly when it is whole and well. Again, I have read in various places that a "Moon" lasts for roughly 27 to 29 days, changing "monthly"; this is patently absurd and totally incorrect as I shall soon explain. Without at least a passing, theoretical knowledge of the basic tides and rhythms of the Moon, one cannot hope to properly gauge how, why, when and where to use them in any given situation. I hope here to give at least a minimum working level of these things, so that the reader may have a firm platform from which to plan their own practices, with knowledge and understanding.

Like the Earth, the Moon is a ball of physical material, made up of many different elements (on many different levels), circling in space. In its particular situation, it both orbits our own planet Earth and, because the Earth does so, necessarily also circles the Sun. For our purposes at the moment, we need only be immediately concerned with the Moon's orbit of the Earth, but it is well to keep in mind that there will also be seasonal variations and differing effects, because of our own planet's orbit of the Sun. These effects are secondary, but no less important than the primary ones.

The Moon orbits at an average distance of 240,000 miles from the Earth, her radius being 1,080 miles, compared to the 3,960 miles of the Earth; a ratio in size of 3:11. The Moon is held in its orbit by the gravitational force of the Earth and, in its turn, also exacts its own gravitational forces on us. Like the Earth, the Moon is not exactly spherical and the Earth's gravity pulls the larger hemisphere towards us, hence we always see the same face of the Moon presented to us, the "dark side" is permanently turned away.

The Moon has two cycles that are most important to us; the *Sidereal* month and the *Synodic* or, more pertinently, the *Lunar* month.

The Sidereal month is the period of time that the physical Moon takes to make one revolution of the Earth and to come back to its "starting point", based on the position of the fixed stars, as viewed from a point on the Earth. The Moon takes roughly an hour to move the distance of its own diameter, covering thirteen degrees in one day. It therefore takes slightly less than 28 days, in actuality 27.322 days, to complete one revolution of the Earth.

The Lunar month, or Lunation, is the period of time it takes from one Full Moon to another, which depends on the relative positions of the Earth, Moon **and** Sun, and is slightly longer, taking 29.53059 days; this is the cycle that is considered most important within magical practice in general.

There are 13.368 Sidereal months in a Solar, calendar year and there are 12.368 Lunar months. This is where the confusion comes in around the number 13; whilst there are definitely 13 revolutions of the Moon around the Earth in a calendar year, there only *may* be 13 **Full** moons, depending on when they actually occur in our date-driven calendar. Most magical/traditional calendars count from Full moon to Full moon and it will depend on the dating in our usual, Solar calendar, as to how many of these there are within any given year. The same holds true for calendars counting from the New moon of course; it just depends on the "cut-off" point, date-wise.

Having, hopefully, shown the difference between these two important cycles, I will now concentrate on the Lunar month, as this is the cycle that most Witches and magical practitioners use, or mean, when talking about the Moon periods. It is certainly the cycle that has the greatest effect on the Earth, its tides and rhythms and humans in general.

The Lunar month can be seen to begin with the *New moon*, a thin sliver of light, a crescent shaped like a reversed letter "C". As each day progresses during the *waxing* period, this grows bigger and "fills out", until it is a *quarter* moon (a half-circle), progresses through the *waxing gibbous* phase (more than half but not full, increasing), until it reaches the *Full moon* phase (a complete, bright, round disc), taking about thirteen days to occur. The Full moon phase lasts for roughly three days - the actual point of Full falling on the middle day - after which the *waning* phase begins. The Moon appears to decrease in size, through *waning gibbous*, to *quarter*, then after about thirteen days again, it appears as a thin sliver, this time appearing as a "C", right way round.

After this, the Moon seems to disappear from view, again for roughly three days, the counterpoint to Full. This is known as the *Dark moon* phase, or the Dark of the Moon (the actual Dark, like the Full, being the middle of the three days and also, confusingly for most people, is the actual *astronomical* New moon). The cycle then repeats with the New, crescent, moon and so on, in a never ending round. The light we see, it should be needless to say, is the light of the Sun shining on the part of the surface of the Moon that is not blocked by the Earth; the Moon has no light of its own - it does not shine independently.

During the period of the Lunar month, the Moon also has a Lunar Day, which is the time between consecutive Moon rises; these are the rhythms that very visibly affect our oceanic tides on Earth and all forms of water and, less visibly, the atmosphere above us and the Earth's crust beneath our feet - these also rise and fall with the tides. There are exactly two Lunar tides each day, taking an average of 12 hours and 26 minutes between each; the Moon rises approximately 52 minutes later each day, hence the progression in the timing of high and low tides. The Moon's gravitational pull lifts the waters of the oceans (etc.), on the side of the Earth facing the Moon (high tide), and these follow the Moon in it's orbit around the Earth; once the Moon has passed a particular place, the waters subside (low tide). High tides will always occur at the same two positions of the Moon in the sky at any given location, these being opposite one another (one position is always beneath the horizon). Centrifugal force causes a similar effect on the opposite side of the Earth to the Moon, hence there are two high tides and two low tides in one day. The highest, *spring tides*, occur two or three days after a New or Full Moon; the lowest, *neap tides*, occur the same period after a waxing or waning quarter Moon.

Finally, in this rather "technical" section, I would like to mention one of the most awe-inspiring of Lunar phenomena, which is the Eclipse. A Lunar eclipse can only occur at Full moon, when the satellite passes from right to left, through the shadow caused by the Earth, extinguishing the Sun's light for up to several hours. Lunar eclipses can be seen by everyone on the night side of the Earth, at that time, and are only possible because of the relative sizes of the Sun, Moon and Earth. The shadow of the Earth passes diagonally over the face of the Moon, cutting off the reflected light of the Sun, the shadow actually travelling from left to right. During the period of totality (i.e. total darkness, full eclipse), the Moon often seems to take on a reddish or coppery hue, because of the refracted light around it, which gives rise to the name "Blood Moon" in some quarters (there is nothing magical or particularly potent about this – it is purely a physical phenomenon). The curve of the Earth's shadow can clearly be seen as it passes across the Moon, proving that our planet is actually spherical in shape and about three times the size of the Moon. On average, there are two Lunar eclipses in a year; however, in other years, there can be up to three, one or none.

Personal Moon Rhythms

Having explained the physical side of things, I would now like to go on to talk about the more non-physical, esoteric effects that the Moon has for us. It is now well-known by Science that the Moon's gravitational pull exerts an influence on just about everything on Earth, however minute. For the Witch, this extends to the invisible forces around us all the time, and is the biggest/strongest effect of all the celestial bodies round us. Within the magical world, it is a given that the Universe is pervaded by energy that the Witch uses in all of their magic, be it spell-crafting, healing, cursing or anything else and this energy goes by many names. Some just call it Energy, to others it is known as Power, Ond, Sprowl, Prana, Ki or Mana. In my own region of East Anglia, it is known as Spirament or simply Virtue. This force is *also* acted upon by the tides of the Moon and these tides are what are utilised in the practice of magic or occult workings in general. It is here that I would like to state the main contention of this section and, basically, what I am trying to get across – it is the **flow** of the energy that counts, pulled by the Moon, **not** the amount of energy. You will read in many books/ publications/websites that there is more energy at the Full of the Moon and less at the Dark of the Moon, and you should time your spells accordingly. This is just not so. There is **no more** energy at any one time of the Moon's cycle than any other, especially at Full and Dark; it is the **flow** and **pull** of the Moon tides in certain directions that counts, not the amount of energy available. It is a known fact within modern physics, that there is only a finite amount of energy in the Universe, as no more can be created and it cannot be destroyed. This is also true for the unseen side of the Universe, within the realms of Virtue or Spirament; a finite amount of this energy also exists, although it is indeed a vast resource to call upon. Therefore, there is no more, nor less, available at any given time than another, it is what it is doing, how it is moving, it's impetus if you like, that counts.

The Waxing tide of the Moon is considered to be the best time for works of increase, for growth, for gain, to attract things to you; this is because the pull of the Moon tide is in that direction. The Moon's effect on the energy around us during this period is in that direction; the flow is to increase. It doesn't mean that there is any more energy to work with, simply that it is better to do that type of working at that time, as you are going with the natural tides of energy, which will add impetus to your work in the pertinent direction. Likewise, the Waning tide of the Moon is considered to be the optimum time for works of decrease, for banishment, to get rid of things and, should it be needed, for cursings, because that is the direction of the flow of the energies. The Moon appears to be decreasing in size – not energy – and is pulling in that direction, so it makes sense to utilise that flow in the work of the Witch at that time. The period of both the Full and Dark moons is a period of stillness, of quietude, even of stagnation if you like, as there is no pull, no movement or flow of energy, in either direction. At these times, works of introspection, meditation, spirit-flight, offerings or worship are appropriate, as nothing is pushing either way and there is no tide to be made use of. This can amply be seen if you are on a beach at either high or low tide – nothing is happening. For a period, the water stays at the same level and neither gets higher up the beach or lower; if you throw something that floats into the sea at that point, it will neither be washed away or brought onto shore, it will just stay there. Once the tide changes, then the sea will flow again and this is just what happens with the tides of the invisible energies and is what the wise Witch takes advantage of. This is part of that knowledge of the Witch, that leads to further understanding, both of themselves and of the world/s around them.

To continue this question of the use of (Lunar), tidal energies, it is also vital for the Witch to be aware of these rhythms within themselves and how they are affected by them. To work effectively and efficiently in bringing about the desired-for results in magic working, the Witch needs to actually feel this Virtue running in their own veins and to feel the flow of it, as it is pulled by the tides of the Moon. Leaving aside the question of when it is the right time to perform any particular rite, not knowing when the *individual* is firing on all cylinders is just as bad as utilising an inappropriate external tide. It is a given that the Moon affects the physical rhythms of the female menstrual cycle – this is one reason that the Moon is linked to the female reproductive cycle and is often seen as a goddess in certain pantheons – and it is also becoming more widely known that it also affects the male body on a similar level, but after a different manner. The serious Witch also needs to be aware of how the energy tides and flows affect them personally, the better to use these effects within their rites. Not every Witch will respond in the same manner to the same tide, be that waxing, waning, Full or Dark and it is extremely advantageous to know when the individual's optimum tide/

time is. Some Witches function best at waxing, others at Full, some at waning or Dark, but without *knowing* when this is, then it is impossible to take full advantage of it. Witchcraft is a particularly Lunar orientated practice, many of its rites and workings being geared specifically to different aspects and times of the Moon, not to mention specific spells and charms which can only be done at certain times. It is of immense benefit for the Witch to be able to utilise not only the actual tide of the Moon, but to couple it with their *own* optimum tide, the better to achieve the best possible results in their workings.

It is fairly simple to discover when any individual's particular optimum time/phase is, but it needs work and dedication, so some effort is required. Try the following exercise on each phase of the Moon (i.e. New, Waxing, Full, Waning and Dark) – and it may need multiple tries for each phase to determine the optimum time, which is where the dedication and effort come in. This is a variation on the old technique of *Utiseta*, or Sitting Out, as practised in the Scandinavian countries and the places of their influence, particularly within the East Anglian magical tradition. This is an important and valuable technique, whereby the Witch "sits out" at night under the stars and other influences, to receive visions, to hear the inner voices and to commune with the celestial bodies and their forces. You will need a secure and undisturbed space where you can sit or lie down outside, where you have a clear view of the Moon. It is better if you can perform this at a local point of power in the Land, such as a barrow mound, stone circle, cemetery or suchlike, but this is not always possible these days, or even strictly necessary. Failing this, try to ensure that there is either a Blackthorn or Whitethorn in the vicinity (your kin tree?), the better to take advantage of any help they may give you. Make sure that you will be comfortable and warm, as this exercise may take some time. If it is impossible for you to do this out of doors, sit at an open window with the interior lights switched off. Your eyes will need about twenty minutes to adjust to night vision, so use the time to make yourself comfortable.

Because this is a very individual exercise there are no instructions other than to enter a light trance state and to go with the flow. However, there is one addition that may help in this practice and that is the use of a traditional Moon salve, prepared especially for Lunar orientated workings, the better to contact the forces you wish to work with. I will give the basic recipe here, but you will see later how it may be adapted in its composition and make-up to be better suited to the individual. In a glazed or enamel pan (not metal), gently warm some oil in which Willow Bark has been infused. (For details on infused oils and related preparations, see my previous work, *Treading the Mill*). Originally, this salve would have been made of tallow, or animal fat, but it is better these days if you can use Coconut oil, as this has a sympathy with the Moon. Failing that, any light, vegetable oil will suffice, but **not** Sunflower oil, for obvious reasons! Add to the warm oil a handful each of Jasmine flowers and Honesty flowers (leaves or seed heads are also fine). Allow these to infuse for 20 minutes or so, being careful not to overheat the oil, so that the plants are cooked! After this time, strain the plant material off through a fine sieve, muslin cloth, or similar, and return the oil to the gentle heat. Add about 10% by volume of pure beeswax to the oil and let this melt. Once all has melded together, take the pan off the heat and put aside to cool. Before the beeswax has set the salve, mix in a few drops of Eucalyptus essential oil and a few drops of Myrrh essential oil. Pour into clean, glass jars and leave to set. You now have a safe, basic Moon salve, which may be rubbed into the sensitive points on the body – temples, inner wrists, inner thighs, back of knees – before beginning this exercise. Because all the ingredients used are held to be under the influence of the Moon, you will have an extra advantage before you start the exercise and this should help in your contacts.

Check on the time of Moon rise and, unless you are working on the Dark phase, you should try to ensure that the Moon is visible throughout your working. For this exercise you are going to let yourself be enveloped in the Moonlight and attempt to feel the effects it has on you, on an energetic level. If you are using the Dark phase, simply gaze up into the night sky above and allow yourself to experience the forces in the darkness.

For Moon phases other than Dark, sit or lay in the Moonlight, watch as it shines all over and around you like shimmering, silver mercury. You can pick handfuls up and watch it stream through your fingers like fine sand or silvery water. How does that make you feel? Reach out with your inner vision and feelings and see what sensations it gives rise to within you.

For the Dark of the Moon workings, visualise yourself slipping deeper and deeper into the darkness. There is no danger here and you can return whenever you wish. Let yourself drift out into the inky blackness; it feels like sinking into beautiful velvet or the softness of unseen feathers. It is gentle, soft and welcoming. Or is it? How do you feel in this black, silent world?

Spend as long as you feel you need to on each of your exercises and, when you feel the time is right or you have experienced all you need to or can on that attempt, gradually bring yourself back to normal awareness. Immediately make notes of what you have felt, thought and sensed, then have a little something to eat or drink to bring you back to full awareness. Take note of any dreams you may have on that and subsequent nights, as they may reveal more information for you.

As I have said, this process may take a little time to complete, as you will need to perform this exercise on each of the Moon tides, probably several times over, to be able to compare successfully the sensations you experience on each and to determine your most powerful/optimum time for working. This will require patience and application, but will be well worth it when you can know in advance when you will be at your best, magical condition and plan your future workings accordingly. In addition to this, having determined your personal "power phase", you may adapt your Moon salve accordingly. Make sure that you prepare it at the time when your personal power is at its height. Collect the ingredients during this phase and combine them together at this time, perhaps whilst softly whispering your own charms into the mixture at the same time. You may then also wish to expose the finished salve to the rays of the Moon, overnight, during your optimum time.

The wise Witch is always aware of their own situation however, and knows that nothing is permanent or fixed. You may find that over a period of time - and I am talking years here, not mere months - that the phase in which you worked no longer seems to be so potent or comfortable for you. This is natural and not unexpected, as all things change. Just as the Blackthorn and Whitethorn may be different shades of each other and grow together, so may the Moon tides exhibit the same for you. If you find yourself becoming less effective or uncomfortable within your personal timings, then perform the exercise above and see what results you get. It may be that your circumstances, time of life, magical abilities/knowledge have changed such that your original "power-time" is no longer appropriate for you and needs to be changed. Be aware and adaptable and your magic and Craft will be the better for it.

Seasonal Lunations.

I mentioned above that, along with the monthly, Lunar tides, there are also annual, seasonal variations in effects and meanings of the Moon's influences. There are many and various "Moon calendars" available to the Witch these days, most of which are totally contradictory and are based on various histories. A lot take the names of Indigenous American tribal moons (mixed together, not from one tribe or Nation) and apply them across the board, with no actual valid coherence. Some mix together these and the names in old almanacs and make a "calendar" that is deemed to be valid across the magical world. Whilst all these calendars have some virtue to them, none appear to be based in a single, actual, working tradition that has relevance. What is appropriate in America, for example, may not be appropriate in Belgium or Greece; different places have their own rhythms and tides which may be completely alien to others. To offset this, I would like to share here a calendar that is rooted in English, magical tradition, which has worked well for Old Craft Witches over many, many years and that I have used in my East Anglian practice to great benefit. This will, I hope, give an example of a cohesive calendar, not put together from disparate parts. It was passed on to me in the late 1970's, from a Family Tradition of Old Craft Witches, in the South East of England. It had been in use within their Family for an unknown period – but a lengthy one – before that. This Family had been living in the same area for at least several generations before this time (they claimed a very long ancestry), and were renowned wood-carvers, passing on the skills from generation to generation, harvesting their material from the local woods. It has the advantage of being both in continuous use for an appreciable period of time and having come out of a knowledge of the natural and magical tides of one area, not a mixture of these from different places and times. As a practical, magical calendar, it has some attributes that others may not have, so I give it here as a working example, which other Traditional Witches may like to take up – especially if living in England or the British Isles where it is most appropriate – or adapt to the conditions in their own country of working, based on local, magical traditions and experiences. (Comparisons with the calendar advanced by Robert Graves in *The White Goddess* will be inevitable, but this has the advantage of working **with** the natural rhythms of the year, rather than being based on fixed, calendar dates, that take no notice of the changing patterns of a natural cycle of progression).

The calendar starts with the first New Moon in January and the name used covers the whole period of that Lunation, i.e. the whole Lunar month. Full Moons – as in other, modern Moon calendars – are named separately and more of that anon. In order, the Moons are named as follows; Snow Moon, Death Moon, Awakening Moon, Planting Moon, Grass Moon, Rose Moon, Lightning Moon, Harvest Moon, Berry Moon, Hunters Moon, Falling Leaf Moon, Long Night Moon. If there is another New Moon in the year – another possibility for the famed "13th. Moon" - this is called the Ice Moon. The year begins again with the New Moon, the Snow Moon, in January. I think the names of the Moons are self-explanatory, so I won't comment further, other than to reiterate that this is based on a British pattern and may not be absolutely appropriate elsewhere.

In addition to this, the periods of the Full Moons are each named after trees. This aspect may, if desired, be acknowledged in Full Moon rites, sprigs of the particular tree decorating the Stang/altar and the spirit of the tree being invoked as part of the work. (If possible, the rite should take place under/near the particular tree but, again, this is not always possible and so should be looked upon as something desirable, rather than absolutely essential). In order from the Snow Moon, the trees follow this pattern; the Ash, the Alder, the Birch, the Whitethorn, the Oak, the Willow, the Hazel, the Apple, the Elder, the Holly, the Blackthorn, the Yew. If there is an Ice Moon in the year, the tree honoured is the Pine or Fir tree.

Coupled with each tree, is a spirit animal and a virtue (there are a lot of "Virtue's" in East Anglian Craft, which is why we also use the term Spirament as well!). This can be quite confusing to simply state it, so I will show all of these in a table for ease of observation and use.

Moon Name	*Tree*	*Animal*	*Virtue*
Snow Moon	*Ash*	*Magpie*	*Knowledge*
Death Moon	*Alder*	*Badger*	*Strength/ Force*
Awakening Moon	*Birch*	*Toad*	*Beginnings/ Initiation*
Planting Moon	*Whitethorn*	*Barn Owl*	*Fecundity*
Grass Moon	*Oak*	*Ram*	*Power/ Spirament*
Rose Moon	*Willow*	*Bee*	*Enchantment*
Lightning Moon	*Hazel*	*Salmon*	*Wisdom*
Harvest Moon	*Apple*	*Goose*	*Exaltation/ Inebriation*
Berry Moon	*Elder*	*Swine*	*Ripeness/ fruition*
Hunter's Moon	*Holly*	*Wolf*	*Bravery/ Heroism*
Falling Leaf Moon	*Blackthorn*	*Raven*	*Decay*
Long Night Moon	*Yew*	*Wren*	*Eternity/ Death*
(Ice Moon	*Pine/Fir*	*Stag*	*Illumination)*

Although this can seem to be quite complex it is, in fact, very simple to use and follow, if utilised as a working pattern that cycles through the calendar year. Within this system, the Witch, knowing their own personal rhythms, according to their own, personal Moon tides can pinpoint the best time, *for them*, to perform any particular magical working, spirit offering, devotional or developmental work. The personal, coupled with the wider seasonal rhythms are capable of propelling the Witch on a working round that encompasses many different aspects of the Craft, which is quite profound in its scope. It also allows for individual development within the system, due to changing tides, both internal and external, and doesn't bind the Witch to a set pattern of working.

The observant reader may, at this point, be asking why there has so far been no mention of deity, of The Powers, of the Gods and Goddesses within this particular scheme of things. The reason for this is quite simple and twofold. Firstly, there is no need for them in this particular system and many Traditional Witches do not actually work with deities anyway, preferring to interact either directly with the spirit world in terms of an animistic relationship or with individual spirits in the form of familiars, the Faerie or other similar Beings. Secondly, unlike modern forms of witchcraft, those Old Craft practitioners that do work with deity, tend to acknowledge the Powers in the forms of the Devil and variants (as previously discussed), the Queen of Faerie (under various names and guises), or both and not in a polytheistic manner, as in modern practice. Names are rarely used (unless dedicated to a particular deity), the terms Him and Her, the Old Lad and the Lass, the Master and the Dame, Witchfather and Witchmother, being much more common. They are considered to be ever-present and not dependant on being Called or Worshipped, and so will be there, within the working praxis, whatever is being done. Of course, this is not to say that Traditional Crafters don't Call upon the Powers, as they most certainly do, but not in a conventional manner. It very much depends on what is being done at the time and who/what needs to be called upon for the work in hand.

Working with the Moon

We have seen above how it is possible to link the Witch's personal energies with the different phases of the Moon, both throughout one Lunation and also throughout the year, working to achieve the best possible times for any type of working and development that they may need or wish to focus on. Apart from purely spell-crafting or charm-making, in what Ways may the Witch practically make use of this intimate connection to the Moon? The first Way I would like to discuss, is the actual gathering of the forces, virtues or energies of the Moon into themselves, which they may then utilise for whatever work they have in mind. This creates a direct link with the desired energies – available at any phase of the Moon – which may also be harboured or stored for later work. Variations of this method are known under various names, but I know it as "Calling Down the Moon". This is not to be confused with the modern rite of "Drawing Down the Moon", as it calls on no deities and is a solo personal rite, performed alone without a group. (When I originally asked one of my Old Craft teachers whether there was an equivalent to the modern rite of Drawing Down the Moon, I was given exceedingly short shrift and was told that Old Crafters "didn't do that sort of thing". It was considered disrespectful to the deities concerned and contrary to Traditional Craft practice).

In his book, "*Cecil Williamson's Book of Witchcraft*", (Troy Books, see Bibliography), Steve Patterson gives an exceedingly interesting version of a rite known as "Calling Down the Moon", as practised by Williamson and Cornish Witches. This is performed as a form of self-hypnosis, seated on the edge of a cliff overlooking the sea, gazing at the Moon and its reflected light pathways on the water. The rite I know of is rather different, deriving from a different source, and is performed as follows.

The Witch first needs to make or acquire (making your own is best), a wand made from Willow wood; if it can be of the type that has a natural spiral grown around it, into the wood, so very much the better. At the tip of this wand, there needs to be affixed a small, polished, piece of clear, quartz crystal, either round or egg-shaped. The wand needs to be of the traditional size, i.e. a cubit in length, measured on the Witch's own body and the crystal should be *no bigger* than half a thumb-size. This wand should be kept wrapped and put away when not in use, as it must never be exposed to direct sunlight, being reserved specifically for Moon-working only. In addition to the wand, the Witch will need a small bowl of, preferably, glazed ceramic, not metal. The inside of the bowl must be plain with no pattern and filled to the top with fresh spring water, that you have gathered yourself from a natural source on the evening/night of the rite. (Alternatively, a wide, shallow, ceramic pan, filled to the brim. The reason for this will become obvious in practice). Place both of these on a suitable tree-stump, flat-topped rock or small table, about waist height, outdoors under the light of the Moon. Wherever possible, position the bowl/table, such that the light of the Moon is reflected in the water in the bowl (hence filling it to the top and/or using a wide, shallow pan). This is not truly essential, but much to be desired. (If the rite is to be performed at the Dark of the Moon, position the table/bowl as if you would be looking up at the Moon over it, i.e. face the position of the Moon in the sky, even though you can't see it). The only other item you may need is a small stool or chair, if you are going to sit later, for further work. The rite may be performed at any phase of the Moon, but it is best to make the first attempt at the time of the Witch's optimum tide, for best results.

When all is in readiness, stand a little away from your table and take some time to calm your mind, attaining that state in which ritual is to be performed. When you are ready, take up your wand in both hands and raise it on high, at arms length, so that, from your point of view, the crystal at the tip is positioned over the Moon itself. The crystal should be in such a position that it is lit by the light of the Moon. In your magical mind, identify the light shining in/through the crystal with the Moon itself; it IS the Moon and all its force and Virtue. Gaze intently at the crystal until this is totally clear and identified in your mind. If you desire, you may softly intone a charm/chant of your composing that encapsulates this, *without* making it an invocation to a deity; we are dealing with the Calling of a Force here, not the summoning of a god. Now, still envisioning the light of the Moon within the crystal, gently and slowly begin to lower the wand towards the bowl of water. As you do so, **see** the shining Lunar Virtue trailing behind it, like the tail of a comet, creating a link in a direct line to the Moon. Slowly and gradually lower the wand, all the time Calling in your magical mind the force of the Moon down with it. Lower the wand further until it finally touches the surface of the water and the tip is immersed in it. At this point, see the energy Called from the Moon lighting up the water in the bowl, until it is shining brightly; the whole bowl is glowing with Lunar power and Virtue. Identify in your mind the water in the bowl with the light in and from the Moon; it IS the Moon and all its force and Virtue. Raise your wand and repeat your actions, Calling down the force of the Moon into the bowl of water, over and over again, until you feel the whole bowl vibrating with the energy that you have Called down.

If working at the Dark of the Moon, the visualisation is slightly different. Raise your wand to the point in the sky where the Moon is positioned, but cannot actually be seen. In your magical mind, see the crystal at the tip of your wand take on a shining, black light; it is infused with a dark glow that, nevertheless, radiates out just as if it was light. Lower your wand gently, as above, and bring it to rest in the water in the bowl. At this point you may visualise the water as turning a deep, shining black, such that it appears to have limitless depths, stretching away into infinity. (You may wish to enhance your perceptions here with a little artful craft. Try coating the crystal on your wand with some, natural, food colouring, such that the water turns dark when you immerse the tip of the wand in it. A cheat? Yes, but it aids visualisation immensely and is a very traditional witch-trick). From this point on, continue as for any other phase of the Moon, repeating the Calling Down until you have the bowl vibrating with the virtue of the Dark Moon.

From this point onwards, there are various Ways in which you may wish to use the charged Moon waters you have just created.

You may wish to use this moment for a period of meditation on a subject that is pertinent to you at this time and tide. In this case, all you need to do is seat yourself comfortably and take up the bowl of Moon-charged water in your hands and rest it in your lap, or simply gaze into it where it sits. Hold the subject of your meditation lightly in your mind. Allow the Virtue you have just Called Down to suggest avenues of consideration for your topic and let the solutions to problems or developments of concepts arise spontaneously within your mind. Allow the Virtue of the Moon to guide you in your deliberations. Finish when you feel that you have come to a natural point of conclusion for this time.

You may wish to allow yourself to become entranced by the light/dark in the waters and use it for the purposes of skrying. For this, seat yourself but leave the bowl on the table. It is considered better if you can orientate both the bowl and yourself, such that there is only a single point of light visible in/on the water (if Dark, then there should be no light, so just focus on "Dark"). This is so that there are not multiple points of distraction to take your mind away from what you are doing. As for meditation above, hold the concept/thing you wish to consider/have resolved in your mind, as you lightly *gaze* upon the surface of the waters. I stress gaze, not stare, as staring will tire the eyes and make you unable to complete the exercise. I tend to liken it to invisible fingers coming from the eyes and just, very gently and lightly, touching the surface of the skrying medium – in this case the water in the bowl. Control your breathing to a gentle rhythm, relax your body and sit comfortably. After a while, what classically happens, is that the surface clouds over and becomes milky white; sometimes it appears as if a mist is arising. It can also seem that the milky white disc starts to revolve. At this stage it is important not to jerk or move too much, else the image will disappear and you have to start again (try not to fall asleep either, as this is also a danger). After a period of this, figures may start to form, either of people, animals, spirits, numbers or abstract shapes or colours, hopefully relating in some manner to the object of your skrying; it very much depends on the individual and their query. With some experience, the Witch will learn the difference between the various types of imagery appearing in the waters at different phases of the Moon. Sometimes these are, indeed, wish-fulfilment pictures or visions, both of the moment and of the future, usually in symbolic form, requiring careful interpretation. Then again there are possible flash-backs to what may appear to be past lives, but much skrying gets no further than symbolic clairvoyance, which itself may lead to erroneous conclusions, so much care must be taken in judging what is seen at these times. It is important that the Witch learn to distinguish "true vision" from mere wish-fulfillment; the latter will get you nowhere and will develop no self-knowledge whatsoever. (Note: as I said above, this is the "classical" manner in which this operation works. For any given individual, their results may be widely different and this is perfectly fine and natural. No one experience is "right" and another "wrong"; all Witches have their own Way of working and the Way in which their experiences happen to them. All are valid: none are invalid). Once the images, etc. vanish and/or it appears that the skrying attempt has come to a natural conclusion, gently bring yourself back to the waking world as is your normal practice. Breath deeply to readjust.

You may wish to allow yourself to become entranced by the light/dark in the waters and use them as a gateway to step through on a journey to the Otherworld/s. This, naturally enough, is likely to involve a journey into the realms of the Lunar energies or spirits and is a good way to explore and gain knowledge of these areas, for each particular phase of the Moon. Although in this exercise there has been no Calling of any deity, it is not impossible that, on this journey, you may encounter any one of the deities, spirits or Powers associated with the Moon. Keep an open mind and do not expect anything/anyone in particular. Different cultures have depicted the divinity of the Moon in many different ways, not all being the commonly assumed "goddess" - particularly when working within the realms of Traditional Witchcraft. Many personifications of the Lunar Power/s are male, particularly in the less Mediterranean cultures, such as the Norse/Teutonic and "Celtic", so be aware that you may not meet what you expected to – if anything! The technique for using the charged waters as a gateway through which you may pass is similar, but different, to that for skrying and so I will give the instructions as I received them from a spirit tutor when I was first learning myself.

> *Sit before your bowl of water, sufficiently large enough to reflect your face. Sit relaxed and consider the purpose of the journey whilst looking at your reflection. Focus your attention to your eyes. Do not stare, rather contemplate them and as you watch you will notice a change in your features. This denotes the first change in consciousness, i.e. the mind is dropping to the deeper level. As your mind is allowed to lower still further, it is probable that your features will become grotesque and you will imagine a demon or such is peering at you from the mirror. Do not waver, for as you progress further the waters will turn black and no reflection will be visible.*
>
> *Hold your gaze steadily at this stage because shortly, commencing as a point of light at the centre of your vision, the waters will become completely illuminated. There will be no reflection of yourself. You will become aware of an open door before you and a pathway ahead. Turn your mind now to the knowledge that you seek, or the entity that you wish to contact and wait for manifestation; or mentally step through the door and proceed along the path. You will experience that which you will. Although the exercise is in no way dangerous, it is best to have a grounding in this world, to call you back when you are done, or the encounter is finished. Before you begin your journey, take in your hand your wand. When you wish to return, rap this on*

> *the table three times. This will call you back from the Other, the waters will cloud over and your reflection will return. Do not move until this has occurred.*

No Witch can say what will happen on these journeys, so try to have a clear idea in mind of what you wish to learn before you embark and be ready for the answer/s to come in many different forms. If you encounter other Beings, deity or spirit, remember to act politely and honourably, but remember that the rules in Other realms are not those of our world so be ready to adapt to any situation that you may come across.

You may wish to lift the bowl and drink the waters within (all of them or saving some), to physically take in the forces you have Called down, in order to perform some magical action, having become the embodiment of the Lunar energies for that time. This can be quite a strange and somewhat mystical experience for some people, especially if they are particularly sensitive to the Moon's influence. The imbibing of the waters alone may help you to drift off into a Lunar reverie or journey, without practising skrying or meditation proper and, indeed, some Witches work better this way. Alternatively, imbibing the waters can act to make the Witch a conduit for the energies of the particular phase of the Moon they wish to work with, enhancing those particular qualities/aspects of their own forces, the better to perform some particular magical working that needs those specific forces. Try it and see what works for you.

On a more practical level, you may wish to use the waters immediately for some forms of magic working, depending on the phase of the Moon at the time and your natural inclinations. One method of using the waters that works well, is with poppet magic, for many different purposes. Once you have made the image for the particular person and identified it with them, it may be placed in the waters, with a charm or chant, or the waters gently poured over it whilst intoning; in this manner, the poppet may absorb the forces conjured by the Witch and transfer them to the subject of the working. This form can be used for either beneficia or maleficia, either working equally as well; again, it is up to the Witch how they wish to use the Virtues summoned. For issuing a maleficia at the Waning/Dark of the Moon, place the poppet into the waters whilst reciting the curse required. You may leave the poppet in the waters for a whole Moon, repeating the curse as often as you wish during that time, then pouring the waters out on stony ground at the end of the Moon. Dispose of the poppet (or keep it), as you see fit. Bottling is also a traditional use of the waters in this case; pour the waters into a suitable-sized vessel and put the poppet in with them, perhaps with a written curse also – as the paper curse disintegrates in the waters, so will the curse take effect on the victim. In East Anglia, this is sometimes known as being "Put in the Waters" and was a greatly feared operation when performed effectively. To remove the curse, the poppet needs to be taken out of the waters and blessings said over it for three nights, at the opposite phase of the Moon to when the cursing was performed. Yet another method of maleficia using these waters is to recite the curse, then take a mouthful of water and spit it in the direction of the victim. Repeat this three times, then cast the remaining waters over your shoulder whilst reciting the curse once more and walk away without looking back (best done if you can cast the waters onto the victims property without them knowing). Certain Bible passages are very traditionally used in these cases, such as Psalms 109, 48, 74 and 79 and also reciting the Paternoster backwards. Of course, all these methods can just as well be used for healing or blessing purposes, the charms or incantations being altered accordingly. Another very traditional and effective use for the charged waters is in anointing objects. I have mentioned poppets above, but this type of Moon water may also be used to great benefit in charging talismans, charms and other forms of magical items. If dedicating certain objects – such as your Moon wand – using these waters will give them an extra charge. It was once very common for a Witch to fill small vials with Moon water, along with other things such as herbs, oils, different types of soils/earths, animal bones or parts to wear around the neck or about the body. These could be refreshed/renewed at certain times of year or phases of the Moon, when their effectiveness was deemed to have run out or diminished – all you need to do is empty out the water, replace with fresh whilst charming the vial again and away you go! Again, the only thing that limits the magic of the Witch is their magical imagination. One other method traditionally employed with Moon waters, was to wash the clothing of the person the Witch wished to enchant. This need not necessarily be anything as large as a shirt, skirt or trousers; a handkerchief, scarf or something similarly sized would suffice. The item was soaked in the waters, whilst suitable charms were spoken – for good or ill – then the item was hung up to dry, by moonlight, either on a Blackthorn or Whitethorn, depending on the aim of the charm, then given to the subject to wear or keep about their person. This worked equally well for either beneficia or maleficia and there was no need to recover or destroy the item once the charm had done its work.

You may choose to save the waters and bottle them for future use, if not wanting to use them (all), immediately. In this case it is advisable **not** to keep them any longer than one Moon's duration, if you have not used them during this time, but to discard them and to create fresh waters again. The reason for this is that, being from a natural source the waters may quickly "turn" and go stagnant or rancid, negating any beneficial qualities therein. It is said to be possible by some authorities to preserve these waters for much longer periods by adding such things as alcohol, essential oils and other ingredients, to keep them "good" for future use. To my mind this is not a good idea or advisable for a very simple reason – you are adulterating and "watering down" the validity, concentration and force of the vital energies that you worked so hard to acquire.

A bottle of Moon water which is 50%, or more, alcohol, or contains several drops of Benzoin oil is not the full, effective, magical materium that you created under that moonlit sky. It no doubt comes down to personal working practice and preferability, but this is the Way I was taught and find best – never adulterate your magic!

As ever, it is possible to use a combination of any of the above that best suits the working methods and manner of the individual Witch. Within some Traditions of East Anglian Craft, charms or spells brought to life using the methods above are sometimes known as "Children of the Moon", because they are birthed of the Virtues of the Lunar sphere. Occasionally the actual Spirits invoked and worked with under these auspices are also known likewise; this can be a bit confusing, but the context will always give the clue as to which is being spoken of. It is in this instance that another one of the connections with Lilith can be seen within the E.A. Traditions; that She is the Mother of the Moon Children, the Weird/Wyrd Folk, half begotten of Herself and Other Powers.

Honour and Respect – Talking to the Moon

As mentioned earlier, it is incumbent upon the Witch to be respectful in all their workings and treatments of the spirits of the natural world, not only as a matter of course, but in this manner they may develop a better relationship, trust and a willingness within the Other to help, guide, guard and teach. As always, there are ways and means to go about this and I would like to share here a method of giving thanks and offerings to the Moon Powers that derives directly from the traditions of my native Suffolk. This example comes from a village close to my home town and was told to me by an associate some years ago, who was then in his early 60's. He learnt this technique from his Grandfather when he was about 6 or 7, his Grandfather then being in his 70's and had learnt it from his Father, so we're going back a-ways here. He was taught that this was the proper way to make offerings and was to be used at all times, but especially when "Talking to the Moon". (He explained to me that, although he was only very young when he was taught this Way, it was normal for the people in his family to do this and was just part of the natural way of things. His folk always did things according to the phases of the Moon, particularly planting and harvesting and still adhered to a 13 Moon year-cycle. When he got older and understood more, he realised that "Talking to the Moon" was a bit of a childish euphemism for working with the Virtues of the Moon and the associated Moon Spirits – as they never addressed a Lunar deity as such – but was probably thought the best way to explain it to a child at the time. The term has now stuck and "Talking to the Moon" it is!).

The technique is very simple, but most practical magical techniques are and need no embellishment. The secret, as always, is in focus, attention and respect.

You will need a bowl/jug of milk (better if it is full fat, but semi-skimmed is fine. However, it **must** be Cows/Goats, etc. milk and **not** Oat, Almond, Rice or other non-animal product). In addition, you will also need a small loaf of bread, preferably home-made, but certainly not a mass-produced, additive-filled one. We are working naturally here!

Slowly and gently, pour out the milk on the ground to make the following shape;

When you have done this, gently crumble the bread around the symbol on the ground, to form a circle around it. If there is any of the bread and milk left, pour/place them out in the centre of the symbol.

Any prayers or thanks should be said whilst doing this. A moment of stillness should be held afterwards in silence, then just turn around and walk away, leaving the offerings for those intended. (Although this form of offering was/is mostly used to thank and honour the Moon Powers, it is also appropriate for use with other Spirits, such as those of the Land, your Guides, Guardians or Familiars).

This simple form may suffice for your thanks and offerings (and it was all that was used by the family of my friend in their case), but you may also wish to incorporate it into a longer form. This form derives from a Witch Tradition from the Suffolk/Norfolk borders area in East Anglia and was a part of their usual Moon workings to honour the Witch Mother, embodied in the shining face of the round Moon. This rite is to be performed *around* the time of the Full Moon, bearing in mind what has been said earlier about tidal flows and personal optimum times – pick the time that feels best to you to give gratitude. Use some of the Moon waters that you have previously created and kept for this working. You will also need some sweet-smelling incense and your offerings of bread and milk.

At your chosen time, go to your working space outdoors, where the Moon can be clearly seen and arrange your ritual items in a manner that suits you. Take your bowl (bottle?) of Moon waters and sprinkle some around the edge of your compass/working space, using the following words, or similar:

"Waters run calm, waters run deep,
Rivers and Seas awaken from sleep.
Waters run calm, waters run deep,
Let the Moon rise, its bounty to reap."

Repeat three times then return to the centre of your space. Turn to face the Moon, whichever direction it is in, lift your face towards it and say the following words, softly, but out loud:

"I claim what is mine by ancient right,
As Son (Daughter) by Blood and Child of Night.
By Hound and Cat, Hare and Toad,
I walk the Way of the Moon Road."

Now, light the incense. Take it round the edge of your space three times, reciting the following as you do so:

"I call the Old Ones, Come stand by my side,
As the Moon's light spreads far and wide,
In this place, a welcome to find,
I do honour to you and your kind."

Replace the incense and go to the centre of your space. Make the offerings as in Talking to the Moon above, keeping in mind your reasons for doing so. When you have done this, go to stand in the North of your space and turn your face up to the Moon again, in whichever direction it is. Take some time to give your thanks, then simply "bathe" in the moonlight. Let the light and virtue wash over you, staying for as long as you feel necessary. Let yourself go and feel whatever comes to you. You may wish to speak to the Moon from the depths of your being, in which case follow that impulse and see what arises afterwards. The Moon has strange and unusual energies and who knows what you may receive in return.

When you feel that this time of communion has come to a natural ending, place any remaining offerings/water in the centre of the symbol on the ground, collect up your items and walk away without looking back.

As I think should be fairly clear, this rite may be adapted to the individual Witch's tastes/needs. If you have made a connection to or work with a particular Lunar deity, then they may be included in your offerings and prayers. Likewise any specific spirits or animal familiars that aid you in Lunar rites, may also be included. Work with what feels right and best to you, within the parameters of this practice.

Seeming To Be

"There is a spiritual power in masks, hints of other things that remain unspoken, stylised yet ideal images of ideal qualities, otherworldly substances, ritually activated."
Nigel Pennick – "The Spiritual Power of Masks".

When interacting with other people, quite a lot of the energy of the Witch can be spent on the arts of Illusion and Enchantment; this may be directed outwardly at other people, or may be directed inwardly to the Witch themselves. By using the term illusion, it may seem that I am implying the use of trickery and falsehood; whilst there may indeed be a larger or smaller element of trickery involved, there is certainly no falsehood implied here. The Witch uses valid arts to achieve their own ends and these should never be false. To some extent, this may be seen as an aspect of the role of the Lapwing, as mentioned in Chapter 1, as part of the Ways of Witchery. The Lapwing, being the Trickster, leads the unworthy away from those things that they are not (yet) ready for and preserves the sanctity of the Mysteries. Whole areas of the Witches Craft may be devoted to these arts and, indeed, some people, like the late Magister Robert Cochrane (Roy Bowers), are known to have spent a great deal of time on this particular aspect of Witchcraft. An individual Witch's reasons for practising this art may be many and various and may not agree with another Witch's reasons, each being at a different stage of their own development of self-knowledge. However, there is one area in which most would share the same attitude in that there are some things that not everyone may see or know, until they are ready and it is their obligation and task as a Witch to preserve these for the worthy to discover for themselves. Such is a right and proper use of the art of trickery. In other situations, the art of Illusion can vary from simply misdirecting a person's gaze, focus or attention, to creating a complete visual image that may, or may not, actually be physically present. This is the use of the art of Enchantment and can, in itself, take many forms. It may be used in its normally understood form to "enchant", to cast a spell or make a charm, depending on the Will of the Witch and the need of the time. This art may be used to both hinder and help, to both conceal and reveal, whichever is needed. In some forms it may be used to change one thing into another, again either in an illusory or actual manner – to Shape-Shift the form of an object or the nature of a thing. In one of its forms it may be used in the creation of a Glamour, but more on that anon.

In using the art of Illusion, the Witch may often start on themselves, before attempting to project anything onto others. This is initially simply to practice the arts in their training, but also to cultivate confidence in their practice – not everyone starts out with supreme confidence in themselves and Witches are only human after all – at least to start with!

Masks and Veils

The use of both Veils and Masks has ancient pedigree in magical practice and can be traced back to our oldest ancestors. Images can be seen painted on the walls of pre-historic cave-dwellings such as at Lascaux and La Caverne des Trois-Freres in France, amongst many others around the world, of masked "shamanic" characters, performing what appear to be ritual dances and other magical acts. Coming forward in time, the tombs of the Pharaohs in Egypt depict masked priests at their ritual work; the goddess Isis

Herself was imaged as veiled and declared that no man had lifted Her covering and gazed upon Her face. Celtic and Germanic magical practitioners are known to have used totemic, zoomorphic masks during sacred rites and the Norse god Odin has as one of his alternative titles the name "*Grimr*", meaning the Masked One. In 7th. Century Britain, Archbishop Theodore fulminated and issued prohibitions against those who wore the heads of stags and bulls at the kalends of January, presaging the wearing and use of the Dorset Ooser mask, of which more below. More recently the Guizers of Mediaeval Europe preserved the traditions of animal masking from their pre-Christian forbears, dancing in these forms at significant times of year, invoking the powers of the animals they represented.

These may have been the ancestors of the folk who employed masks such as the Dorset Ooser, mentioned above. This was a horned mask, which used to be kept and used in the Dorset village of Melbury Osmond for ritual parades and dances and was owned by the Cave family, who appeared to be the hereditary guardians of the item. It was a very rare example of an English, humanoid mask, about which much has been written and speculated over the years which now, unfortunately, has been lost. The first mention of it was by Canon Charles Herbert Mayo, in 1891, writing in the *Somerset and Dorset Notes and Queries.* I will reproduce his description here, as it is an exceedingly interesting, first-hand account of a genuine, historical tradition. He describes it thus;

> *"a wooden mask, of large size, with features grotesquely human, long flowing locks of hair on either side of the head, a beard, and a pair of bullock's horns, projecting left and right of the forehead. The mask or Ooser is cut from a solid block, excepting the lower jaw, which is movable, and connected with the upper by a pair of leathern hinges. A string, attached to this movable jaw, passes through a hole in the upper jaw, and is then allowed to fall into the cavity. The Ooser is so formed that a man's head may be*

> *placed in it, and thus carry or support it while he is in motion. No provision, however, is made for seeing through the eyes of the mask, which are not pierced. By pulling the string the lower jaw is drawn up and closed against the upper, and when the string is slackened it descends."*

One of only two known photographs of the original Ooser, taken between 1883 and 1891 by J.W. Chaffins and Sons of Yeovil and reproduced with the original article in Notes and Queries.

At some point after 1897 the mask disappeared, never to be seen again, its whereabouts having been lost. However, in 1975, using available images such as the one above, the Weymouth Morris Dancer, John Byfleet, made a replica for his local Morris Side, using a penknife to carve it. On May Morning in 1978, the new mask was subsequently taken to Giant Hill at Cerne Abbas for the traditional ceremony of Dancing Up the Sun in The Trendle earthworks. However, the mask was so heavy that it was never used ritually again, and now resides in the Dorset County Museum.

In modern times there are still many branches of traditional Morris Dancers who don masks, tatters and other forms of disguises to depict archetypal forms during their performances. One well known example are the Black Face dancers of the Border Morris, which now cause so much controversy, because of the lack of understanding of the reasons behind the "disguise". Blacking the face, both in dance and ritual, has several meanings and uses, only one of which is purely for disguise, to make it more difficult for onlookers to recognise the individual. Blacking can be seen as a type of veil that ritually hides the actual intent of the wearer; it is intended to throw the observer off the scent, so to speak. In British Craft lore, the Magister of a coven would often Black his face, both in honour of and to personate the Horned One, the Devil being known to be black-faced through contact with the transformative fires of the Underworld and in His role as the divine Blacksmith, forging the spirit of the Witch with/from the same fires. Conversely, in certain situations, the face may be Whitened, instead of being made black. This whitening conveys a different meaning, but also related to the black, in that it depicts the shining radiance and dazzling light of divinity. We are used to seeing pictures of saints with halos around their heads (copied/borrowed from pre-existing pagan originals, such as Mithras, Apollo, Selene, etc.), but this is a 2D version of what was meant to be a 3D reality – the whole of the face/head was meant to be understood as shining with an inner, divine light or flame. The whitening of the face during ritual or dance is a personalised form of this, intended both to depict this to onlookers and to bring about a heightened spirituality within the "performer". In an alternative form to this meaning, White may also encompass the corpse-like pallor of the spirits of the Dead. To whiten the face is also to bring forth within the subject those ancestral attributes that they wish to work with, or even to allow the dead full use of the body, as in some branches of Voudou or in the secretive Order of Bonesmen, said to still be active in East Anglia.

All these images may be seen as examples of an artificial or created *persona* (ironically, from the ancient Greek for "mask"), or personality, which the individual may put on or off at will. Within Witch magic, the persona is a magical personality that the individual learns to assume, normally during ritual practice, but not always, when attempting to become "more" or "other" than themselves. This is one of the reasons for assuming a "magical name" upon beginning to practice the Craft, in that this name represents and embodies the magical attitudes, abilities, knowledge and powers (aspired to) of the individual Witch. In addition, a magical name often helps to allow the inner Witch to emerge, it helps to bring the more secret and magical identity to the fore and can help the Witch to leave the everyday world behind and enter Other realms more easily. Finally, but not the least in importance, having a magical name allows the Witch to be recognised on other levels of existence by other forces/Powers and identified as One who is seeking to learn the Mysteries.

When taking on a magical name, it is important to chose one that accurately describes the true personality and (desired) characteristics of the Witch. For example, there is no use choosing something like "Night Owl", if you have a deep-seated fear either of flying or the dark - it just wouldn't reflect the inner personality and could actually affect the magical abilities in a detrimental manner, by conflicting with the inner nature of the aspiring Witch. It would also be patently ridiculous for a Witch who was either a vegetarian or vegan to take on the name of a meat-eating animal, such as "Bright Wolf" or "Strong Bear"! Many things need to be considered when taking on a magical name; our natural skills, any animals or birds that we feel a particular (and appropriate) empathy with and our physical capabilities, as well as those things and qualities that we aspire to. It is also considered *very* poor form, at least in British Traditional Craft circles, to assume the name of a God or Goddess.

The magical persona may be assumed at important points in working practice, or when dealing with non-Witches, the better to access those abilities desired. Initially this can be very important, as not everyone can achieve the required mental states, focus, attention and vision required for magical work straight away, and assuming a magical persona – as contained in a name – enables the Witch to become the person desired, if only for a short while. By putting on this personality, the Witch becomes the person with all the abilities needed, even if they don't quite possess those abilities without assuming the persona. It has often been said that it doesn't matter if the gods exist or not (which, of course, They do), the Universe acts *as if* They do. It is this *as if* that is the important point here. By putting on the magical persona and acting as if they have all the powers and abilities that they need, the Witch will acquire them eventually. Acting in this manner, the Witch creates a channel or conduit for the Virtue to flow through and create the actual fact; the Illusion becomes the Reality. In some Magical Orders, this magical persona is known as the Body of Light and highly complicated instructions are given for its creation. The Witch knows that simplicity is always best and so acts as if it were true, creates the illusion and lets the force come through to create the actuality. As Ignatius Loyola, the co-founder of the Jesuit Order, once said; "*If you place yourself in the attitude of prayer, you will soon feel like praying*". If the Witch, by donning this name/persona *feels* like a powerful and knowledgeable magical practitioner, then they are much better able to become so. Once the practitioner becomes proficient, this personal "illusion" may no longer be required, but it is a useful tool in the meantime. Alternatively, by this time they may actually have become the powerful Witch they aspired to be and so the name actually represents them in truth and reflects a reality instead of an illusion.

Whilst it is perfectly possible to assume the magical persona mentally or figuratively - and many Witches find this perfectly suitable and practical - this technique may also involve the putting on of a physical mask or other form of face-covering, the better to image-forth the desired attributes. This may take place both during solo workings and also in group ones, such as coven meetings. It was not unknown in times past that the whole of a large gathering of Witches would be masked, the better to preserve their anonymity, even between people that knew each other well. I have been told by one of my Old Craft teachers that, in the recent past, even amongst family groups of perhaps 20 or 30 people gathered, masks were still worn. This was not only to preserve anonymity, but also to build up a certain magical tension, as no one (apart from the Magister), was quite sure exactly who was there and this all led to a better working situation. Everyone working with their magical persona was able to create a much more powerful ritual than if they had been there "just" as themselves. To put on the mask, is to enter the ecstatic state of magical consciousness, where this world and the Other conjoin and interact. Wearing a mask is to invoke the powers of both the inner Witch and the Other, as the mask may manifest both in a most direct and tangible way. To both the Witch wearing the mask and to the beholder – be they Witch as well or not – it is a Way of overcoming normal "ordinary" perception and slipping between the worlds into non-ordinary perception or reality. The mask thus enables both Illusion and Reality to be present at the same time. It is another example of overcoming the limitations of perceived duality and allowing the "two" to become "one", combining the best of both elements within the magical practice.

Martin Duffy in his highly informative book "*The Devil's Raiments*" (see Bibliography), puts it like this;

> *"Herein we encounter the crux of the mask's power, for in wearing it we blur the line between our own persona and that of the thing we wish to become until the two are as if one, for unlike the scientist who would seek to understand his subject by examining its external form, the witch instead gains their knowledge by overcoming the barrier that separates the observer from the observed, becoming the perceived itself".*

To create this Other state, the Witch must possess and don a fully empowered mask, depicting the condition that they wish to embody, or the Being they wish to ensoul. In past days, these masks would have been carved/created from natural materials by the Witch themselves, or someone practised in the art from within their coven or group, in just such a manner as the Dorset Ooser above (if not quite so large and heavy in general). This would have been a highly skilled task, involving not only the fashioning of the physical mask itself, but also the ensouling and embodying of the forces and virtues that it was meant to bring to reality. Examples of this type of mask are still to be found on the European mainland and in other places around the world where such items are still part of a vibrant and living tradition. However, after the Protestant revolution in Britain, the exoteric side of the craft died out, as it was seen to hark back to both a pagan and Catholic past, which was shunned and forbidden. The skills and crafts involved went underground and were carried on in secret by those practising the esoteric side of the arts and masks of this type are now exceedingly rare and hard to find. If wishing to embark on the use of a mask within their own magic, the Witch needs to create their own and imbue it with the required energies. This, in fact, is always the best way to go about creating one's own magical items/regalia. If using something created by another person, be they Witch or no, it is never possible to know exactly what virtues have been put into the item. Whilst these may be fine and appropriate for the original creator and perfectly harmless in themselves, they may be totally the opposite of what the subsequent owner wishes to work with and could be positively detrimental or negative to their own magical work. Unless a mask is made specifically for the individual Witch by an experienced practitioner who knows exactly what is required, it is better to create a mask of your own, with whatever skills you may have.

A mask need not be an incredible work of art – it is not intended to be so, as it has a magical function to fulfil (if it does, however, end up being one, then so much the better). As long as the individual Witch is satisfied that the image depicted therein embodies those qualities and virtues that they wish to assume or become, then the mask has satisfied its purpose. These days, not all of us have the manual skills and abilities that our forbears possessed and we may not be able to carve, plait, weave or stitch/embroider something suitable. However, there are things available to us that were not available to them! Many toy or craft shops sell simple, blank face coverings, that are used for parties or Hallowe'en and are meant to be decorated accordingly. If your skills do not extend to making something from scratch, one of these basic shapes may be purchased and decorated to your own designs. Alternatively, if you are feeling a bit more adventurous and have the help of a fellow Crafter, then the medium of papier mache also makes an excellent base for creating a mask. To do this, you need to make up the mixture to your satisfaction and, before putting it on your face, apply a thin layer of something like Vaseline, to enable the mask to be detached easily once dry. Simply apply the papier mache mix to the face, following the contours of your own features and maybe enhancing certain aspects – or even creating them – to make the image of your desire. You will need to then wait for some time whilst the mixture dries sufficiently to be taken off without altering its shape, then it can be left to dry out completely before working on it further. A light sanding to smooth the surface and a few coats of white (?) paint will create an excellent ground on which to work.

At the simplest level, it may be painted or coloured with pens, fabric stuck on or other items added. If feeling a bit more adventurous, you may add feathers, fur, bark, moss, corn, flowers...the list is endless. Whatever you may conceive of to depict those qualities and attributes that you wish to bring through can be incorporated in the design – this is **your** mask and is designed to work for **you**, so it doesn't matter how it looks to anyone else. (If working with an established group, this may not be strictly true as there may be common attributes that need to be incorporated, such as group spirits/animals/familiars, etc. In this case, all may work together to create suitable designs that all can be satisfied with, at the same time as retaining individual expression and personal qualities). There is, however, one thing to remember before you get too carried away – it must be practical, i.e. you must be able to wear it comfortably during ritual work, without it actually hindering what you need to do!

One way to check on the progress of your mask, is to occasionally put it on and look at yourself in the mirror whilst wearing it. Keep the lights low, or at least not bright, and just see how it both makes you look and feel. Don't be alarmed if at some point, looking out of both the mirror and your eyes reflected in it, you see some totally alien individual to yourself; this is a sign that you're getting it right. If you get a decidedly "Other" feel to your reflection and maybe a little quiver or vibration in your solar plexus, than it's a sure sign that the mask is beginning to work for you. This is how it **should** feel – it is useless otherwise.

Once you have reached this stage and feel that the mask images forth the being or qualities that you wish to become or embody, then it is time to empower it. There are several ways in which this may be done but, as ever, the simplest is usually the most effective and may be developed by the individual Witch as and how required.

Take your mask into a fully hallowed compass and stand it on your altar, facing towards you, or hang it upon your Stang – again, facing you. Stir up the energies and call upon the virtues that you require to be embodied by the mask, in the form that suits you best. Some Witches find that treading the mill is the right way for them, others prefer to chant, drum, sing or a combination of these. You must really whip up the forces you require, until they are a tangible, physical presence in the compass with you. However you do this – and it will be different for each one, just as every mask is different – once you feel the virtues stirring around you, stop and face your mask directly. Place your hands on either side of the mask and stare deeply into the empty eye holes. As you feel the energies swirl around you, focus them through your body, down your arms and into the mask; really feel the flow as the virtues pass along your arms and into the mask. At some point you may see a light, glow or flicker from within the depths of the eyes. At this point, or when you believe that the mask is "saturated" with intent, state strongly and clearly words such as the following:

"I name thee X (magical name).
Thou art X in form and spirit.
I name thee X!"

Take up the mask, put it on and sit to meditate for a while. What happens now will be unique to the individual Witch; ideally you should feel the energies that you have just invoked into the mask and become one with them. Some people will be taken on a journey, others may receive words, pictures or insights. Just accept what happens and go with it. Once you are happy that this experience has completed, stand and - as your magical persona - immediately perform some small, magical task that you know you are capable of. You may like to anoint a candle and light it for a specific purpose; possibly plait a cord and knot it for some desired end; perhaps simply cense your compass with words of hallowing or blessing. Anything that you know is currently within your magical abilities. This is to firmly fix a positive identification with your mask and those abilities that you wish to work towards acquiring in the future. It is very important that you create a positive and comfortable association with your mask immediately, so that you may work beneficially with it in the future. Once you have finished the task, take off the mask and replace it on your altar/Stang, where it will now remain when you are not using it. End your ritual in your normal fashion, remembering to give thanks.

A fully empowered mask can generate a powerful presence of its own, often seeming to be a kind of guardian and becoming a focus for spirit activity in the compass. This will become even more concentrated when you are wearing it. It will aid in intensifying inner concentration and the focussing of consciousness in those areas desired. It will aid in the detachment from normal reality when worn in ritual and help in the internalisation of awareness into Other realms. If fully and properly empowered it will help to subdue normal, everyday awareness and bring through those deeper spiritual abilities, of which the mask is a symbol and living reality. It will become, in truth, the face of your spirit, neither illusion or reality, but something that can transcend both.

(Note: whilst I have spoken here of making/assuming a mask for the purposes of putting on the magical persona, a mask may be made in many different forms and used for widely differing purposes as well. It is perfectly possible and traditional to make a mask in animal form, the better to communicate with your familiar, guide or guardian, at one end of a spectrum, or to don the mask of a deity for specific work at the other. As ever, it is up to the individual Witch as to how they use any specific technique, depending on the need they have for it in their work. The thing to remember is to adhere to the basic principles and then make suitable adaptations that work best for the individual).

Glamouring

If it can be said that the *taking/putting on* of a magical name or personality is the assumption of a powerful (magical) persona, then it can also be said that the art of Glamouring is the *projection* of that power to influence others. This can also be seen as part of the art of Enchantment, as mentioned above and I would first like to deal with this art, in brief, before going on to discuss glamouring itself specifically.

The term "Enchantment" comes from the Latin "*cantare*", meaning to sing. It has the same roots as the word "charm", from "*carmen*", a song, verse or incantation. It is clear then that the essential practice involves the use of words, either sung, chanted or intoned in a certain manner. (On the subject of the derivation of words, I was once soundly castigated by one of my mentors for giving the dictionary definition and origin of a term that was being discussed. The final remark was: "Since when has the Oxford English Dictionary been a magical reference work"! The point that was being made was that – at least in Old Craft – words can take on a magical meaning of their own for the Witch, independent of their dictionary definitions. It took me some time to internalise and understand what was being taught me then and it is, indeed, a valid point. However, I still think a knowledge of where a word comes from, its origins, to be a useful piece of knowledge in itself). In this case, it is the voice that is the starting point for enchantments and, while I think it is obvious that it may go far beyond just the voice and encompass many other forms of "projection", it is true that a spell, an actual "enchantment" needs to be verbalised in certain situations and this verbalisation can be very important. The manner of projection and use of the voice can work in very different manners, depending on the need at the time. In certain situations, the enchantment may need to be howled at the Moon, under an open, starry sky, putting all the power and force of that magical persona behind it. At other times, the charm may need to be whispered into the gentlest of breezes, to be carried off to its ultimate destination. On other occasions, the spell may need to be chanted repeatedly in a certain tone, whilst projecting the virtue into an object, such as when empowering a talisman, poppet or other form of physical charm. In this instance the breath may also carry the saliva of the Witch onto the physical medium, in the form of spit or moisture in the breath, to further empower the object. Essentially, the force of the magical persona – whether wearing a physical mask at the time or not – is carried by the voice into the enchantment and released upon the breath to carry out its work. Initially, this must be borne in mind the whole time that the Witch is performing the enchantment but, like anything, with practise this need not be constantly held in mind; the "magical gears", so to speak, take over and the force of the magical will is automatically projected with the spell (although any act of magic should NEVER be done purely by rote, but with full attention and focus, else it will fail). This obviously takes time and practise and doesn't come easily to all, but hard work brings its own rewards. The voice as a magical tool is a powerful vehicle and one that it would do well for every Witch to develop to the best of their abilities.

Many aids can be used to influence the mind and to remind it that this is the time when it needs to project that force during a working, and one of the most potent of these is smell, hence the use of incense during ritual. Our sense of smell is one of the most primitive senses that we possess, being focused in the Limbic area of the brain, what is sometimes called the "lizard brain", located at the back, at the base of the skull and is hence one of the most powerful senses that we possess; it bypasses rational, cognitive thinking and relies purely on feelings and emotions. There are many thousands of recipes for incense for countless different purposes in specific workings, but it is sometimes useful to have an all purpose incense, purely for spell casting of any type. The main benefit of this is that, once you have got used to working with it, then as soon as you smell it, it automatically keys the mind to "spell-casting" mode. It will put you instantly into the right frame of mind for putting on that "mask" and projecting the required virtue into your working voice. Here is an incense that I developed many years ago for just such a use and it still works well for me many years later. As soon as I smell this particular aroma, I am immediately ready to perform what needs to be done, with little preparation and no lengthy "warm-up" exercises. The recipe is as follows;

8 measures Hawthorn berries or wood shavings
2 measures Frankincense resin

4 measures Jasmine flowers
4 measures Rose petals
2 measures Cinnamon (powder or bark)
4 measures Damiana
2 measures Dragon's Blood resin
4 measures Orris root powder
1 pinch Camphor crystals
2 drops Sandalwood (white) essential oil
2 drops Orange essential oil
2 drops Clove essential oil.

Grind up the Hawthorn and Frankincense together to a fine, gritty consistency, then place in a separate bowl. Mix and grind the rest of the dry ingredients together, leaving the Dragon's Blood, Orris root and Camphor till last. Mix all these into the Hawthorn and Frankincense base, then add the essential oils. Stir until all are mixed well together, pour into a suitable vessel/jar, screw on the lid and leave to mature for at least a couple of days. To use, simply place a small amount on burning charcoal to release the aroma, topping up as necessary. Incense is peculiar to each and every one of us and each Witch likes to create their own particular signature smell, but I can recommend this mixture as at least a starting point from which you may then like to make your own adaptations.

Before I move on from discussing the voice as a magical medium, I would like to relate a tale from the lore of my own region, that describes the powerful use of this method. This concerns the memories of the witch Bet Cross, from Longstanton in Cambridgeshire, who was active in the late 1800's. A woman who used to run errands for her as a girl recorded the following in 1921;

"Then there was that business with young X. He was walking down the lane by the church one Sunday afternoon, and there he saw Bet Cross ridin' on a hardle.(Note – a hardle is a hurdle, a section of wickerwork fence). I don't rightly know which way

> *up the hardle was, but there she was, and young X he said to her: "Ah, Bet Cross I see ye. I'll tell on ye. Yer a-riding on a hardle." And Bet Cross she give 'im a queer look and she says: "Young man", she says, "you can tell on it when you think on it." And the funny thing was that it went right out of 'is 'ead, and he never did tell on it till 'e 'eard the bell goin' out for 'er death, and that wasn't for years. And when 'e 'eard the bell 'e said: "Why, if that isn't for old Bet Cross that I met ridin' on a hardle. Funny thing, I never thought to tell on it till now."*

An example of a powerful, verbal enchantment, I think you'll agree.

Continuing on from this example, the reader will note that along with the verbal command, Bet Cross also gave the unfortunate victim a "queer look". This is highly likely to be one of the rare examples of a recorded, historical occurrence of a witch using the art of projection of power, via the eyes, or with a glance. Whilst this art is generally known by the name of the Evil Eye, it has many others, including the Romany term "Maloik", Overlooking, Eye-biting and Owl-blinking and is usually viewed as a form of maleficia in itself. However, this form of projection of power has a great many other uses and should not be purely confined to delivering curses. It is simply a method of delivering a burst of energy, which could "contain" anything that the Witch may wish to deliver to their subject. It is one of the old arts of Witchcraft and very little practised these days, but is worth preserving as it is a very versatile technique, adaptable to many uses; again, only the imagination of the Witch limits its application. Whilst it is obvious that the eyes are used to receive light and images, it has long been an occult understanding that they are also a vehicle of projection of force and were well understood to do this in the past. The whole "science" of Mesmerism was based around this principle and it is still applicable today. Our eyes express our emotions more than any other part of our bodies and it would be a shame if this particular old art were lost in the past.

The first thing to remember when using this technique, is that the power or virtue must be built up in the Witch first. The aim of the charm must be held firmly in the mind, whilst accumulating the virtue within, usually with the face averted from the recipient or the head lowered. Once the virtue has built to an almost overwhelming or intolerable level, the Witch raises their head and makes a swift and penetrating eye contact with the subject, a forceful glance, that takes them by surprise. This is normally accompanied by a muttered remark, that subtly encapsulates your purpose. As you make eye contact, you project a bolt of virtue which will send a shock through the recipient. Do not gaze at them or hold the eye contact. Do not wait for them to react, but walk away without looking back, before they have time to recover or question the look that you have delivered. Keep what you mutter very short, but make the pronunciation very clear and definite, but quiet, so as not to be clearly heard by the recipient. The whole impact can be heightened if you accompany the look with a slight gesture, just a small movement of your hand, as if casting something in their direction – which, indeed, you are. Make this subtle and not too obvious, as you don't want to either show off or attract more attention than needed, but a gesture sometimes helps to "deliver" the charm, for both the Witch and the subject. It is not a good idea to make a habit of this form of magic and it should be reserved for the rare occasion; the impact will be lost if you go around doing it at the drop of a hat. Nevertheless, it is a useful technique to have at your disposal but, like all valid techniques, takes time, effort and practice to master.

Having briefly looked at the arts of Enchantment using the voice and the eyes, I would now like to turn to the art of Glamouring itself, which may be the combination of these techniques, plus a little bit more.

Like many of the older arts, this is another technique that is not often addressed in more modern traditions, yet it forms an integral part of Old Craft training. It is not something that can be taught to all and much of its success lies in the individual Witch's natural abilities and craftiness. The value of the art of glamouring should not be underestimated, for in it there is true power. In fact a large part of a Witch's ability to influence others lies in the ability to cast a glamour. This is not to suggest that the art is necessarily used for any nefarious purposes, on the contrary, there are times when it is very important for all concerned that the Witch can convince others that they have an abundance of certain qualities. For example, if someone approaches the Witch with a difficult problem that needs magical aid to solve, and the client is lacking in faith in both themselves and, perhaps, the Witch, then the projection of a glamour depicting both confidence, knowledge and ability would be a vital necessity. Alternatively, if the Witch finds themselves in a situation where they themselves, or someone that they are with, are confronted with possible physical threat or attack, the projection of a glamour suggesting that it would be overwhelmingly stupid to tackle them would be exceedingly advantageous. (This actually happened to my husband several years ago. He and some friends were coming home from an evening out, when they were confronted by some potential muggers, who stopped them and "requested" their valuables. Far from being cowed by this situation, my husband stood his ground, put forth his energy and threatened them all with being turned into toads. Such was the force of the glamour that he delivered, that the group of vagabonds turned tail and fled!!!). When we put this art to use magically, we are literally manipulating our images to give the impression that we are indeed imbued with rather impressive magical (or physical), abilities. (This, of course, needs also to be true and the Witch needs to have the actual magical ability to back up the glamour if so needed).

One thing to remember is that there is no such thing as a typical Witch because we come in both/all sexes and all shapes, sizes and ages. The true magic within the art of glamouring lies *behind* the eyes, for we *know* who we are and what we can do. The glamour filters through our confidence and our abilities and the magical persona that we have built up over a period of time. Another simple example to give of glamouring would be to take a cross section of people at a social gathering. Imagine a varied mix of people from all walks of life relaxing and enjoying themselves. There are bound to be some who appear to be physically beautiful or handsome, some who are less so and then perhaps others who would not consider themselves to be particularly good looking. If one of the latter happened to be an Old Craft Witch and they had a reason for gathering attention from the others there, then by working a glamour they could gain and hold the attention of the people that they desired to attract. This may be for any reason, not necessarily romantic, business or "political". It is no secret that speaking confidently is very magnetic if done in a subtle way, but glamouring is the art of creating a subtle image that overrides this and creates a much more lasting impression on the Witch's "audience".

To create a successful glamour the Witch needs to use the arts previously mentioned above, both of voice and eyes (but not delivered in a blow this time), combined with the magical effect of the magical persona. There is no trick to this, but it is the result of solid hard work and practice. As with the projection of the Eye, above, the Witch needs to build up the virtue within themselves, but not to such a breaking point as before. Slowly build and increase the energy within – in whatever manner suits you best, which you will have developed by now – and gradually feel it gently flowing out of you as you interact with the recipient/s. Visualise or feel the virtue colouring your voice and being projected from your eyes as you engage with people. At the same time, feel the energy sort of "oozing" from your actual body, as if giving off an enticing aroma. Some people like to colour or charge their personal energy field and mentally expand it to include the person or people surrounding them. Some people imagine a sort of "glow" around them, which affects their "audience". This is not as difficult as it sounds, but needs practice to perform efficiently. The glamour involves a slow and sustained release of energy over a period of time, unlike releasing a bolt of energy with the Eye, and can take a while to master. (Unless you need to use it in an emergency, as in the above example, then you need to be quick about it!) Some practitioners, if they know that they are going to need to cast a glamour beforehand, take with them some form of pre-charged charm or talisman, whose energy they can draw on and that will help them sustain the glamour over a period of time. Whilst what the Witch is doing is essentially creating an illusion of what they want the other person/s to see, feel or think, it is actually a real manifestation of power, in that it has an actual physical effect on the individual recipient/s and their actions. The extent of this is entirely up to the ability and strength of the Witch. Some are able to cast a glamour that completely alters their physical appearance; others may be more adept at mental manipulation – it all depends on individual ability.

As a "warming-up" exercise without projecting any magical virtue, try visiting a shop where you are not known. Speak, dress, act, etc. as someone very average, almost nondescript. Appear hesitant or shy and pay close attention to how people react to you and how you are treated. Return a few days later with a different appearance and attitude, make eye contact and project a little virtue, speak slowly, drop your voice a pitch and project through it. Be confident but not pushy or loud and arrogant. Note the differences in the way you are treated – you may be very surprised. This exercise can go a long way to increasing your confidence in the early stages of glamouring and confidence in itself goes a long way in magical practice.

A Spell to cast a Glamour

This is based on an old charm that was passed to me many years ago and I include it here more for interest sake than for anything else.

"When the Moon is Dark and the night is only lit by the stars, then shall you go unseen to stand beneath the boughs of an old Whitethorn tree. With lowered head whisper these words;

"By the magic of Darkness I whisper to thee
Oh Ancient One of the Whitethorn tree
Touch me with the secrets known to thee
Vouchsafe thy cunning this night to me
For I shall be you and you shall be me".

The words are a little bit strange and you could be forgiven for thinking that you may temporarily turn into a Whitethorn tree, however, to the best of my knowledge, this hasn't happened - yet!

Finally in this section, just a note of caution on this subject. There can be dangers to casting a glamour, but these only exist when the Witch actually starts to believe in the image that they are projecting themselves. It is one thing to use the art occasionally when the need arises, but it is quite another to carry it on all the time. This is when we are in danger of believing our own publicity and this is certainly the slippery road to ruin. This is where we must not let that old demon ego take the reins; it is all very well to appear as something else to others when there is a need, but the Witch should always know just exactly who and what they are; remember the art of self-knowledge also. Use the art of glamouring skilfully and it will serve you well; abuse it and you may live to regret it – many a budding Witch has been overtaken by their own glamours and suffered because of it. Glamouring is essentially much more than a convincing acting performance. It is the practical application of magical knowledge and, like any acting performance, one has to totally believe in it *whilst on the stage*. Once the "performance" is over, the mask needs to be taken off again and put away.

"Shape-Shifting"

Many years ago, when I was between the ages of about ten or eleven, until I was in my early to middle twenties, I used to have a recurring dream. Initially I would have it a couple of times a week, if not more, but gradually as I got older, the frequency decreased until I stopped having the dream completely when I was about twenty-five. Although I no longer have this dream, I remember it vividly and can conjure the feeling and experience in my mind to this day. It was a simple dream, with no great happenings in it, but it had a profound effect on me which has lasted up to the present day. In my dream, I was in the form of a great, black shaggy hound; this was so alien to me at the time when I first started having the dream, that it took me some while to realise just exactly what it was. However, once I got used to it, I thoroughly enjoyed the experience and revelled in it. In the form of this hound, I would be running, just running, along the roads and lanes near where I lived. It was always night and dark (I never noticed if it was any particular phase of the Moon, or if it changed) and there was never anyone else about. I never seemed to be actually going anywhere that I could detect and I never got to the end of the journey, but the thing that stayed in my mind was the sheer joy and exhilaration of the running. I was aware of being in this animal form, with shaggy fur and the great muscles bunching and pushing me along as I ran. It seemed to me that this was the most marvellous, simple and easy way to travel and I just couldn't understand for the life of me why humans would want to get around standing up only on two legs – it just didn't make sense! (I even tried running on four legs in the waking world occasionally, but a human body is a poor substitute for a four-legged hound). I remember making great leaps and bounds across the land as I was running in this form, seemingly just for the sheer joy and pleasure of doing it. I seemed to have a sort of "split mind" at the time; I was aware of being a human and thinking how marvellous this was, but also there was a wild and bestial side to my nature at the same time – woe betide anyone who tried to stop me or get in my way, as I would have ripped their throat out with my huge jaws and sharp teeth in a trice! I was quite sad when these dreams stopped coming and remember them very fondly; I've never quite given up hope of them reoccurring one day.

Now, by describing this dream I am not saying that I was deliberately shape-shifting into the form of a hound at night, but this experience is a classic example of historical descriptions by Witches who have transformed deliberately and I think myself lucky to have had the experience spontaneously. This example shows what **can** happen when the ability is developed to a practical level. Shapeshifting is one of the classical arts of Traditional Old Craft that is much talked about, but very difficult to do deliberately and, like others previously mentioned, not much practised these days. This art is not merely a matter of a visionary journey in animal (or non-human) form, as it requires a very definite skill in astral projection and controlled thought forms. Nor does the Witch physically transform into an animal – that is an impossibility, however much desired or claimed. Not everyone has the ability to perform this type of magic and it is difficult to teach to another – you either can or you can't and it's very much a question of having an innate ability and learning by yourself as you go along. Some parts of it depend on the ability to project the spirit of the Witch, others on the ability for communication and empathy with the animal involved. However, there are traditional methods and explanations that can be passed on, so I will attempt to get this form of "Illusion" conveyed as best I may. I say "illusion" here, as it is initially a form of deception practised by the Witch on themselves, which becomes a reality in the doing of it. Essentially, it can be seen as taking the essence of Enchantment and Glamouring and casting them on yourself, with practical results. Hopefully this will become clear as we go on.

As a magical technique or art, shapeshifting, skin-turning, extruding the fetch in animal form, call it what you will, basically divides into two different, but related, types. The first is where the Witch sends out their own spirit (also known as the Fetch in some traditions), in the form of another being; this is usually that of an animal (although it may be other), normally that of their animal familiar – if they have one – or that of an animal that they feel intense empathy with. The second form is when the Witch takes over, or "rides", the physical body of an animal – again, usually that of a familiar but sometimes other – and experiences the world through their senses. The former technique may involve journeys in both this world and the Other, the latter is usually confined to this world. The reasons for doing this are seldom addressed, let alone discussed, the emphasis mainly being put on the actual fact of being able to perform the act. In times past, the reasons, although various, centred around the Witch spying on their neighbours and seeing what they were up to, or alternatively performing maleficia in an undetectable (supposedly) form. Occasionally, as in my involuntary experience above, it was done for pure fun and enjoyment. There are also accounts of Witches using these methods and techniques to travel to Otherworldly Sabbats for celebrations and learning from their Mentors; these, however, are usually done in human form and are part of the lore of astral projection proper. These days, there are as many reasons for attempting it as there are persons doing it, but the main one in my experience is to gather information and knowledge, both of the Witch themselves, the animal forms, the natural and Otherworlds. What the Witch then does with this information is, as ever, up to them, but be aware – this is magic that transforms in more Ways than one and you may not come out of it the same person. This form of magic is not without its dangers and it takes a strong and stable mind to perform it successfully. Many a Witch has left a part of their soul behind, either in the Otherworld or with their animal contact and has never been the same again.

Be very sure you wish to perform these techniques before embarking upon them.

The first method of "going out" as an animal in spirit form is an ancient and well-attested Witch technique, going back centuries, if not thousands of years. Examples can be found in Ancient Greek literature, the Norse Sagas, Old Irish tales of Druids and Heroes and is described in the "voluntary" confessions of the 17th. century Scottish Witch, Isobel Gowdie. In the records of her trial there are recorded several charms she supposedly used to transform herself into various shapes, to go out and perform her various nefarious activities. The original transcriptions are not complete and some words appear to be missing, but here are the wordings that she gives, as near as can be ascertained.

To change into a hare, say thrice over:
I sall gaw intill a haire,
With sorrow and syt and meikle care;
And I sall goe in the divellis nam,
Ay whill I com hom againe.

To change into a cat, say thrice over:
I sall goe intill a cat,
Wi' sorrow and sych and a black shot;
And I sall goe in the divellis nam,
Ay quhill I com hom again.

To change into a crow, say thrice over:
I sall goe intill a craw,
With sorrow and syt and blak thraw;
And I sall goe in the divellis nam,
Ay quhill I com hom again.

To change back:
Haire, Haire, (catt, craw) God send thee caire,
I am in a hairis likness just now,
Bot I sall be in a womanis likenes evin now.

Or alternatively:

Catt, cat (crawe, craw), goe send the a blak shott or black thraw,
I wes a catt or craw just now,
Bot I salbe in a womans likenes just now.

The modern Witch may wish to use these as a basis for their own charms of transformation, when journeying out in animal form.

To practice this art it is advisable to first hallow a full compass in which to work; this is for a couple of reasons. It is only sensible, especially when first attempting this type of magic, to have a safe place in which to work, in which to leave your body whilst you are out. As mentioned previously, this practise is not without its inherent dangers and a safe place in which to leave one's body is obviously a good idea. The second is not often mentioned but, I think, is even more important and particularly practical. A fully hallowed and empowered compass is already at least half-way into Otherworlds by its mere creation and is therefore an ideal place from which to go-out. The Witch has already detached themselves from the everyday world of normal reality and that effort goes a long way to putting them into a suitable frame of mind for the attempt, right from the beginning.

There are obviously many methods for performing shapeshifting and it is advisable for the Witch to find the one that works best for them – as ever – but here I would like to suggest a method that has been found to work well and which may be adapted for personal work.

For this particular method, you will need several important items. Some of these will be standard tools for the Old Craft Witch, some may not be.

Firstly, your Stang. This is now such a ubiquitous item for those practising Traditional Craft that it needs little comment here. Suffice it to say that, apart from any other meanings or connotations that it may have for the individual, in this rite it stands for the World Tree of animistic lore and tradition. Upon and up and down this tree the Witch may travel to

Other worlds and dimensions in their search for knowledge and wisdom. Its use here is particularly apposite to going forth in a shape-shifted form.

The next item you will need is a mask of the animal (or other being), you will shift into. This is a completely separate mask from that of your magical name/persona and needs to be kept purely for your exercises in shape-shifting. For many Witches the form of this mask is often in the shape of their familiar animal, but also very often not. The familiar animal is not a part of the Witch's soul (for more on this aspect of going forth, see the next section), whereas the shape-shifted form often is – maybe as in my experiences with the Hound as detailed earlier. The Fetch is a term used by Witches to describe the animal part of their own soul, often perceived to be a separate being. Strictly speaking this is termed the "Fylgja", a Norse term meaning "double" or "follower", which is conceived of as an animal form, living separately from the human mind, but sharing the same body. This is what is often thought to be the form that is projected during sleep. However the animal form is conceived of, the mask must be made in as much detail as possible. It is wise to chose an animal that is native to your Land and, hopefully, region, so that you may study it in detail in its natural habitat. Try to learn as much as you can about it, its habits, food preferences, mating rituals, etc. the better to understand and appreciate the animal. Make the mask as detailed as you possibly can, incorporating also any signs or symbols that you associate with the animal in question. Once made, it should be hallowed in the same manner as detailed previously and kept on your altar or hanging also from your Stang when not in use.

In this method, you will also need a cord with which to "anchor" yourself in this world and aid in your return from going out. There are many different types of cord used in Traditional Craft with many regional variations in their construction and dedication; this one is specifically made with the purpose of being a "safety cord" when venturing forth into other dimensions, whether shape-shifted or not. This form of making uses the principle of what you do magically in the physical world is reflected in the spiritual realm. From the lore of my own region, here is the method of making and dedication.

Take a piece of cord, three times as long as your body is tall; measure it against yourself and cut it accordingly. The cord should be of a natural material – cotton, hemp, wool, etc. - and red in colour. Tie off the ends with red thread, making a small loop at one end. In your compass, using the gaze and the voice, enchant the cord with thirteen knots. As you tie each knot, breathe in a charm of safety and home. Tie each knot securely. When you have done this raise your cord before your Stang and intone; "*Within this cord, within these ties, does safety lie. Darkness surround me: Light surround me: Powers surround me, with all the strength of Witchery. This is my ward, this is my guard. So be it.*" Place the cord around your waist, one end through the loop and sit now to meditate upon the security it gives you. Perform this dedication at dusk on a Saturday evening, for 13 weeks. After this time you will be able to use the cord as your way back, when going out.

Obviously this will need to be prepared beforehand, but can then be used in any operations you need to make in the Other worlds.

In addition you will need some form of inducing trance. Some people like to drum or use a rattle, sistrum or other rhythmic sound inducing instrument. Others prefer to dance, pace or use a form of rhythmic breathing, either whilst using a chant or not, or a combination of several of these methods. The point is that you should be familiar with trance-inducing before attempting this practise, or it will be highly unlikely that you will succeed. You may also use the enchantment incense mentioned above for this, or your own adaptation. Some people find that taking an infusion of Mugwort and/ or Wormwood herbs before starting also helps to loosen the spirit from the body. Use what works best for you.

If it is suitable and safe to do so, hallow your compass at the site of your Whitethorn kin-tree, the better to use its energies for going-out. If this is not possible, with permission, take some of its wood, berries or leaves and place these around the edge of your compass before hallowing it, in the manner of Thorning the Ground described in Chapter One. In the process of hallowing, make sure you call upon your guardian spirits and any familiars that you work with, along with your deities and any Powers that you honour, asking them to open the ways for you and protect you on your attempt at going-out. Make offerings to these spirits before continuing the rite and making the attempt. Once you have completed the hallowing, place your Stang at the northern point of the compass, put on your mask and commence your trance-inducing procedure. If this involves being seated, sit at the foot of your Stang, with your back up against it. If you will be pacing, dancing or moving around, sit at the base of the Stang once you have entered the entranced state. Wrap your safety cord around your waist, one end through the loop and tie the free end to your Stang; this is your route home. Should you become lost; simply think of and/or take hold of your cord in your hand and follow it back to your compass (the cord will, of course, stretch to any length in the Otherworlds – or the astral counterpart of this world; simply follow it home). Continue your verbal chant or charm until you achieve as deep a state as you are able and then continue it mentally. At this point, you need to achieve separation from your body, in the form which you have chosen to go out in. Lie yourself down on the ground (or stay seated if this is better for you – neither is right or wrong; go with what feels/works best for you), with your head in the north and your feet to the south. In your mind, form the shape of the animal (or other), that you have chosen to go out as, standing directly in front of you. Visualise this form as strongly as you possibly can, in as much detail and clarity as you can manage – continue your chant, gently, the whole time. When you have completed the image as best you can, slowly and gently project yourself into it, like you did when you were "oozing" your power out in glamouring, only this time your mind is going with your virtue and you are becoming a different shape. This may take many attempts before you achieve success and some may never achieve this. However, once you are successful, it will be immediately obvious. Some say that their perception and consciousness changes in subtle ways – not that you forget that you are human, but that you become human and "other". Some say that there is an audible "ping" sound, or similar, and you are just there. Others say that there is no great difference, but that you just "know" that you have changed and are able to go off in a different form. It will not be the same for everyone, but you WILL know.

Having achieved separation into your different form, you may now travel wherever it is you will and for whatever purpose you chose to go out. It is best to have decided this reason well beforehand, as achieving success in projection can sometimes be such a shock or a profound experience, that you forget what you are doing and why you are doing it. However, like with many things, practise will make this easier and you will be able to go where you will with ease. Remember on your travels always to be respectful to any other Beings you may meet, particularly those in the same form as you, as you are now one of Them, in spirit at least! Once you decide that it is time to return, there are several ways to do this. You may begin a "return charm", as in the manner of the ones given by Isobel Gowdie previously above; this should take you back fairly quickly and safely. You may simply retrace your steps and awaken in your body. Some find that merely by thinking of being back, that this is enough. Others may have difficulty and that is what the cord is for; simply take it in your hand and will yourself to return to your body and you will find that it is so. However you make your journey, on your return, give yourself a few moments to adjust to your new state, take off your mask and cord and replace them where you normally keep them.

Give thanks and more offerings to those spirits and Powers that you called upon initially, then dismiss your compass in your normal manner, taking especial care to ensure that the ways between worlds are fully and properly closed down.

The second type of Shapeshifting I would like to discuss is slightly different to that described above and involves the deliberate working together between the Witch and their animal familiar to facilitate shape-shifting. True shapeshifting is an extraordinary act of magic when fully accomplished and is one of the old "five skills" that mark an Old Craft Witch; the others are divining accurately, summoning the spirits, hexing and healing (two sides of the same coin, as we have been discussing already) and the art of "telling the maze" (trance and mediumistic work – which are necessary for much of the other Ways of Witchcraft generally). As previously mentioned, it is difficult to fully convey the actual nature and essence of this art, as it partakes of true magic and this cannot be taught but must be experienced. This is as it should be after all, as true magic is elusive and not of this world as such and is the reason why many Traditions rely on personal experience in their training. Developing and becoming proficient in the art of shapeshifting is very much a matter of faith and belief – faith in *your own* abilities. Absolute faith is essential to develop any of the Ways of Witchcraft and the Witch is only limited by their own self-doubt – which is why the creation and absorption of the magical persona is such an important part of magical development for the Witch.

This particular form of the art of shapeshifting depends almost entirely on the level of affinity the Witch can develop with the animal world and, in particular, with their animal guardian or familiar. It is assumed here that the reader has already acquired and developed a relationship with an animal familiar or guardian and has worked with them for some time. Once your animal friend has shown itself to you on the inner planes, you can then make the effort to learn all you can about its habits on the physical level. Not only will this understanding strengthen the bond between you, but it is vital if you want to shape-shift into this particular type of animal. For example, it will be useless trying to run like the wind as a fox, if you have no idea how foxes run at full tilt. As mentioned previously, you must study the animal's movements and habits down to the last detail. Take note of any seasonal changes in the animal's coat or plumage and note whether its habitat changes. Try to learn all you can, right down to the way the creature smells – this is how the old-time Witches would have learnt, from practical experience and observation in the wild. No tiny detail should be overlooked as being insignificant, however mundane it may seem to be. This is why I mentioned earlier that you need to chose an animal from your Land, if not your actual region; if it is too exotic you would be highly unlikely to encounter it naturally, even if symbolically, in your daily life. It is necessary to interact with creatures that are native to your own landscape to truly appreciate and understand them and their ways – book learning is not enough! Having established a strong bond with your animal familiar, you can begin to experiment with this form of shape-shifting, by becoming it.

Create your compass as previously detailed above, going through all the stages, up to and including the trance inducing work. Once at this stage, put on your cord of safety, around your waist, looping it as before. However, this time instead of tying it around your Stang, tie a Hagstone onto the free end and hold this tight in your hand during the rest of the rite. As a naturally protective item, the hagstone will keep you safe and you can use it to call you back again, just by squeezing it in your hand, if you need to, when you are ready to return. Sit comfortably, or lie down, and mentally call out to your familiar; if you have a close bond, after a few moments it should arrive. (Depending on the closeness of your bond, the animal may arrive in its actual physical form, or you may receive a visitation from its spirit form – more likely if you are working indoors; either is appropriate for this rite). Gaze deeply into its eyes and gently begin to exchange minds with it. This sounds simple but is actually very difficult to do and takes much practice; it is not possible to describe the method any better than this and you will know once you have achieved it, as you will be looking at the world from a completely different perspective. It is important to remember that this exchange is every bit as risky for your animal as it is for you. In this instance, you are leaving your body for a temporary dwelling place in theirs and it is important that you place yourself in a sacred and protected place first. It stands to reason that when shape-shifting, you do not loose your physical body entirely and if anything should happen to the physical body of the animal, there may be a risk of injury which will leave its mark on your body, which will only become apparent when you return to it. This is the phenomenon known as "repercussion" in a magical sense.

Not everyone has a natural talent for this type of magic, but it is something that can and should be attempted by anyone seriously hoping to work the old Ways of Witchery. The ability to leave your body and assume different shapes is a liberating experience; it can open up so many possibilities and lead to so many opportunities for learning new knowledge that it is well worth the time and effort expended in learning the technique. Patience is a virtue, but do not be surprised if your first success happens by accident; it is often the case with magic that we may need a bit of a jolt to shake us out of our normal patterns of thinking but, as long as our protection and faith is strong, we can survive.

When you are ready to return, do not simply disengage from your familiar. Let it know that you are ready to go back and help guide it to your compass as best you can – your minds being linked. Gently relinquish your hold/contact with the animal's mind and awake to everyday reality. Don't forget to make some form of offering to your friend and the other creatures of the wild after your practice – however successful or not – as this shows appreciation of their efforts on your behalf and strengthens the bonds even more. Finish as above and as is your normal practise.

Before I finish this section, I would like to add that there is a variation on the above technique, that works the other way around – whereby the animal spirit shape-shifts or takes over the human mind. This is the origin of the legends of such folk as the Berserkers and Ulfhednar of Norse practice. By deliberately allowing the animal spirit to "ride" the human body, the animal gains a completely different perspective on the world/s and is able to communicate with other humans. It is not necessarily all blood, rape and murder, as much useful and valuable information and knowledge may be passed on in this manner. The technique is exactly the same as the above, only the animal spirit takes the upper hand and "controls" the Witch for a time. Again, this is an extremely difficult thing to master and can take many years, if success comes at all.

Conversing with The Other

"When you work with a spirit of the dead you are assisting that spirit in its spiritual evolution, as well as working for the further development of your own spiritual nature."
Martin Coleman - "Communing with the Spirits".

Whilst the modern definition of the word "Converse" is usually taken to mean talking to someone or something and normally implies a two-way interaction, a more archaic definition is "to maintain a familiar association with" someone or thing; this is precisely the sense in which a relationship with "the Other" is maintained by the Witch. The "familiar association" - which of course includes two-way conversation/ communication - is one that is normal and natural to the Traditional Witch and it is by and through this association that much of their work is accomplished. Working with Beings other than themselves, the Witch gains great benefits in both knowledge, understanding and power, but also enables these Beings, or Spirits, to maintain a position in our realm of reality, the better to perform their own works and achieve their own development. This is always a reciprocal arrangement, however strange the arrangement may seem to an outsider looking on and is something that is often forgotten these days. That Spirits also have "work" to do is not something that is generally considered or discussed, but is one of the main reasons that they enable contact with the Witch; just as we have things that we wish to achieve, so do they. More on these arrangements, or pacts, later.

In using the term Other within this situation, I mean to describe what is traditionally held to be the realms of the worlds of Spirits; however, these are not really Other to the Witch. Just as I have been using the images of the Blackthorn and Whitethorn to infer opposites that are not really opposite throughout this work, the Witch doesn't see the Other as Other; to them these realms are perfectly normal and are places that they enter, explore and have converse with the denizens of on a regular basis. These realms are viewed by the Witch not as Other, but more as different realms within the whole of the fabric of the Universe. Just as we, as humans, inhabit our part of the Universe, so too do other Beings or Spirits inhabit their own parts of the Universe. That these realms are not normally discernible to humans at large makes them no less existent, just more difficult to get to. Consider; we all know that Australia exists, but not everyone has been there or finds it easy to make the journey. Unless we possess the skills (i.e. access to appropriate transport and the money to finance the journey, not to mention the time to spare on making the trip), then we are unlikely to be able to visit that "realm". Likewise, the Witch trains hard in acquiring the skills to make the journey to different areas of the Universe that are populated by different "people". In turn, they also enable the Spirits to make the journey to where we are, thus reciprocating the effort on the part of the Spirits that aided them. This is another example of the appearances of duality within our perceptions; these realms are not really Other than ours, they are just less familiar and take a little more effort to get to – it is just a question of perception.

A large part of the work or operations of the Witch is in having familiar discourse with the Spirit worlds and, hence, are perfectly familiar to them. When setting up the area in which to work, the Witch very often creates their compass, which both enables them to cross boundaries into places not commonly accessible and also allows the virtues and denizens of those places to have access to our realm, for however short a space of time. The creation of a fully functioning compass creates pathways to whole areas of reality that it is not normally possible to perceive or work with, but it is really just a question of shifting the awareness of the Witch to a different level or aspect, the better to interact or converse with these realms.

I have touched on the interaction between the Witch and the Spirits earlier in this book and also in others of my works, but here I would like to focus in more detail on a few specific areas and go into some of the practical details and techniques of conversing with these (not) Other realms and Spirits.

Traditional or Old Craft is essentially animistic in nature, in that it perceives or considers that all things possess their own inner life force, virtue or Spirit. This applies as much to a house, a car or a sideboard as it does to a human, a horse or a tree; an object does not have to be animate to be possessed of a living Spirit. In the forms of Craft that I am familiar with, this virtue or Spirit is considered to be part of the divine Flame of Life, gifted by the Witchfather at the beginning of all things; He sent forth part of his own essential, divine nature into all things and, hence, engendered Life. We all partake of this nature and therefore there is an essential unity and commonality between all things. There is no essential division, opposite or Other. However, this is not always immediately apparent to everyone and can sometimes take a lot of work to shift the perception enough on the part of the Witch to enable converse to take place. Whilst it is true to say that communication is possible with all types of Being - and I will go on to describe some different types later in this book - it is usually considered easier, at least at first, to attempt communication with those Spirits that either are, or were, most like us. In general this usually means the spirits of the Dead, Ancestral Spirits, and those Beings variously known as The Good Folk, Faerie or the Elven races.

Dealing with the Dead.

I have talked about how the Dead are viewed in Traditional Craft and described some methods of contacting and communicating with them in an earlier work ("*Treading the Mill*", see bibliography), but here I would like to discuss some different perceptions and approaches. Whether one is an initiate of a particular lineage of Traditional Witchcraft with set Ways of working with the Dead, or a solitary worker practising on their own and developing their own rites, the Ancestors are generally an important part of that work. They may enable contact with other Spirits and can bring forth types of knowledge that are not readily available by others means; through them, the Witch has a direct line back in time, stretching through all past relatives to very remote periods in history. In the final analysis the line can be said to go back to the First Parents, the Witchmother and Witchfather, who are often viewed as the ultimate Ancestors. A close working relationship with the Ancestors is therefore greatly to be desired and developed. There are many and various ways of working with the Dead, but the initial contact is an important part of this and should be carried out carefully and considerately. Most Old Crafters will usually have either a separate altar set aside for Ancestor work, at which offerings, etc. can be made, or a representation of the Ancestors on their main altar. However this is set up one of the things that is most often included is what is known simply as an Ancestor Pot. This is a vessel containing either soil from the grave/s of the Witch's dead relations, or some of their ashes (if they were cremated and it was possible to obtain some), or a mixture of both. This acts both as a focal point for concentration during ancestral work and also as a point of contact, that enables two-way communication to take place more easily. If it is not possible to obtain either soil or ashes of the Dead for whatever reason, some symbolic item such as crushed bone, soil from places Ancestors were known to have lived, photographs or even slips of paper with names written on them are included instead. However, the best substance to have – if not actual cremation ashes - is undoubtedly soil from an Ancestor's grave. There are varying methods for obtaining this from different traditions, but here is a Way from the traditions of East Anglia.

Initially, the Witch needs to obtain a pot that feels comfortable for them and is acceptable to the Ancestors that will "live" in it; intuition plays a great part in the choice. A ceramic pot is the usual choice, one with a cork top, maybe similar to a witch bottle. This may be bought or handmade by the Witch themselves, which always creates a stronger bond. Size is a personal matter, but not overly large. Likewise any decoration is very personal, but normally a sigil, sign or decorative representation of the pot's purpose/use is placed on it. It needs to be clean and free from all previous associations and "contaminants", so a good wash in thieves' vinegar is appropriate. Having prepared a suitable vessel, the Witch needs to obtain grave soil, from as many of their Ancestors graves as they can. This can involve long trips for some people, but that is all to the better, as the more effort put into obtaining the soil the better will be the end result; effort is greatly appreciated and rewarded by the Spirits. Put the soil into the pot all together, so that it mixes well.

In addition to making journeys to where the Ancestors are buried, the Witch needs to obtain the soil in a very particular manner. The Witch needs to enter the "*inner life*" of the graveyard to obtain the essence of the Ancestors' spirit, as this is where it has its being. There is a procedure for doing this, which entails calling on the Guardian of the Graveyard and gaining its support, help and permission to enter this inner side of the cemetery. It is well acknowledged that all graveyards have their spirit guardian. In days gone by, this was created deliberately by sacrificing an animal, usually a dog, and burying it in the graveyard before anyone else was interred, with specific instructions to act as its guardian. When this practice died out, it was considered that the first person buried there took on this role and remained in situ, until such time as some other spirit voluntarily took over. Bearing this in mind, the procedure is as follows.

At a liminal time of day (i.e. dawn, midnight or dusk), go up to the entrance of the cemetery and knock three times on the left hand gatepost with the left hand. Quietly announce your presence and request entrance into the spiritual side of the graveyard from the Guardian, saying that you have a right to be there as your blood is buried there (i.e. an Ancestor of yours), and state why you have come and what you wish to do there. Place an offering for the Guardian; traditionally this is bread and milk, although some people like to leave some whiskey or brandy as well. Pause for an answer, which may be felt either as an acceptance or rejection within. It is rare for the request to be rejected if made sincerely but, be honest and, if it is, walk away and try again another time. There is usually shown to be a good reason for the refusal at that time, so do not be deterred and come back on another day. Once accepted, enter with respect and reverence and locate the specific grave that is needed. Kneel down beside the grave and ask the Ancestor there to have some of their essence in the soil you will take and ask that they be willing to help you in your work. Wait for a response in the usual manner. If it is negative, depart with thanks and without rancour and try another day. If the reply is positive, as is normal, gauge the approximate position of where the heart of the person would be, lying in the grave and take one or two teaspoons-full of soil from over that place – no more. Place this directly into the pot which you should have with you. Express your thanks to the Ancestor and make an appropriate offering. If you knew the person in life, make a small gift of the things they liked to eat whilst alive wherever possible. If you do not know what they liked, or did not know them personally, make offerings of bread and milk, but add some honey and a small amount of alcohol (unless you know that they were teetotal). Return to the entrance and knock three more times on the gatepost, giving thanks to the Guardian for granting access to the spiritual life of the graveyard. Leave without looking back and perform a spiritual cleanse as soon as possible, in case any unwanted influences accidentally attached themselves to you during your time in the graveyard; although you only intended to attract the energy and attention of your own forbears, you also entered the inner life of the whole graveyard, and others may have been attracted to you, which may not be appropriate. This procedure needs to be followed each time you gather any graveyard soil and you should visit as many of your Ancestors as you can.

Once the Witch has obtained soil (or ashes), from as many of their Ancestors as they can manage, the Pot is then placed on their altar and is ready to work with – no other special ceremony is needed, the Ancestors know why they are there. It is now time to make the initial contact, open up communication and begin working with your Ancestral Spirits.

As is usual, there are various ways in which the Ancestors are contacted and each Witch will normally have their own preferred method, but there are some generally accepted ones. It is usual to make and leave offerings to the Ancestors at certain, regular times; daily, weekly or monthly – whatever suits the particular situation. These offerings can vary from simply a glass of water, incense, some flowers, a small cake and/or some wine, to a full meal of favourite things to eat, if known. The latter is generally only given after specific workings or on special feast/holy/anniversary days, etc. and generally, the more normal bread and milk are given, with perhaps some honey added. These offerings are always given before any results from working with the spirits have been obtained, as it shows a measure of trust and belief that the Ancestors will be there to aid you; this is only polite, respectful and is appreciated by Them. Obviously the Ancestors don't physically eat the food, but derive nourishment and sustenance from the virtue contained therein. The energy expended in making the offering and the thoughts and prayers that go with it are also gifts that are appreciated, in some ways even more so. The length of time the Witch leaves the food on the altar is a matter of personal choice, but usually at least overnight, sometimes for several days, or even up to a week. After this time the essential essence will certainly have left the offering and it may well begin to smell and/or rot – not a good thing to leave out as an offering! Change your food gifts regularly and often. In addition to food, most practitioners will also make prayers or speak words of welcome and encouragement when giving these gifts, inviting the Ancestors to come and make contact and aid the Witch in their work. These words need not be lengthy or overly flowery, just simple words of invitation and welcome or gratitude for work accomplished or intended. Always leave a quiet period of a few minutes after making the offerings and prayers for any response to be given.

(Note and personal rant. You will often read that certain things **must** be done with/on an Ancestor altar and that you **have** to have this or that present and you **must** offer this or that at given times. Why? Most of these writers are coming from certain cultural backgrounds and are writing from their point of view – as, indeed, am I – but none of these things **must** be done, only that they can. I feel that a lot of people are missing the point entirely in developing a personal and intimate relationship with their Ancestor/spirit by insisting that certain things must be done entirely inappropriately. Feel your way, develop your relationship individually and you will get a lot further. For example, the Tobacco plant – often cited as a must-have offering for the Ancestors – is not native to Europe and, indeed, is toxic to much natural life here if left out in the wild. My Ancestors certainly wouldn't appreciate an offering of this, especially as most were non-smokers anyway and at least two died from lung cancer! Use what is native to where you are and that which is liked or preferred by the spirits you are working with and you will develop a much better, intimate and more rewarding relationship than trying to slavishly follow methods that are unsuitable for your own situation).

Over a period of time, the Witch will begin to develop a feeling or sensation of when the Ancestors are present. This may simply be a sense of not being alone, or of someone watching them when making the offerings, or a more developed sense of an individual or individual's presence. Sometimes the atmosphere may "thicken" and feel charged or it may be that a sensation of heat is felt. However this works for the individual, the Ancestors will make themselves known when they are ready. It is from this point onwards that the Witch will be ready to start working practically with the Ancestors and can expect them to give help and aid, advice and counsel in their magical work when asked. Eventually, it will be possible for the Witch to request the Ancestors to bring other spirits to them, to take part in their work, but this is quite a developed practice and best left for when they have been working well together for a period of time. Like all associations, contact and communication needs time to grow and develop.

Once this association has developed the Witch may start to ask the Ancestors for advice and information on various aspects of their magical work and the other projects that they are involved in. The way in which the questioning takes place and the manner in which the advice or information is given will vary from Witch to Witch and each will develop their own preferred methods, but here are a few suggestions that are used by many.

Initially, the Witch may find that the answers to their questions are received via dreams, or during meditation. If using the latter, after placing the offering to the Ancestors as usual, state the subject that needs clarification, or the situation that would benefit from advice, then sit calmly before the altar and compose yourself for meditation. Enter a light trance state and simply hold the question in your mind. Don't concentrate overly hard, but just hold the thought lightly and turn it around and around, looking at it from different viewpoints. Think of it like an object – a statue maybe – that you are holding in your hands and turn it around and around to see the different sides. As you do so, be open to accepting different thoughts about it, new considerations and viewpoints that you hadn't come across before. If the Ancestors wish to communicate with you, it is likely that you will suddenly get a flash of insight or suddenly perceive something that had never occurred to you before about the situation. If asking about how to resolve a magical problem, a spell, charm or rite might occur to you in a manner not normally thought of. Accept this as it happens and remember it once you come out of meditation. Don't forget to give thanks afterwards. If attempting to get information from the Ancestors via dreams, the method is similar. Make your offering and request of the spirits before retiring to bed, then compose yourself for sleep, holding the question or subject in mind as you drift off. If you find it simpler or an easier method, compose a sigil of the question and visualise this as you go to sleep. This is a powerful method of dream influencing, as we are mostly visual, rather than verbal, animals and signs and symbols have a great impact on the psyche, making it a much more direct method. You will need to have a pad of paper and pen beside the bed for this, to record your dreams the moment you wake, both in the morning and at any time during the night. Alternatively, use any recording device for ease of storage. As we all know, dream images can vanish very quickly, so it is imperative that you record them straight away. If you used a sigil to ask for advice, it is likely that you will receive an answer in symbolic form also, that may need careful interpretation. This will be a very personal thing and will need careful consideration and skill to interpret correctly. Keep in mind the type of Ancestors that you have managed to make contact with and what manner they are likely to reply in. Time and practice will make this easier and you may well find that you develop a whole dream symbol language with the Ancestors that you can both use. If asking a more direct question, the answer is likely to come pictorially, but also in a form that will need careful interpretation, so develop discernment and don't take the obvious route; Ancestors can be devious and the obvious answer isn't always the right one!

Another form of contacting the Ancestral spirits is via divination. This may be by using any of the well-known forms, such as tarot, oracle cards, runes or other forms of casting, or via such devices as the pendulum, the spirit board, the crystal or the mirror. In all of these situations, make an offering as above, requesting the help and aid of the Ancestors for the particular problem, then turn to your chosen method of divination. Hold the question lightly in your mind whilst you are spreading the cards, casting the runes or scrying in your chosen medium, then make your interpretation accordingly. If using a pendulum, you need to frame the question such that it can be given a "yes" or "no" answer, or alternatively design a pendulum chart that has several possible alternative answers; always remember to include an option for "other" or "unknown", as it is not possible to give an answer to all questions and some outcomes may not yet be seen or known – even to the spirits (see Chapter Six for further information on the technique of Pendulum dowsing and other forms of divination). If using the spirit board, I would advise that just a single spirit or Ancestor be petitioned at one time. This device is best used when you have developed a good contact with a particular spirit that can be relied upon not to give misleading answers, as it is very easy to deceive oneself using this method. As usual, make your petition – but to a single, named, spirit – and hold the question in mind throughout the operation. Write down the letters as they are received and then apply sense and discernment to the result. If you are in doubt, ask again and check the result; the Ancestor in question will not mind if it is genuine.

Another method that is worth considering using here is that of automatic writing. It is a skill that will need work – on both sides – to develop proficiently but, once mastered, is exceedingly useful for quick accurate and detailed responses. Again, this should be used with a specific, named spirit that you have developed a good rapport with and that has proved itself accurate and truthful in the past; remember – Ancestors have a sense of humour too! The technique is very simple but, like most simple things, is quite difficult to do and takes time and practice. To start with, I would suggest that you attempt this and do your initial sessions in a fully hallowed compass. The reasons for this are that it is much easier to focus in an enlivened, magical atmosphere; it cuts out distractions from other energies that are not appropriate at the time and it is easier for the chosen spirit to manifest/make contact within this environment. Once you have both become proficient, using a compass will no longer be necessary, but it helps to start with.

Having created your compass, made your offerings and stated your reasons for attempting contact, sit down comfortably and relax. I would suggest that if you are not comfortable sitting on the ground for possibly lengthy periods of time, that you bring a comfortable seat into the compass with you; something that you can relax in, is supportive of the body and that gives free movement to the hand, resting on a pad of paper, possibly on your knee/s for some time. You need to be able to relax both your mind and your body and not be thinking how uncomfortable you are – be practical! Once you have achieved this, clear your mind and enter a light trance state. Call the Ancestor spirit by name (it should also be obvious by now that most of these techniques can be used with other "familiar spirits" as well) and re-iterate your question. Hold your writing implement loosely, but firmly enough that you don't drop it inadvertently, with the point at the top of a blank page and allow your mind to drift over the question. Unless you are particularly gifted in this area, it is initially difficult to get a balance between writing something yourself and allowing the spirit free rein to write its message. The urge will be to move the pen yourself and see if it will "take off", so to speak, but this must be resisted. It may take some time and several sessions before you achieve results, but these will come with dedication and tenacity. The first result will be a shock and you are likely to end the session yourself, as you will immediately be tempted to hold the pen tighter and take control, being so surprised that the implement is apparently moving by itself. This is natural and normal but must be overcome if any progress is to be made. Relax, still your mind and start again. Further initial attempts will probably produce what looks like a child's scrawl or something completely illegible, or both. However, take heart, you're getting there. Develop this progress over however many sessions it takes, and you will finally achieve legible and intelligible answers.

The next step is to decide who wrote them. Always exercise, caution and discernment; don't just accept anything that appears on the page as "gospel" truth. Just because you had no *conscious* intention to write something, it doesn't mean that another part of you didn't. Look at the reply and try to determine if you would already have had access to the information; does it make sense; is it of any use; does it answer what you asked? All of these need to be considered if you are to accept the reply as valid. Only you will know this, so self-honesty is essential and is, after all, one of the keystones to magical practice – self-knowledge. If you can honestly say that you didn't already know the answer, that it presents new, workable and valid information, that is verifiable by empirical means (if, for example, asking an historical question that can be fact-checked), then you have achieved your initial goal of practising automatic writing. You can now continue to converse with your spirit and ask further questions that will help you with your magical and, perhaps, other work. It is also wise to check replies from the spirits gained in other manners as well; don't be too credulous and just accept anything given – scepticism is a healthy magical attitude to take!

(Just a short example from personal experience here. Once contact has been made, don't expect it all to go your own way; as mentioned above, the spirits also have their own reasons for making contact with us, and they don't all follow our agendas. Many years ago I was learning my Craft from a teacher I respected very much, who was in contact with a familiar spirit and they communicated via automatic writing. This spirit purported to be a priestess from a temple in ancient Egypt and used to give advice on questions of magical ritual. They were in regular contact and had been for several years and knew each other well. However, this spirit had one personal foible, in that she would always start personal communication with a severe castigation of my teacher for not having followed temple procedure in his daily activities. From her point of view – and presumably her position in time and space – she didn't understand why my teacher hadn't made the morning sacrifices, hadn't accepted the offerings from the local populace to the temple, or set aside the required 3 hours for meditation and ritual in the middle of the day. Trying to tell her that things just weren't like that any more in this day and age were to no avail and she found it very difficult to understand. That things like public temples with priesthoods and servants no longer existed and that we had to follow a 9 – 5 regime was totally incomprehensible to her. So do be aware that sometimes the spirits' attitudes may be very different from ours).

Having reached this stage of proficient contact with the Ancestral spirits – or an individual spirit – the Witch may feel that there is no need to go further and this is perfectly acceptable. However, there may be occasions when it *is* felt necessary to have a deeper and more direct level of contact, perhaps to request/receive some extra knowledge or information that can't be communicated in any other manner, and this may be achieved by performing a full conjuring or summoning of the spirit/s. By using the terms "conjuring" and "summoning" I do not mean to imply any imposition of force or control upon the spirits, any constraint or servitude, as is normal within some of the Solomonic Traditions or those based on the mediaeval grimoire systems. Within Old Craft, certainly as I know it, the whole aim is to work *with* the spirits, as equal partners in shared operations, designed for the benefit of both parties. There is no use trying to get information from a spirit that you have spent months building a relationship with, only to threaten them with fire and damnation at the final moment – they're not really likely to be forthcoming with advice in that situation. A better term for this operation might be a "Calling", or a "Calling Forth", which better fits the nature of this rite and so I shall continue with this term from here. The purpose of this rite is to Call Forth a specific Ancestor spirit, either to visual or semi-visual manifestation, or to a strongly felt presence, in order to make a request that would not otherwise be possible under other methods, as deemed valid by the individual Witch. The response may be seen, heard or felt immediately if a direct question is asked, the answer received later via dream or vision work or, if a practical result is desired, to be manifested at a later date.

This rite needs to be performed in a fully hallowed compass, so all the usual things the Witch would use for that need to be present, and also food and drink for a shared meal afterwards, but some additional items will also be needed. The first of these is a bone skull of a human, or representation of the same. It is obviously not that easy to get hold of a human skull and digging up Granddad would also be both difficult and illegal, but these things are available if sought for – why not ask the Ancestors for help beforehand in procuring one. If you do manage to find one, it is obviously highly unlikely to be the skull of one of your own, direct Ancestors – certainly not a specific one – but it is the representation that matters here. We all have shared ancestry, no matter where we come from, and the further back in time we go, the fewer Ancestors there are, until we go right back to a common or shared ancestry in the First Parents, the Witchfather and Witchmother, however or whatever They are conceived of as being by the individual Witch. The bone skull is intended both to represent the Ancestors – common and individual – and also the Witch themselves as a living continuation of the line of Life. The skull represents the ancient power of the Ancestors that resides in the Witch's own, living body. The chain of life that led from them up to and within the Witch themselves. It is used to open up a gateway whereby the spirit may pass through and manifest within the compass when Called. It is a representation of the shared Life of us all, both living and dead, as we all possess our own skulls as well and it is through this shared bone that we may interact at a very deep level of connection. It is another example of there being no "Other", no Us and Them, no Dead or Alive; in this operation, all are the same – literally – there are no opposites.

So, wherever possible, it is most desirable to obtain a human skull – in a *legal* manner – for use in this rite. If this is not possible, an anatomically correct, artificial skull should be obtained and used. In this case, the skull needs to be marked with a little of the Witch's own blood, in the compass just before the rite of Calling begins. Just a drop will suffice, obtained from a small pin prick and smeared onto the skull. This is to "enliven" the skull and to give it that essential connection with both the living and the dead, without which it would be difficult to form a connection and, hence, a gateway for the spirit to manifest through.

The next item that is needed here is a triangle made from three lengths of Blackthorn, each roughly a foot to 18" long (big enough to place the skull inside), placed on the altar if using one, or on the ground, in the middle of the compass. The wood should be taken with permission from your kin-tree. The use of the Blackthorn here makes use of several different aspects of the tree itself and the work that you will already have done. Because it is from your kin-tree, you will already have developed a relationship with the spirit of the tree and can call on its aid in performing this rite. The triangle created will already be a thing endowed with spirit, which will make it easier for the Ancestor spirit to manifest. The Blackthorn wood itself is also of a powerful nature, full of vitality and virtue, so will add it's strength in the manifestation of the Ancestral spirit. The use of a triangle of this nature is also important, in that it is not used for containment, but for *manifestation*; the triangle is the strongest and most stable of the basic shapes and actually aids in the spirit manifesting itself.

The final extra item is a wand of Blackthorn, again made from your kin-tree. Just as we availed ourselves of the attributes of Whitethorn in the previous chapter for its abilities in enchantment and shapeshifting, so now do we use the Blackthorn for its strength and energy and ability to aid in shaping and guiding the forces invoked during this operation. It is valuable in focussing and directing the virtue of the rite into the desired areas for manifestation. (If your kin-tree also happens to grow in a graveyard or cemetery, then there are also much stronger links with the dead there too and this will aid in the rite of Calling).

Having now obtained all things necessary for the rite of Calling, this is the manner in which it needs to be performed. (I have deliberately given fairly loose instructions here, so that the individual Witch may adapt the rite to their own particular circumstances and situation. It is much better to personalise a rite of this kind than to slavishly follow a set of directions that are not appropriate to the individual or their spirit connection. The timing of the rite is also up to the operator; use the time and tide that seems most appropriate to all parties involved).

The Calling Forth of the Shade

Have the Stang standing in the north of the area, at the edge of the compass and the altar in the middle of the space, if using one, otherwise place the items on the ground, on a black cloth. Position the triangle of Blackthorn in the centre of the altar/cloth, with the long edge to the south and the point at the top, facing the north. Place the skull in the middle of the triangle, along with anything else associated with that particular Ancestor spirit (picture, mementos, flowers, etc.). Place a lit beeswax candle to either side of the triangle, outside of the "thorned-area", but close to the edge. Set a censer of appropriate incense just inside the top point of the triangle (a suggested blend of incense is detailed below); this is both an offering to the Ancestor spirit and an aid to manifestation. Light the charcoal and put on some incense at the start of the ritual. Lay the things for the shared meal (wine/ale, cakes/bread, etc.), below the bottom edge of the triangle. If you are working with a known, named Ancestor, place the Ancestor Pot, opened, inside the triangle, beside the other memento items; if you do not know the Ancestor, or the name, place it outside of the triangle, but still opened.

Place a large Hagstone, as large as you can find (but small enough to lift comfortably), at the south of the area.

When all is in readiness, hallow the compass as is your usual practice, remembering to call in all the other spirits you normally work with, to help with this rite.

Raise the Stang in the north and invoke the Horned Lord as Father of All, and ask that the Ancestor be allowed to attend. Replace Stang.

Raise the Hagstone in the south and invoke the Witchmother as Divine Ancestress, and ask that the gateway may be opened. Replace Hagstone.

Return to the altar/cloth. It is now time to anoint the artificial skull with your blood if you need to do this, before the rite progresses any further. There is no need for any words to be said, as you know what you are doing and why, but feel free to express this verbally if you feel you want to. Either way, focus clearly on what you are doing, while you are doing it.

Add more incense now.

Take up the Blackthorn wand in the left (or non-dominant), hand and state the reason for the rite in simple terms. You must now Call on the Ancestor spirit directly; use this form of Calling, or use it as a basis for your own words. (Use the name of the spirit if you know it, otherwise just say "Ancestor" (but keep in mind who you are Calling).

> *"Spirit of X, in the names of the Witchfather and Witchmother, divine Ancestors of all Folk,*
> *By the powers of the Light and the Dark, of the Day and of the Night, I Call upon thee to appear before me in comely form now! By the spirits of the Blackthorn and the virtues they possess, by the virtues of the Blood that binds us, by the virtues of the Four Winds and in like manner of the virtues of Above and Below, I Call Thee Forth! Come hither and appear, I Call Thee! I Call Thee! I Call Thee Forth!"*
>
> (Say this three times in all).

Still holding the wand, begin to tread the mill widdershins, focussing on the skull in the centre. Use a chant of your own composing, or use the following as an example, tailoring it to your own circumstances. Gently intone as you pace;

> *"Hear my Call and rise,*
> *Ancient One of Kith and Kin;*
> *Hear my Call and come,*
> *From thy home within the Land."*

Continue until you feel a shift in the atmosphere, both within yourself and within the compass.

Stop pacing and stand/sit before the skull. Place more incense on the coals. Begin to gently tap the wand on the skull at a beat of about twice a second, whilst softly chanting the following;

"Awake X (name of Ancestor),
Arise X.
Come, Come."
(If you don't know the name, say "friend").

Find a beat that suits you, but try to keep closely to this timing. This regular, sonic vibration helps to create a gateway between yourself and the Ancestor, through which you will be able to converse. This vibration makes it easier for you to connect and communicate, without further resort to other techniques or materials. Continue this for as long as you feel is necessary, whilst visualising the Ancestor as standing in the place of the skull (close your eyes for this if it helps, or look through half-closed eyelids). Continue for as long as you feel necessary, but don't drain yourself – success is not guaranteed in any rite and it is as difficult for the Ancestor spirit to make contact from their side as it is for you to Call them. Once you feel that contact has been achieved or the spirit takes visible/semi-visible form before you, stop your chant and tapping and gently ask your question or make your request. This may be verbally or mentally, whatever suits you best. Wait a little while for them to reply back to you – remember this is hard work on both sides. Continue with the questioning as is appropriate.

Once you have received your replies and/or you feel that the connection is breaking, it is time to hallow your meal. Do this in the manner that you are used to and dedicate it to the Ancestor spirit, giving thanks as you do so. If you are outdoors, pour/place some of the meal directly onto the ground in front of the skull. If you are indoors, leave some on the altar/cloth (in a bowl) overnight as an offering in gratitude. Don't forget to eat and drink some yourself, as this is a communion in the true sense of the word. Finally, say your thanks and bid the spirit depart in peace, but ask that they may be ready to communicate again, if you feel that this is needed and/or appropriate. Do not forget to bid the spirit to depart as, however friendly the exchange has been, the gateway must be specifically closed down; open doors are dangerous and leave opportunities for entities not deliberately Called to also come through. This should never be neglected.

End your rite in your usual manner, not forgetting to give thanks to those other beings and spirits that you have asked to be present, including the Witchfather and Witchmother.

Incense for spirit manifestation and Calling.
2 parts Frankincense
2 parts Benzoin
2 parts Dittany of Crete
1 part Balm of Gilead
2 parts Wormwood
1 part Rosemary
1 part Blackthorn leaves
1 part Parsley leaf
1 part Henbane leaves.
A few drops of Cinnamon pure essential oil.
A small amount of pure Honey.

Grind the gums to a rough shingle, then mix in the dry ingredients; grind all together to a pleasing consistency. Add the cinnamon oil and then just enough honey to bind all the ingredients together loosely. Allow the mixture to dry thoroughly before using. Store in a cool, dry place in a dark jar. Use freely for spirit manifestation.

Before leaving this section, I would like to include an alternative rite for contact with the Ancestral dead. It is simple, but relies on the Witch having access to the relatives' grave, which, obviously, is not always possible. However, I include it here for those that are able and willing to perform this rite. It is derived from a Family Tradition in East Anglia of unknown age.

When wishing for information on a certain subject, or directions as to what to do in a certain situation, perform the following. Go to the cemetery at night, on the day of the birthday of the person you wish to enquire of. If this is not possible, then the anniversary of the day they were buried will suffice. Along the top of the grave, dig a smaller, replica grave, into which you should pour a bottle of red wine and a single drop of your own blood. To the north of the grave, create a circle big enough to lie in, by Thorning the Ground (as described earlier) and surround this with earth taken from the grave, mixed with dried bread; scatter this around outside the edge of the circle. Next, dribble some fresh, spring water from the edge of the grave, up to the edge of the south side of your circle and light a red or black candle there (traditionally a beeswax candle mixed with soot or red ochre is used). Stand inside the circle in front of the candle and call out the Ancestor's name three times, quite clearly. Ask them for the information that you need, or the answer to your question, then lie down and compose yourself for sleep. (Opinions diverge as to whether the candle should be blown out or not at this point; some say yes, some say no. Chose whichever seems right to you at the time). Spend the night in the circle and, when you awake in the morning, take careful note of your dreams, for they will reveal the information that you require.

This technique *may* also be used to contact one of the Elven-kind at a burial mound, or similar, but comes with increased risks of safety. I would suggest you read the following section first and then consider carefully before undertaking the rite in this situation.

Associating with the Faire Ones

As with the Ancestral Spirits, I have previously discussed the origins of the Faire Folk or Elven races elsewhere (see "*Treading the Mill*"), so I do not wish to repeat myself here, but would like to look at the subject from a slightly different perspective. I have described earlier in Chapter 2 of this book, the theory that the Fair Ones were the product of the matings between Lilith and Samael (Lucifer) and that they may have been the (magical), progenitors of the Witches of yore, or at least of the proposed witch-blood that flows in many veins today. Taking this point it can be proposed that the Witches, or at least the Old Witch Traditions, stand as a meeting/joining/crossing point between both the Ancestors and the Faerie races – Blackthorn and Whitethorn once more, whichever way round you may wish to describe each grouping – with the Witches taking the place of the Light between the Horns. This replays the concept of non-duality discussed earlier and combines both strands of traditional lore concerning the subject (Ancestors and Faire Ones). The Witch stands in the middle, between both parties and partakes of the nature and essence of both the Ancestors (naturally) and also the Faire Ones, by virtue of magical blood and association. It has long been known that Old Craft works intimately with the Ancestral spirits, but also that initiates are known to associate closely and derive much lore from, the Elven folk. Indeed, there are traditions that state that Witches are the spirits of Fairies, reborn into a physical body. However that may be, there are many recorded instances in the lore of Witches gaining knowledge and magical powers from the Elven races themselves, either directly, by visiting Elphame or going within the Hollow Hills, or during trance states where these Folk are encountered. In the lore, these Beings are treated variously as both corporeal and non-corporeal and, indeed, they appear to be able to be either, depending on the situation or how they wish to interact with us. However, for the purposes of this work I will treat them as non-corporeal, as spirits, as that is the way they appear mostly, in my experience and research.

Let me just say here, before I progress, that as far as the difference between "Fairies" and "Elves" is concerned, I consider them to be one and the same race, albeit viewed through different lenses. The "Faerie" race derives much of its lore and magic from the Gaelic traditions and peoples, whereas the "Elven" lore is derived mainly via the Germanic/Norse peoples and they tend to become one in English lore, magic and tradition. One can argue endlessly – and many learned people have done – about the derivations of the names, characteristics and attributes of the two magical races and, indeed there are many, but there are obvious and undoubted similarities between Fairies and Elves, however much they vary. However, I consider that the differences are the result of these Folk being viewed and recorded from different cultural viewpoints, with all the baggage that that always brings. That they are the same race is self-evident in my view and I shall treat them as such in this work from now on. The reader is, obviously, entitled to disagree!

As an example of the association and interaction between the "races" - human and non - I would like now to present a remarkable interview that I obtained with a modern, practising Witch from my own area of East Anglia, which demonstrates some of the concepts discussed already. It gives many details of the lives of the Faire folk and some of the manners in which they may work and interact with us. This person first encountered what they call the Elves, after suffering a sudden, life-threatening situation and was recovering in hospital. A Being turned up to help them in their recovery and has been with them ever since. My informant did not call upon the Elves themselves, but always assumed that they had been sent to help them by someone else. However, from that time onwards they were able to see and converse with these Folk and this has lasted over a period of more than ten years to date. I will give the interview in full and then examine some parts of it, but much is self-explanatory and needs no further exposition.

"The spirits I work with are best described as Elves, although the words they use are different and very hard to pronounce, particularly their names. It's not really English and I suppose that I communicate directly mentally with them in any case, so language doesn't really matter. The Elves I know are very much attached to a wood where I go and will sort of fade back into the trees when they don't want to be disturbed, have finished communicating, or just don't want to communicate, although

they are not *tree spirits themselves. This fading back is very much based on the fact that they have been ignored for so long, that they are unwilling to put themselves forward and approach people. They live a communal life and have a council that they take their problems to, for help in making decisions. It's a sort of Council of Elders, who will give their opinion, based on experience, but the decisions are always made jointly by everyone.*

In appearance they are human shaped and have a nutty brown tone of skin and dress in similar shades of clothing; a bit like typical camouflage colours, but not in those patterns. They can vary in height from about waist high on a human, to taller than us, but are generally seen around waist height. There are men and women, but I haven't seen any children; they tell me that when more are needed, they emerge fully formed from the Life all around us. They are quite shy and gentle and can't bear anything being hurt, never killing anything for food. They don't eat like we do, but subsist on the energy around us all. They are usually quite active during the summer months, but become less so during the winter, perhaps reflecting the trees and the natural life that they are so close to.

To work magically with them, they generally let one become attached to a person, sort of like a familiar spirit – as in they become familiar and work with you – and can be very helpful. I don't know exactly how they work their "magic", but if I ask for something, like healing, or for help for someone, or to make sure we can pay the bills, then they just go and do it. It needs to be something possible though, not like, I want to find a thousand pounds today – they just laugh at that! If the person that needs help is not near, they will either send someone to help them, or get in touch with one/some of their folk who are nearer and get them to help instead. Offerings are much appreciated – I give them bread, honey and almond milk, which they seem to prefer to cow's – but these are not essential; a heartfelt word of thanks is more than acceptable.

They don't appear to have any leaders, other than the Council I've mentioned, and I've not seen or heard of a King or Queen who rule them. They appear to have a very "natural" form of religion, but don't make a big deal about it, taking it very much as a given and it's always just there in the background. It's a bit like a form of what we know as paganism, in that there seems to be a Green Man/Horned god type of figure and also a form of goddess. They say that they (the Elves) are part of the gods and that the gods are part of them, so there's no need to make a big thing of it. The goddess figure is quite abstract and never personified or shown in anthropomorphic form, but seems to be something like our concept of an Earth Mother or Gaia figure. She is very maternal and caring and very immanent, so much so that she is just accepted for being there all the time and not much is made of it. There's nothing like a Maiden and Crone, just the Mother figure. They don't seem to have religious festivals like us, but they do wish me a happy whatever, when it's one of ours. They just accept the turning of the times and seasons as part of themselves and everything around them, which they are a part of."

There is much in this description that correlates with and is borne out by the traditional lore; the close association with nature, lack of children, subsisting on energy rather than physical food, living in a sort of twilight world between humans and a spiritual realm, the size descriptions and their ways of working with humans. What is interesting is the point about there being no King or Queen and being led by a Council of Elders. Most stories of these Folk make the point that they are ruled by either a King or Queen or both and that it is these beings that transmit magical lore, teachings and knowledge to Witches. It may be in this case that my informant has contacted a group with a slightly different communal set-up than normal, or that different groups have different ways of organising themselves anyway. I also find their description of their religious attitudes very interesting and it bears out a salient point that Lee Morgan makes in his book, "*Sounds of Infinity*". He quotes Robert Kirk's statement from "*The Secret Commonwealth*" that, "*religion is not known among them*", and then goes on to say that;

> *"the faith of the fairies is far more a matter of direct experience much more akin to the direct gnosis of the mystic than blind belief. There is enough...........to make us ask if the term "Fairy Faith", meaning the faith humans place in fairies, should instead be taken to mean the faith* shared with *fairies."*

In this case I can do no other than agree wholeheartedly, as the description given by my informant closely matches much that would be shared with Traditional Witch practice today.

When describing the offerings that they give, there is a difference from traditional lore. It is normally stated that the Folk will not do anything unless they are given payment, usually in the form of the traditional bread and milk, although other versions are known. Here it is stated that these are not needed and that heartfelt thanks are sufficient. Normally, when thanks are given in the traditional tales, the Faire Folk disappear and are never seen again – it is the physical offerings that are much preferred. It is interesting to speculate here as to whether the Folk derive nourishment from the energy behind the "heartfelt thanks" in a similar manner that they take the essence from the physical offerings. This may be supported by my informant offering almond milk rather than cow's milk. The Elves say that this is preferred because of the way cows are reared/treated in milk production these days and they don't like the energy – food for thought here, not just about milk, but in offerings in general and in attitudes in magical working.

As a working practice, I am told by my informant that there is nothing particularly formal about it. Now that they are in contact with the Elves and can associate closely with them, all they need to do if they want something done, is to walk in the woods and ask them. I have seen this happen myself and the requests are usually answered in a very short time; either the thing required is done, or the answer comes back they they are not going to do it this time, for whatever reason. Whilst this method of contacting the Folk is not unusual, other methods and practices are certainly more common and I would now like to turn to some of these.

Unlike working with Ancestral spirits, it is not usual to summon, conjure or formally Call the Faire Folk, within Traditional Witchcraft. Methods such as these certainly do exist and are used by some, but are not originally traditional and come from the mixing of Witch lore with the Grimoire traditions of ceremonial magic, beginning around the 16th. Century. This mingling can be seen in such works as the *Book of Oberon, The Grimoire of Arthur Gauntlet, The Discoverie of Witchcraft* and *A Cunning Man's Grimoire* (see Bibliography). These, in turn derive from the associations of English Cunning Men, inheritors of much traditional Witch lore, with their more literate and "bookish" companions, the ceremonial magicians of late Elizabethan times and onwards. Many Witches – or those about to become Witches – often had "chance" encounters with the Faire Folk, the Fay initiating the contact themselves, no doubt for their own purposes. The more normal methods used by Witches for calling or communicating with the Elven Folk are much less formal and rely mostly on attracting their attention and waiting to be contacted by them. This was not without danger in itself, as to draw their attention was traditionally a decidedly chancy thing to do, their attitude towards humans being deemed ambiguous at best. However, there exist procedures for gaining the attention of the Faire ones and I shall describe a few below.

Alongside the traditions of what may be termed Woodland or Sylvan Elves – an example of which may be assumed to have been given by my informant above – there is also the lore of the Mound-dwelling Elves or Fairies. These Folk are sometimes thought to be the same as the Dwarves or Svartalfar of Norse tradition and legend (often also themselves considered to be spirits of the dead), but bear a marked similarity to the Hill Folk or *Sidhe* of Irish legend in appearance and actions, and therefore can be considered separate from the Dwarves. These Folk are described as tall, fair in colour and attitude, mostly indifferent to mankind, but can be contacted if treated with respect and fairness in return. In my home region are located the well-known burial mounds of Sutton Hoo, thought to be the last resting place of the East Anglian King and one-time Bretwalda of England, Raedwald. These mounds are still visited and used by magical practitioners, but are also considered too public and inaccessible by many who prefer to make other arrangements. East Anglia was once home to several stone circles which over time, alas, have been destroyed and are no longer available for magical working – the nearest one to this region being the Rollright Stones in Oxfordshire. However many other, much smaller, burial mounds are still in existence, more accessible to lone practitioners and less public than those at Sutton Hoo. This region is also home to many "tumps" or artificial mounds, thought to delineate the paths of the leys or spirit lines within the Land, often topped with lone or a small clump of Scots Pine trees. In addition, particularly in the coastal region known as the Sandlings, there are many heathlands dotted with large hillocks and odd-shaped mounds that have yet to be excavated and are of unknown age, use and origin. All of these are viable access points for contacting the Elven-Folk.

A traditional method used to attempt converse with the dwellers in the mounds is as follows.

This may be used for contact with an Elven being that you already know and have communicated with before and also if you desire to initiate contact in the first instance. Take three Hazel Wands, all of one years growth, each one cubit in length (the distance from the elbow to the middle finger of the Witch). Strip the bark cleanly from all of them and, if known, carve the name of the Being you wish to contact on each of them. Rub the carvings with some of your own blood, so that the name stands out clearly. (If the name of the Being is not yet known, either carve three X's in a row or the name *Sibylia* – thought to be the Queen of Faerie in some traditions). At dusk on a Friday evening, during a waxing Moon, bury all three wands at the base of a mound of your choosing, known to have Faerie associations. Leave a hagstone at the place to mark and protect the wands in your absence – also to absorb the essence of the mound. The following Friday, at the same time, return to the mound and dig up the wands, retaining also the hagstone which you should hold in your right hand when performing the Calling. Holding the wands in your left hand, raise them over the mound and make a simple Call to the Folk, to the effect that you wish contact and association with them. If you know the name of the Being you wish to contact, call this out three times at the end of the Call, otherwise use Sibylia. This procedure should be repeated three times over and then you should wait silently for any response. The hagstone may be held up to the eyes to look through the hole for any visible manifestation, as it is both a protective amulet and is also valued for its ability to convey the Sight temporarily, to enable the viewer to "look between worlds". If your Call is answered – visibly or in any other manner - remember to treat the Elf with honesty and respect, but do not fawn; They also respect dignity in others as well as in themselves. State what it is you wish to know or have Them do for you and proceed as the situation dictates. (If a pact or oath is required, see below for advice on this subject). A gift is usually appreciated and you should ask what They require, but do not agree to something you are not willing to give, or you think ridiculous – They are quite capable of testing you and this may be such a situation. When the encounter is over, give thanks, turn and depart without looking back. This whole procedure may be attempted three times in the same place, on separate occasions, if not effective the first time. However, if after these attempts no results are obtained, a new site should be sought, as it is clear that the Folk of this place are not willing to converse with you. Discard the hazel wands and the hagstone – suitably! - and begin again with fresh ones in another location.

Another method of attracting the attention of the Folk at a mound, is to lay out a special meal for them. This is usually done on top of the mound at night, but specific locations might dictate otherwise. As ever, be practical in your Craft. This method is sometimes called the White Meal, as opposed to the well known Red Meal, which has a different use. There are differing directions for setting up this meal, coming from various Witch Ways – one in particular is given in "*The Grimoire of Arthur Gauntlet*", derived from traditional sources – and I shall describe the one that I know best.

Before attempting the contact with the meal, you must prepare an essential ingredient. On the night of either the Dark or Full Moon, clean and freshen your hearth (or equivalent), whilst asking the blessing of the Faire Folk, *silently* and never looking behind you. Place a bowl of fresh spring or rain water on the hearth and leave overnight. You must be the last person up in the house and do all this without being observed. The next morning, you must arise first in the house and check the bowl of water – if anyone else sees the water first the spell will be broken. If the operation has succeeded, there will be a kind of skin or thin film across the surface of the water. This must be very carefully removed and kept in a small box either of tin or silver, until needed. If the skin has not formed, try again another time. Once you are successful, you may proceed with the meal. On a night which you deem suitable, go to your chosen mound and place a white cloth on the ground. On the cloth put a bowl of ale or mead, a small bowl of fresh cream, a cup of freshly drawn spring water and a choice piece of lean meat. Set a smoking bowl of sweet smelling incense (something simple like Rosemary, Lavender or Balm), and sprinkle all with water of Roses. This must all be done in total silence. Sit now and place over your eyes the film that you took from the water on the hearth. Stay in utter stillness and silence, blinking as little as possible less you disturb your vision, not looking directly at the meal, but have it within sight of the corner of your eye. This is another form of the technique of "sitting out" that we encountered in an earlier chapter. Wait silently and patiently for any contact. If you see any of the Folk arrive to partake of the meal, do not look directly at Them or speak to Them, but you may incline your head in acknowledgement of their presence and wait for them to initiate contact. If They do – and it is by no means guaranteed that they will – remember the attitude of respect and honesty and proceed accordingly. Once all is finished, whether the Folk have appeared or not, give thanks and pour out the (remains of the) meal on the ground and leave without looking back over your shoulder or turning around. If no contact occurs, then you may attempt this working three times but, again, if it does not work after the third attempt, seek another site.

(On an interesting historical note, there is a recipe for making an oil for putting on the eyes to enable one to see the Fairies, from a manuscript dated 1600 in the Ashmolean Museum in Oxford. I think it is appropriate to reproduce it here for those that are interested in trying it.

> *A Salve to Enable One to See the Fairies.*
> *"(Take) a pint of sallet-oyle and put it into a vial glasse; and first wash it with rose-water and marygolde water; the flowers to be gathered towards the east. Wash it till the oyle becomes white, then put into the glasse, and then put thereto the budds of hollyhocke, the flowers of marygolde, the flowers or toppes of wild thyme the budds of young hazle, and the thyme must be gathered near the side of a hill where fairies used to be; and take the grasse of a fairy throne; then all these put into the oyle in the glasse and sette it to dissolve three days in the sunne and then keep it for thy use.").*

With all of the above workings, it is never possible to say beforehand how any of them will come out. Apart from anything else, the Faire Folk are traditionally known to be a very fickle lot and love having fun at our expense, if they deign to acknowledge us at all, so patience is definitely a virtue in these situations. However, contact between Witch and Faerie kind is both traditional and rewarding to both parties and has occurred repeatedly over hundreds of years, so success is something definitely to be hoped for, if not totally expected always. In addition, some people are more naturally gifted in the realms of psychic vision than others, so where it may be possible for them to perceive a full "manifestation" of another Being, or at least a transparent figure – and be able to communicate with it – another may see nothing at all. Some people are adept at dream-working and derive much of their information and inspiration therefrom, after performing a working of this type – indeed, with mound working, it is traditional to spend the night on the mound, often asleep, and derive contact that way. As discussed above, each Witch has their own preferred method and area of expertise and should develop most what comes best naturally to them; none is inherently "better" than another. There is one other method of associating with the Faire Folk though, which I would like to discuss now, and that is one that can be both very enlightening and also one to be cautious of.

Taking Possession of the Situation

In my experience, possession is not a topic much discussed these days, but it is one that has a long history within the Craft and is also a very traditional arte, in all senses of the word. It is a technique of contact and association with an outside Being that can be very richly rewarding for both parties, if willing, each gaining something that they would not otherwise be able to experience. For the Witch, it gives direct insight into the workings of different realms, from a "native's" perspective; they may be changed spiritually and magically in ways not otherwise practicable and they can also gain in magical knowledge and ability. For the Being possessing the Witch, They gain a foothold – however temporary – within the physical world and experience it as we would do. It also gives them the opportunity to pass on, verbally, instructions, teachings and other directions, that it may otherwise be difficult to deliver and receive direct communication back in turn. They may gain other things on levels that we are, as yet, unable to comprehend also. Everyone wins – or so it would seem.

Possession, whilst seeming to be an excellent medium for communication, also has its drawbacks. It is not a technique that it is advisable to be practised by an individual alone, but is best attempted within a group situation. Whilst it would be unthinkable – and totally stupid, not to mention magically irresponsible – to voluntarily let an unknown entity take over one's body and senses, this does sometimes accidentally happen – and I have seen it occur. If this is the situation, untold harm may be caused to the subject's psyche and mental health, not to mention scar them to a greater or lesser extent and put back their magical development immensely. If this were to occur whilst the Witch were alone, then they would have no recourse to help or aid in getting rid of the unwanted "passenger", which is why this technique is always best attempted in a group, with experienced practitioners available to watch, guide and help if things go wrong. Even within a group situation, it is not unknown for certain individuals to fake possession and attempt to pass off their own "teachings" and actions as those of an exalted Being, without repercussion for their actions, so participation by experienced and trusted practitioners is essential here. Before I give instructions for how this practice may be attempted, I would like to give an example of an involuntary – albeit benign – form of possession from personal experience which, I hope, the reader may find interesting and informational.

Some 35 years ago I was visiting a Witch in Germany whom I used to work with in England. She had moved abroad and had begun to work with a new group of people in her new location. On this occasion, some 5 or 6 of us were visiting a group of megalithic remains known as the "Sieben Steinhauser", near Bergen-Hohne, Lower Saxony.

These are a group of five, capped dolmens, dating from the third millennium BCE, the largest being designated "Grave D", which was where I had my experience. We had entered the chamber and I had begun by dowsing the site, to see if I could get any impressions of the original users. It seemed to me after a while that I was being wrapped in cotton wool or in a cocoon, everything became very quiet, still and insulated. I closed my eyes to see what I could pick up and gained the visual image of a dark interior, lit by a fire in the centre. Around the fire sat a group of people who appeared to be banging on skin drums with bones, whilst a woman was dancing around the fire; chanting was also taking place but not by the people drumming. The feeling was of some form of ritual, possibly a funeral rite. At this point, I got the sense of a great space, like a large hall, which I was part of and that I was rising higher and higher within it. I seemed to be being pushed up into a small space right at the top and out of the way of the rest of the space. This felt like it was being filled with something else, but I couldn't tell what. I was no longer aware of the tomb I was in, or of the people that I had seen, only of being pushed into a smaller and smaller space in what felt like the inside of the top of my head, which at the same time was also this great hall. At this point I was beginning to become somewhat concerned and was wondering what to do and how to get out of the situation, when my normal vision began to re-assert itself and I gradually found myself sitting on the ground, inside the dolmen, surrounded by several rather relieved faces. When I asked what had happened, I was told that all had seemed normal when I began dowsing, but then I had stopped and gradually slumped down to sit on the floor, with a rather vacant expression on my face. I had apparently then started to try to speak, but nothing much – or coherent – was coming out. In view of the situation and location, the leader of the group decided that it was time to bring me out of the trance-like state and so had carefully brought me round and back to normal reality. I described the sensations that I

1. The damaged figure of Pan, originally in the Manor House gardens, rescued and cared for by a childhood friend. (Photo (C) Ticky Wright).

2. Blackthorn blossom; top. Whitethorn blossom; bottom.
Shades of magic and duality.

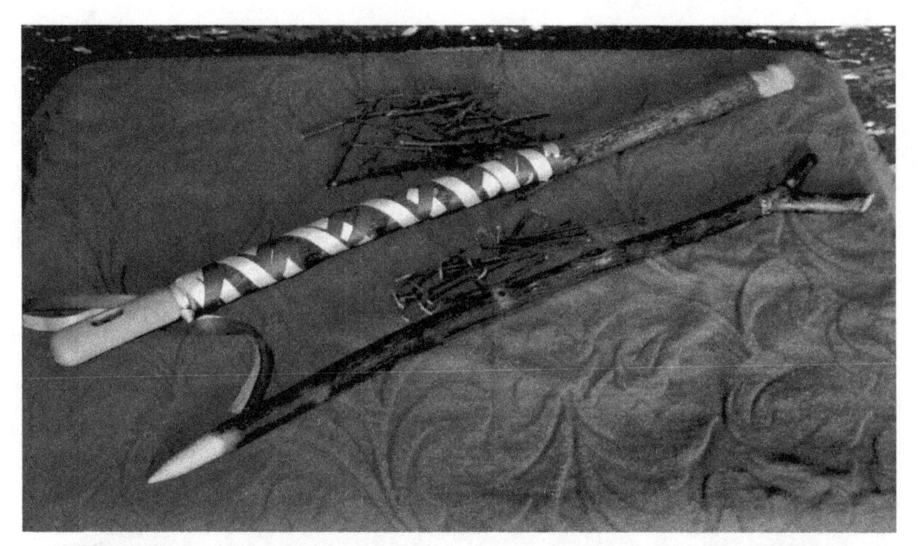

3. Top: Whitethorn wand and spikes. Below: Blackthorn wand and thorns. Two shades of the same Virtue.

4. "Roamers Road"; a passage to non-duality in the East Anglian countryside.

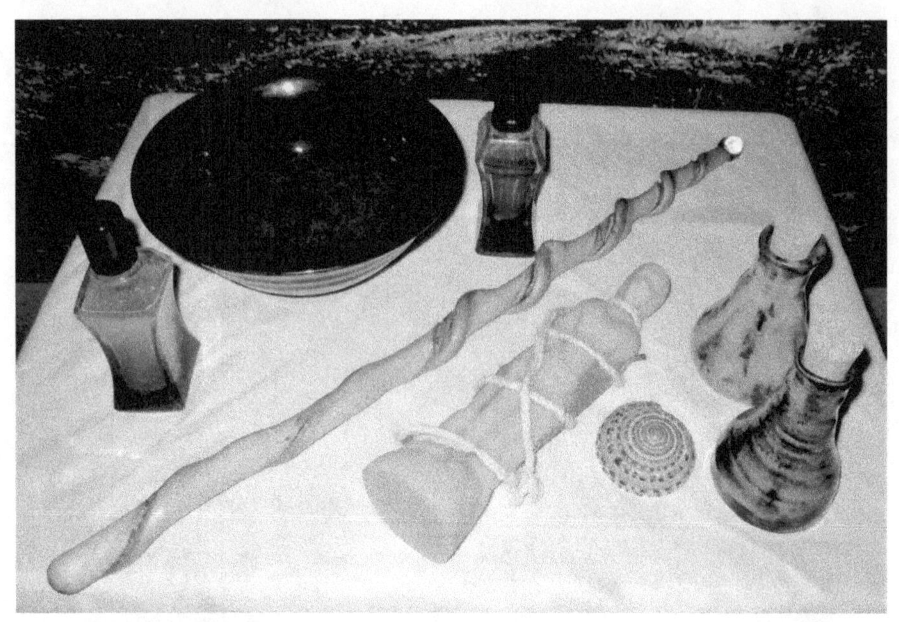

5. Items used in "Calling down the Moon". A lighter form of magic is here depicted, using the bottled waters for healing via a poppet.

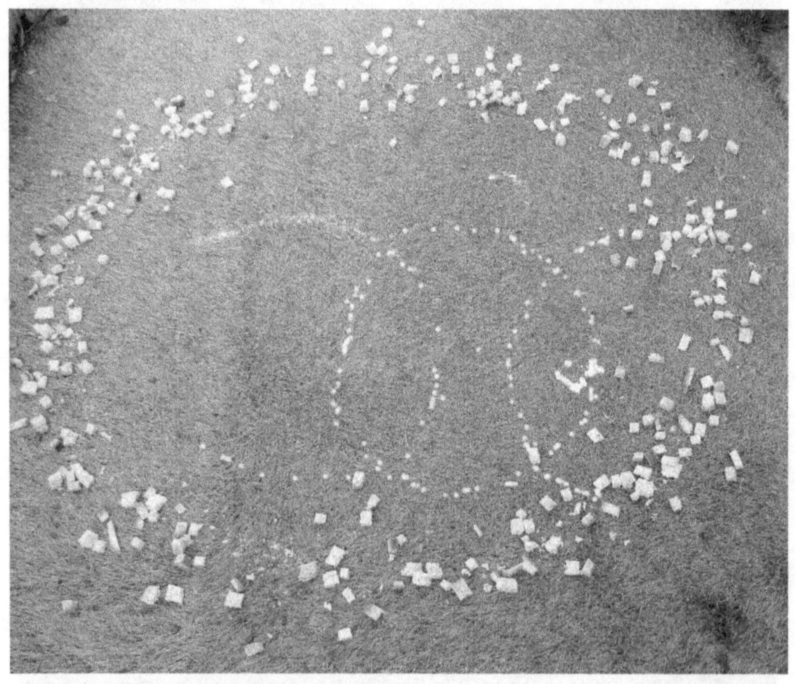

6. "Talking to the Moon"; the traditional layout of offerings to the Moon and Land spirits, as described to the author by an East Anglian resident.

7. Ritual Masks, used in the performance of shape-shifting, self-knowledge and Illumination. In the autor's collection.

8. Reconstructed replica of the helmet discovered in Mound One at Sutton Hoo. An ideal image for connection to Ancestral and Spirit energies within the Land of East Anglia. (Replica on display at Sutton Hoo Museum, Woodbridge, Suffolk. Photo by the author).

9. "Calling Forth the Shade". Example of the ritual preparations and layout for Calling on Ancestral and Otherworld Spirits.

10. Pole Hill. A burial mound dating from the late Neolithic to late Bronze Age, situated at Foxhall, Suffolk. Once part of a cemetary grouping of similar mounds, it now stands alone, topped by Scots Pines, a feature in the landscape. Known to be visited for purposes of Ancestral contact.

11. The River Gipping, at Bramford, Suffolk. The Spirit of this river has identified itself as "Gippiswealha" to the author and requested offerings at the New Moon in March.

12. "Putting in the Waters" – a "darker" form of working than used in "Calling Down the Moon"; using a thorn-pierced, bound poppet, placed in a north-flowing part of the Gipping River.

13. Genius Loci; an individualised manifestation of the wider Anima Loci. Dunwich Forest, Suffolk.

14. "Owl Stones". Discovered by the author some 20 years ago and believed to be the site of ritual workings to honour/invoke the Anima Loci. Suffolk.

15.Gifts of the Woods. Virtue-full wood, taken from local trees and crafted into ritual objects. A double-headed serpent representation of the Spirament in the Land; A contorted piece of timber housing a Familiar Tree Spirit; A handle for a copper blade, used for herb cutting; Two versions of Keppens, both crafted from Oak. From the author's collection.

16. Black Mary:White Mary. Representations of the feminine Anima Loci in perceived dualistic manifestation. Author's collection.

17. Sea Cave. Site of the rising of the Serpent's Breath. North Cornish coast.

18. The twin Holy Wells at Walsingham Abbey, Norfolk. Renowned for their healing properties.

19. Walsingham Holy House. Original site of the wooden house, inspired by the vision of Richeldis de Favarches, upon which the later Walsingham Abbey was based. Norfolk.

20. St. Clether's Well. Named for the sixth century saint, Clederus, whose spirit is said to manifest inside the Chapel attached to the Well upon occasion. A site of great healing properties and a confluence of local lines of Virtue within the Land. Nr. Launceston, Cornwall.

21. Asking the Land. Tools of divination; Geomantic tokens, dark and light pendulums, horse brasses.

22.Amanita muscaria. Fly Agaric mushrooms, used by those of the Dark Orders to cross the boundaries and partake of the Virtue within the Land.

23. Himself". Light and Shade, Fair and Foule; the tutelary, male Power of the Witches. Variously known as The Devil, Old Scratch, Witchfather, The Old Lad or simply "He". Carved Oak representation, commisioned by the author and in his collection.

24. "She". The tutelary, female Power of the Witches, called by some Witchmother, Providence, Old Fate and Wyrd. Original, colour painting, executed by the author, in the style of a mediaeval icon.

had felt myself and, with what the others had witnessed, we concluded that one of the ancient inhabitants of the area had probably tried to take over my physical body and start communication with the other people there. This may well have been a beneficial experience but, not having planned it, nor given permission for it to take place, it was not deemed a very good idea. We had no more pertinent contact with other spirits from the site that day and, as other people were now arriving, we called it a day and went home.

Not all possession experiences go like this of course, as most of them are planned and arranged, as much as possible, beforehand. They usually take place between a Witch and their patron deity or with spirits that the Witch has a close working relationship with and both are very familiar with each other. In the case of a deity, this is usually a very formal ritual situation (although it may be spontaneous, and I have witnessed several of these), but is usually less so with a familiar spirit, such as an Ancestor or one of the Faire Folk. These sessions are usually planned with mutual agreement beforehand and the "audience" of other Witches is gathered and ready. The techniques involved are quite simple, but are based on a very close working familiarity between the two parties – whoever they may be – and a certain level of competency in trancework on the part of the Witch involved. Although spontaneous possessions *do* occur, as I have said, these are much more difficult to control beneficially for all parties and don't tend to yield much useful information. It is much better if things are arranged in advance with both sides being aware of what is required and the outcome sought. One of the things that can be of great benefit in these situations is the use of masks, as has been discussed in a previous chapter. If the Witch has a good working relationship with a particular spirit that they wish to make a deeper contact with, a special mask can be made to enhance the contact. The mask is created using all the creative abilities of the Witch and incorporating everything that they know about the spirit. This obviously will include the shape of the face and the features, as well as colouring and any other obvious items such as charms, feathers, leaves, etc. but it will become a magical work in itself. By the creation of the mask, the Witch will already be transcending normal barriers and drawing some of the very essence of the spirit into the mask, such that when it is donned, it makes contact that much easier. Obviously, it will be visually much more representative for other Witches present, which will again feed back into the energy available for the possessing entity to make use of.

Both of the techniques I am about to describe rely on familiarity with trancework and the ability of the Witch to, both literally and metaphorically, step aside or outside of themselves for a period. Both techniques should ideally be practised in a fully hallowed compass, with experienced Witches attending.

For the first method, the operative Witch should be seated comfortably and put on the mask if wearing one. They should enter a light-to-medium trance state (as control is still needed) and open themselves up to outside contact, dropping personal barriers. Next, they should either mentally or verbally Call their Spirit Co-worker, who should already have agreed to and been primed for the working. Once the presence of the Spirit has been felt and/or contact has been made, the Witch should mentally take a step to one side, or outside of their body, leaving a space for the Spirit to inhabit. Alternatively, the Witch may use the imagery I have described in my experience at the megalithic tomb in Germany and "rise up" in the space of their minds/skulls, leaving room for the Spirit to enter. (Obviously these descriptions are not literal; I am using imagery here that I have found to be useful in practising this technique and would suggest be adopted when attempting this working). Either way, contact with the body is maintained throughout. At this point some signal or sign needs to be made, either by the Witch or the Spirit, that possession has been achieved and converse may now take place. The Spirit may begin to speak through the Witch and announce its presence or the Witch may raise their hand, or similar, indicating that their companions may begin to ask questions, if that is what has been agreed on beforehand. The session will continue as long as is felt necessary for the work in hand, or the Witch and their Spirit are able to maintain the state of contact. As I have mentioned before, this requires much effort and practice on both sides and can be a great strain. Possession should not be overly prolonged because of the enervating effect that can be had on both parties. I would suggest that half an hour should be the maximum time allowed, after which the contact should be broken. At this point the possessing Spirit should leave the body of the Witch voluntarily, or the Witch should gently re-enter or "re-fill" their body (depending on which technique was used) and end the working. Thanks should naturally be given to the Spirit for attending and allowing the converse to take place and for the information that was imparted. In this case, a shared meal with offerings being left for the Spirit is most appropriate.

The second technique is a progression on the first and usually produces a much stronger connection between the Witch and the Spirit and enables clearer communication between all parties involved. Verbal interchange between the Spirit and the other Witches present tends to be more coherent and more information is likely to be passed. The Witch undertaking the possession should begin as above, being seated in the compass and donning a mask, if desired. This time, a much deeper trance state should be invoked and, once achieved, the Witch should mentally journey or project themselves into the familiar Spirit's own environment. If the Spirit is not already waiting there for the Witch, they should be Called. Once both parties are present, they should stand face-to-face and take each others hands in their own, forging a "physical connection". From here, it is up to the working parties as to how close and/ or strong a possession is required. The closer together they stand, the stronger the bond and flow of energy. The closest bond is achieved by each party stepping into the other and merging completely. Remember, this is all happening in a non-physical, liminal realm and so is perfectly possible and practicable. However, this must all have been agreed with both parties beforehand and not be a spur of the moment thing. Much damage can be done – on either side – if advantage is taken of the other in this situation. This is why there *must* be a very strong working bond, the result of trust and shared experience, between both sides, before any working of this nature can be contemplated. Anything else is tantamount to spiritual rape.

Once this direct communication has been achieved, the working may progress as above, with perhaps a shorter time frame, the strain being greater on both parties. From personal experience, this technique can be somewhat disorientating – to say the least – as the Witch is aware of being in two places at one time, quite fully, and of everything going on around them. One can hear and see the working taking place within the compass, but at the same time, one can also see and hear the home environment of the Spirit companion, to a greater or lesser extent, and it takes a lot of practice to remain stable. When it is time for the working to come to a mutually agreed end, the two parties involved – Witch and Spirit – should gently and carefully back away from each other to arms length. When this is reached, they should slowly disengage hands, back away and, in the case of the Witch, return to their own state of normal reality. As above, a shared meal should be hallowed and partaken of by all, thanks and offerings being given and left for the spirit Co-worker.

Pacts, Oaths and Vows

Throughout this chapter I have stressed the development of a close working relationship between the Witch and the Spirit involved, be that an Ancestral spirit or one of the Faire Folk. This can take quite some time to come into being, as friendship, let alone trust, is something that is won out of shared experience. These experiences can be tentative at first and depend on a willingness, from both parties, to participate in shared actions and communication. Once this has developed to a certain level, it is normal for pacts to be made between the parties, each stating what they would like out of the relationship and what they are willing to give in return. They are not absolutely necessary and many Witches never feel the need to make them, but they can be helpful in setting boundaries in a relationship, so that everyone knows what is – and what is not – expected of them. It helps to avoid confusion and mistakes that may offend, hurt or wound either party. Don't forget that we are dealing here with communication between two very different – albeit related – Beings and the clearer that communication and relationship can be made, the less room or likelihood there is of making mistakes.

There are many different definitions of what exactly an oath, a vow, a promise or a pact is and the differences between them all, but what it all boils down to in the end is, what are you willing to give in order to gain what you want? Once both parties have decided this, or these things, and agreed upon them, then you have a pact. However, there are things to consider – at least from the Human viewpoint – before agreeing to any pact with a Spirit, as you *will* be held to it and could suffer if you break it. Now, I don't mean here that you need to pledge your soul for servitude from a spirit and will lose it if you fail, but some points are worthy of consideration before the Witch agrees to a pact.

Firstly, what do you want out of the relationship? This could be many different things and everyone is different, so what is meaningful and important to one could be trivial to another, but it needs careful consideration first. Woolly thinking has no place in magic! It may be that you require a certain piece of information as a one off, or a continuing feed of information. You may need a particular task achieving, such as a healing or getting a new job, or maybe you want to develop a certain magical ability with the aid of the spirit. How long is the pact to last for in this case? Is it for a one off thing, several months, years or a lifetime? Consider this carefully first and be clear about it; just as woolly thinking has no place in magic, neither does woolly and ambiguous language. One very important point to consider also is to make sure that the thing/s you want are within the realms of physical possibility – don't go asking for a yacht in the Mediterranean if you're on minimum wage!

Secondly, what are you willing to give in return? Requests from the Spirits can sometimes seem strange to us, as their value systems are not the same as ours, just as their Ways are not always ours. You may be asked to do no more than make offerings at certain times of day, week, month or year. You may be asked to do something, such as look after a piece of Land and care for it, or devote some time or money to a charity or particular cause. You may be asked to make/have made a piece of artwork or statuary which needs to be anointed with oil or smoked at certain times. Any of these and many more things may be asked of you and you need to decide what you are willing to give/do for the things that you want.

These may seem to be obvious things to consider, but it is surprising how little thought goes into these things sometimes and the Witch is then surprised when what they thought was going to happen doesn't. I am not saying that the Spirits will deliberately try to trick you (although some might and you should either watch out for this or not have that particular one as a friend after all), but as I have mentioned several times, the rules, morals, customs, Ways and actions of the Spirits are not ours and values differ greatly. Clarity in any relationship is something to be valued!

Once both parties are agreed on terms that they can both accept, how is the pact made? Well, just by agreeing to it, the pact comes into existence really, as this is based on trust and a word given is a bond in the magical world. Simply this; nothing more is actually needed. However, most Witches prefer to have something written down that they can refer to and keep, if only just as a reminder. If you wish to do this, obviously the spirit will not be able to sign it physically (unless you can get them to do it by automatic writing), but they will be able to give you a sign or symbol to place on it, which represents their agreement. Ask for this and include it on the written pact.

Having done this, you *must* stick to the agreement. This sounds obvious but is worth saying, as humans can be frail and forgetful creatures and cause offence without even meaning to. A bond with one of the Faire Folk is a serious thing and to break an agreement could leave you open to some unfortunate retribution. However, the reverse is also true; if your pact-companion fails to keep up their side of the bargain – say, you don't get that promotion within 6 months as agreed, or the healing is not performed – then you are under no obligation to keep to the terms of the pact and can cease doing whatever it was that you promised to do. All pacts work both ways!

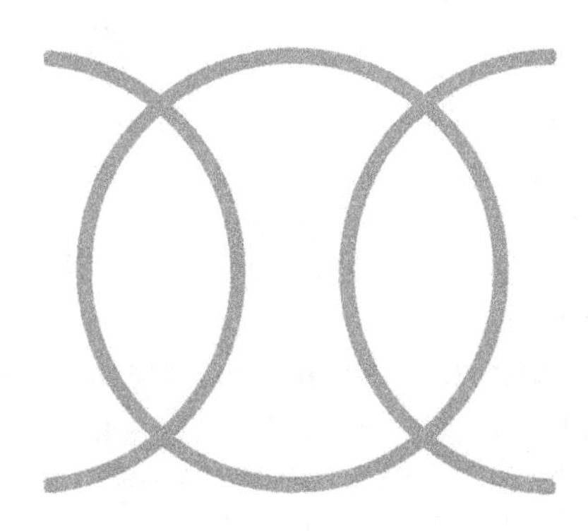

Living Within the Land

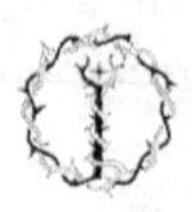

"The eldritch world is a place redolent of the quality of strangeness and wonder..........; something glimpsed from out of the remote past of human experience, seemingly immune to the passing of time, filled with beings of that state of timeless continuity that is ever present within us and manifesting also as an external presence.
Nigel Pennick - "The Eldritch World".

I have described in previous chapters some of the Beings that the Witch encounters and works with in their magical acts and Ways. Many, if not most or all, have their origin and existence rooted within the Land around us. This is the bedrock of the Ways of the Witch and from which all else comes. I have said before that however far the Witch ranges in their knowledge and work, the origin of their Ways, their Powers, their magic and their "faith", all comes from the Land upon which they live and walk. Whilst much magic is focussed on the Moon, the Stars and the Planets within our Solar system (and maybe beyond), without the, literal, Earthing that the Land gives the Witch, all would be in vain and their work come to naught. In addition to this, the landscape is multi-dimensional. It exists in the here and now yet it contains places which are gateways to other landscapes and worlds. We too are gateways into other worlds, but while most people live in the here and now, the Traditional Witch, bound by their attachment to the natural world and their service to it, is forever part of those other worlds and stands with one foot between this reality and all others. They stand, as it were, in the open doorway, belonging fully to both realities. To illustrate and explain this, I would like to begin this chapter and "set the scene", so to speak, with a description from Nigel Pennick, the well known East Anglian Cunning Man and practitioner of the Nameless Art.

> *"As human beings, we are rooted in the earth, but urban civilisation is verb-effective in obscuring the fact. Most people appear to be unaware of it. Traditional wisdom recognises our relationship with subtle qualities in the land. This is expressed in the relationship between each individual and the land: it manifests its spiritual nature in different places by differing spiritual qualities. We can have a personal spiritual relationship to these qualities. Ultimately, landscape is the basis of human culture. We are so held to it by myriad links, that without it, physical life, culture and consciousness are inconceivable. When we walk our own land, we are part of the landscape, and its total nature is present within our inner body knowledge. As part of our own country, we do not need a map or any external representation of the land. We know the names of our local places without recourse to written or printed records. Walking is the primary form of understanding the inner nature of our own earth, the Goddess of the Land. Each place has its own anima loci, its own history, geomythic qualities, legends, stories and anecdotes. Every part of the land has a name. The whole body of the land is infused with the names of deities, people, sprites, events, qualities and numinosity. So long as the names and form of the land remain within the consciousness of its inhabitants, the land is alive. As participants, we have a personal and collective cultural relationship to the landscape. Our imagined individuality is no longer so important; we are not separate. The reality is what we walk upon, see, touch, smell and experience. We are present, and this is the essence of the Nameless Art." (Quoted, with kind permission, from "Secrets of East Anglian Magic" – see Bibliography).*

To **know** the Land where you are is essential within the practice of Old Craft and every Witch of this persuasion will be intimately involved with and a part of their locale and its places of importance. It takes time, effort and dedication to know the Land intimately, but richly rewards the Witch that goes to these lengths with insights that are otherwise unobtainable. There are various techniques involved in gaining these insights, but all essentially boil down to one practical procedure, known by different names in different places, however it is performed.

Witchwalking

I have briefly mentioned this technique earlier and described it under another name in my book *Treading the Mill*, (cf. Wight Tracking), but I would like to take a more in depth look at it now. Witchwalking, in the form in which I know it and wish to describe here, is a totally immersive experience, in which the practitioner gradually becomes one with the Land, not a separate entity apart from it. As Pennick states above, "*Our imagined individuality is no longer so important; we are not separate.*" This reiterates the point that I have been making throughout this book and is one of the main themes, that there is NO Other; the Land and the Witch are one – all else is illusion. Just as the Blackthorn and the Whitethorn appear to have different characteristics but, in reality, partake of the same, essential, identity and the Roebuck is in actuality the Witch themselves on their quest – as seen in Chapter 1 – so too the illusion of separateness with the Land. By walking with intent and attention, the boundaries between the inner and outer blur and can disappear, leaving the Witch as an intimate part of the life all around them, as in reality they actually are. Once this state has been reached, profound realisations may be achieved. This involves a type of merging of the senses with the Land around, such that there is no distinction between the Witch and the Landscape; for that time there is no "I" and "Other", but a continuous stream of consciousness that transcends differentness. Existence is felt to be in a mytho-poetic state of awareness, where many things that were not previously, are now apprehended as being, clear and possible. It is similar in concept to the search for the Grail in Arthurian mythos – the King and the Land are One, except that this applies to everyone if they took the trouble to realise it. Once this state is realised, the Witch is in intimate contact with the Life in the Land around them; contact with the Powers and Spirits that inhabit the Land is made much easier and interactions may take place that were not previously possible. This is the state in which individuals are enabled to enter and visit such places as Elphame and the realms of the Underworld, which house the spirits of the Ancestors and the Elven kind in their own environment; there are no barriers preventing this, as there is no longer any separateness to be overcome.

So, how is this mystical state achieved, what is the technique involved? Walking – simply walking. However, it is walking with a purpose and attention and allowing the senses to be flooded to their full extent, such that they "overload" and artificial barriers are overcome. Remnants of this technique exist in popular religion and culture to this day in the practice of Pilgrimage. This involves going on a journey, by foot, along a certain path, with a stated aim in mind and performing certain acts along the way. It is found in many cultures around the world and is becoming increasingly popular again today, as it brings meaning and insight into peoples' lives. The Witch, of course, will do this with a different purpose in mind, but the technique is the same at root.

Witchwalking is best done in a natural area that the Witch is already familiar with and, although certain Traditions advocate doing this at night, it is best attempted during the day, to begin with at least. (Once the Witch is familiar with the technique and its results, then performing it at night may be attempted, but, safety first!). The terrain needs to be out in nature – as pristine as is possible in this day and age – and the length needs to be appreciable - several miles would be ideal. The type of terrain is not important – it may be heathland, woodland, seashore, rocky/mountainous, or a combination of several – just as natural as can be found. (For those that live a totally urban lifestyle and absolutely cannot get out into the countryside, a park or arboretum may be used, but is obviously not ideal). If possible, it is very useful to begin the Walk at a significant point in the landscape. Traditionally this may be where two Oak trees grow, with a gap between them; an Oak an Ash and a Thorn tree standing together; at a deserted crossroads or at a holy well or standing stone. This is why it is best for the Witch to perform this exercise at a place that is known to them first and in daylight.

Beginning at this significant place, enter a comfortable trance state, bearing in mind your reason for this working – that of entering into communion with and becoming part of the energetic life of the Land and its denizens. Pass between the trees (a liminal gateway), or acknowledge the starting place in some other manner (reverently touch the stone, anoint the forehead with water from the well, leave an offering at the crossroads, etc.) - such is indicative of entering into a relationship with the Land not normally undertaken. Stepping forward lightly but with intent, the journey begins. As you Walk, try to keep the conscious mind in abeyance, try not to actively think of anything in particular. Be aware of everything around you, but don't describe it or categorise it to yourself; stop the internal dialogue – this is key to the practice. We are all guilty of persistent, mental "gabble" all the time, constantly reaffirming and re-creating the normal state of the world around us, as we are used to seeing it; this needs to be switched off, or as much as is possible. Just look, be aware and absolutely open to all around you; let your senses be flooded by sight, sound, smell and hearing, without naming what you experience. Withdraw to a high-up place in the hall of your interior mind – as previously described – and let your mind be filled with everything around you. Unlike in the exercise in Wight Tracking, you don't want to focus on just one or two senses becoming super-sharp, but in expanding all of them; let everything flood in. Continue in this manner for as long as you are able and the journey lasts; if you can make this a circular Walk, such that you end up at the point where you first began, so much the better (which is why it needs to be a long enough Walk, several miles, to give you time and space to achieve your objective). Don't rush or hurry, just Walk at a gentle pace that allows you to take everything in. After a while, you will find yourself naturally sinking into a rhythmic pace that is suitable for you. Having found this pace and become comfortable with it and having allowed your senses to be as overwhelmed as possible, you may start to notice a change in your mental attitude. It shouldn't be as difficult to shut off the internal dialogue as it was initially and you will find yourself not being so fixated on it (the initial trance-inducing that you began with will have gone a long way to helping with this). A sense of calm and peace will begin to overcome you and you will find yourself just enjoying the journey – going along for the ride, so to speak. Initially, this is all that can be hoped for or expected, but as you continue to practice this technique, over several or perhaps many journeys, all manner of things may begin to open up for you. Some people begin to sense the life in the Land around them, to feel the virtue coming off the Land in waves or flows. Some people may become aware of the life in the trees or the plants that they are passing on the Walk and may start to perceive the spirit-life there, both in general and specifically. Some may become aware of the Life in the rivers, streams and other bodies of water, perhaps perceived as Meremayds or other anthropomorphic forms. Others may encounter the Folk in the Land, the Elven or Faire ones, just as my informant above, and be made aware of the life that they lead. Once the barriers that separate you from the natural life in the Land begin to fall and you truly begin to realise that there *are* no barriers, you are *not* separate, then all manner of things may begin to unfold for you. If any of these things happen, just accept them as a natural part of what you are doing and go with the flow, so to speak. It would be unwise in your early experiences to stop and start to examine things minutely, as this may well cause you to loose the state of mind that has been so developed to perceive the phenomena; just mark it and carry on. Unless, of course, you encounter one of the Folk in the Land, in which case follow the rules of politeness and respect and react to the situation as is appropriate. (If you are at any point invited to enter fully into Their realm, remember the traditional prohibitions; do not lie but always speak truth, do not partake of the food and drink there and never look back when leaving). Once you have finished your Walk, take some time to just sit and contemplate what you have experienced and to gradually emerge from your trance or altered state. It may take several, or many, Walks to fully achieve what you set out to do, but each time will bring you so much closer and each time you will come back that little bit more changed, just that little bit more aware.

On these Walks you are highly likely to come across notable features that attract your attention – numinous sites and places where the Spirit of the Land is most strong or more concentrated; certain trees, glades, stones, wells, hills, rivers, caves and possibly many other features. I would now like to look at some of these and the ways that the Witch may learn from and interact with them.

Rivers and Streams

As moving or flowing bodies of water – in contrast to the more static bodies like lakes, pools and wells – rivers and streams can be seen to carry the energetic life in the Land, the spirit-energy or Virtue and, possibly, move it around from place to place. Still bodies of water have their own life, but of a different kind and I will look at these later on. Sometimes rushing torrents, sometimes gently meandering, sometimes overflowing and destructive, rivers – be they large or small – are the most obviously and immediately "alive" features in any environment. The Witch who is a part of their own landscape and intimately aware of the inner life of it will know how to make good use of the energies that these bodies of water contain. To many other people, rivers can be ambiguous creatures, sometimes benevolent, very often not. There are many well-known rivers, such as the Dee, the Severn, the Wye and the Derwent amongst many others, that are known in folklore to demand sacrifice each year; i.e. they take the lives of one or more humans to appease their hunger or need for extra life-force. Of the River Dart in Devon, the tradition claims: *Dart, Dart, cruel Dart, Every year thou claims't a heart.* While of Cheshire's Dee and South Yorkshire's Don it is said: *Bloodthirsty Dee, each year needs three, But bonny Don, she needs none.* Many mothers even to this day keep their children away from their local rivers – if they are known to demand sacrifice – until the tithe has been taken. Alternatively, it is deemed that they demand these payments in return for continuing to flow benevolently and not flooding, possibly taking more lives and properties with them. However it is understood, there is still the knowledge that these are powerful Beings and will do or take what they please, irrespective of human feelings, customs or situations. These tales may possibly be reminders of the times when most rivers were revered as deities or great Powers in their own right and were offered gifts as their due, in order to continue to provide the life-blood of many communities that relied on them – be that fresh water, trade routes, or food in the form of fish, wildfowl or plant materials. Perceived as mostly feminine in nature, many of the names of these Powers remain known to us today; *Verbeia* for the Wharfe, *Tamara* for the Tamar and possibly the Thames, *Sabrina* or *Hafren* for the Severn and *Clota* for the Clyde, amongst many others. These Powers were known to be strong and fierce, not essentially antagonistic to humans, but like all Powers and Spirits of the natural world, to be honoured, respected and treated with a certain caution. In my home county of Suffolk there is the River Gipping, that flows through much of the county, as a gentle, meandering watercourse. When reaching the county town of Ipswich, it widens and deepens and becomes the River Orwell, before heading out to the coast and joining the sea between the major ports of Felixstowe and Harwich. The Gipping has long been a force to be reckoned with and notorious for containing the dreaded *Merewife* of local legend. James Bird (a local man born in Earl Stonham in 1788), wrote in a poem from 1837 about his boyhood in the area and his mother calling out to him;

> *"Make haste and do your errand. Go not nigh*
> *The River's brink, for there the mermaids lie.*
> *Be home at five!"*

However, in my experience, if dealt with in a respectful manner, the presiding Spirit of the Gipping can be very helpful and the source of a good deal of useful information. I have experienced Her on many occasions when performing Walks by Her and She has always been willing to interact with me. I have been given the name "*Gippiswealha*" to call Her by and She has asked that I make offerings of bread and wine into Her waters at the New Moon in March. Other than that She has made no demands and remains a close and generous ally in my magical work. (I have been unable to trace any known meaning of the name given to me so far. The river takes its name from the village of "Gipping", near Stowmarket, which is so small it has now been absorbed by the nearby and larger village of Old Norton. So I suppose that She is happy to be known by that derivation!). She helps me with any spells where I need to make use of water which flows and also in getting rid of items that need casting off or away. I may also ask Her to empower items for magical working, either by leaving them submerged (if materially suitable), for a while in Her waters or else washing them/pouring water over them, so that they may gain Her virtues. Many Witches use rivers and streams in similar manners, having got to know those in their area well and I shall now describe a few Ways in which these methods may be employed below.

As flowing water is known to contain the vital force of life, the Virtue, it is usually deemed best if the flow can be disturbed as little as possible. Therefore it is considered that if taking water from a river or stream for magical use, it should always be done in the direction of the flow, not *against* it, to retain as much virtue as is possible. The direction in which the flow is going is also of much importance, different directions being used for different works, the flow being considered to carry certain qualities depending on the direction. Each particular Tradition of Craft will naturally have their own associations and these will vary around the country, but these are some of the associations that I have found to be used in East Anglia, although there are others.

North flowing: the Black path of midnight and the spirits of Air, of the sky, the stars, the heavens and, in particular, the Pole Star. The Skull, Bones and Stang are associated with this direction and communication with the Ancestors. Cursing and binding, blasting and hexing avail themselves of this flow and also workings of Knowledge. The part of the body associated here is the head, neck and shoulders. Water taken from a northern flowing river can therefore be used to wash the Skull before any works of attempted ancestral or spirit communication, as described in the previous chapter. In the East Anglian Tradition, particularly in the Cambridgeshire Fens, the famed toad bone is washed in north-flow water to further enhance its properties. Cords used for knot magic or in the binding of poppets to stop or contain an enemy can be soaked in northern water before use, as can the poppet itself. Charm bags likewise may be washed and left to dry out before being used. A Witches Ladder, once knotted, may be steeped in a north-flowing river before being placed to do its work and items used in a banishing rite may be cast into the river itself. Conversely, this water may be used to take away headaches, either by soaking a poultice in it and laying it on the forehead of the sufferer, or by washing the head with it. If studying or working to acquire knowledge on a subject, a cord or ribbon soaked in north-flow water may be tied around the head whilst reading or working on the subject. Of course, if it is felt safe to do so, the water may also be drunk to aid the same conditions.

East flowing: the Red path of dawn, sunlight and the spirits of Fire, both those of the Sun above and of the fires in the Earth, those of the Cunning Master and the Light between the Horns; volcanoes and thunder/lightening are associated here. It is also the flow of the inner fire within the body of the Witch and the quality of ultimate Understanding (Illumination). Here is associated the Knife and all bladed tools and the part of the body is the right hand and side. Workings aided by the virtues of east-flow water include all martial pursuits, energising activities such as fitness and sexual vigour, cleansing of negative places/situations and those to uncover secret or hidden things. This water may be used in similar ways to the above in the appropriate situations, drunk during meditation and prior to lengthy rituals for vigour, used in washes and cleansing sprays for hauntings or ill-wishings and used to hallow and strengthen bladed tools for magical or practical work. It is a good base for a scrying medium if seeking out hidden knowledge, things that have been lost or stolen and for charging spell-casting items with extra virtue.

South flowing: the White path of midday, the spirits of Earth, the Sacred Land and of Sovereignty. Here are associated the Godstone (phallic pillar/standing stone), all magical Stones, including the Hagstone and the Offering Bowl. The whole physical body is associated here, but particularly the stomach, genitals, legs and feet. Magical operations concerning Power, herbs and healing in general, material and physical gain, practicality and stability are aided by south-flow water. In addition to the above suggestions, this water may be used in the making up of any magical or purely physical healing potions or medicines, to wash any herbs used in magical or mundane workings and to immerse the whole body in if needed. South-flow water may be used in charms for abundance and wealth and for spells of success in such things as lotteries and games of chance. It may be poured on sick or ailing plants to give them added vitality and used as offerings to the Faire Folk in the Land. If making or crafting any magical tools from scratch, hallowing them in south-flow water will give them an extra charge.

West flowing: the Grey/Blue path of sunset/evening and the actual spirits of the Waters, of Seas and Lakes, Rivers, Wells and Streams. Human emotions, blood and the left hand and side of the body are associated here. The Cauldron and the Cup are especially connected with west-flow water. Magical operations associated here are Wisdom, love, all emotions, Moon magic, dreams, shapeshifting and transformation. The healing of internal and psychological wounds may be aided by west-flow water. This water is excellent for use in all forms of scrying, especially such as working with the Moon, detailed in chapter two; a strip of cloth may also be soaked in the water and bound about the head whilst scrying to aid in the process. Scrying may also be done at the site of a west-flowing river, at night under the light of the Moon, without recourse to extracting the waters. All rites associated with the Moon in general; it may be used in the Cup for both offering and communion. Love philtres may be worked using this water as a base and also added to food offered to a loved one. Masks or other tools used in rites of shapeshifting, glamour or other forms of transformation may be washed or hallowed with this water to great value.

For all directions of flow, any objects, such as stones, plants, animal parts, etc., taken *from* the waters will obviously be imbued with the quality of that direction. In addition any magical items deposited *into* the waters and left there with magical intent, will partake of the respective associations. For example, from my own Tradition, there is the following practise. Make a libation into the River of a whole bottle of wine, ale or mead. Then, next to the River's edge, where the flow of the water after rain will cover it over and wash it away soon, dig a hole, large enough to deposit a "message" to the River-spirit. By this I mean a doll of your intended target (be that for healing or other), a charm, sigil or talisman. Make it with care and focus and, before laying it in the hole, kiss it with your heart's desire and whisper what you wish to happen. Lay it in the hole and wait for the waters to carry it away. Once the wish has come to fruition, make another libation into the River at the same place.

I am sure that the reader will be able to think of many other uses for these waters, especially within their own regions and taking into account their own traditions.

Of course, rivers and streams don't always flow in one direction for their entire length, but twist and turn, facing in different directions as they go. For the canny Witch, if their nearest river doesn't flow in the direction that they need for the work they wish to do, it is a simple matter to trace the course of the river and collect water from the part of it that runs in the appropriate direction, carrying the desired qualities. Always be practical in your Craft and work *with* the virtues of your area!

When using the waters, it should be emphasised that they can be used in seemingly contradictory ways. The virtues that they carry may be used both to *imbue* an object with those qualities and also to wash them away. When pouring water over something, remember that it is both the *flow* of the water and the intent of the Witch that creates the desired result. This explains a very old folk tradition that is now little understood as it stands. It is said that a Witch (normally meaning a worker of maleficia), cannot cross a flowing river and will be trapped on one side. What is little understood is that it is not the *Witch* who is unable to cross, but the *energies* that they are carrying with them, the *energetic* body of the Witch. This is because the flow of the river/stream disrupts the energies being used and carries them away, thus voiding any spells being cast. This is why some Traditions of Old Craft use a moat filled with water to surround their working site or compass, or otherwise work by flowing rivers and streams, as the water carries away any antagonistic or negative energies, forces or spirits attempting to disrupt their workings. A wise Witch will be able to use this knowledge in many other Ways.

(For more information, history and practice of water magic, I can thoroughly recommend Gemma Gary's "*Wisht Waters*" - see Bibliography).

The Landscape

Walking away from the flowing rivers and streams, the Witch will be interacting directly with the Anima Loci, the Life in the Land. This frequently manifests to the aware senses as the localised genius loci, the Spirit of Place and can vary greatly in form, depending on the location and type of terrain. The Witch may work greatly with such local and intimate manifestations, others perhaps being barely aware of the phenomenon unless marked in some way. Some 20 years ago early one morning in the woods nearby that I habitually work in, I was taking a walk. As I got to the top of the next hill, I suddenly heard a weird bird call, one that was quite sharp and that I didn't recognise. I turned my head to the left to see what it was and saw something very unusual that I had never seen there before, having taken that path every day for years. Off to one side, at the edge of the woods and by the corner of the adjoining field, someone had set up a small shrine or altar. Two large-ish blocks of chalky stone, possibly from the nearby field; one roughly shaped into what looked to me to be an owl and the other roughly squared off and shaped into a base for the figure to stand on. I had a careful look around without touching anything and noticed that fresh, green branches had been driven into the ground to stand up around the figure, creating a small enclosure. Nothing else was apparent. The only other thing of significance that I observed was that that morning I had met a man that I didn't know, coming down and out of the woods, carrying what looked like two Stangs, but could have been just thumb-sticks. We had nodded, but didn't speak. I had never seen him before. I saw him again the next day, with the Stangs/sticks, at the same time and place and after that never again. The "owl" stayed in place for a few weeks, before it was tumbled and broken by persons unknown, but I have always considered it a strange and significant occurrence. To my mind, this unknown man had been "working" up in the woods and had created an acknowledgement of what he had observed as a manifestation of the genius loci, or something very similar.

This serves as a very good example of a Way in which the Witch may work with the manifestation of the genius loci, by using local, if not immediate, materials to acknowledge the virtues made apparent to them. They will not harm the environment and can fade back into it when the work is done or the need for them is ended. They need not be as obvious or as "sculpted" as the owl image I saw; a log stood on end, or maybe a thick stick planted in the ground to mark the spot, or maybe a small pile of stones placed as a cairn. Anything may suffice to mark and acknowledge a place of manifestation or focussing of the genius loci, in whatever form it is perceived by the Witch.

Having observed and acknowledged this, the Witch may begin to use/work with the virtues manifested there in various ways. Essentially utilising the extra and more focussed energies, spells and charms may be created or left at this spot to further strengthen and enhance their charge. Knotted cords may be left or made there for different purposes. Talismans may be created or charged there; charm bags or pouches may be put together or empowered on the spot, perhaps making use of ingredients from the local area. As ever, the only limit is the imagination of the Witch and their connection with the Spirit of Place. Under certain circumstances, the genius loci may even be persuaded to enliven or inhabit a doll or poppet for specific workings, if it so desires. This takes a lot of focus and attention and work on the part of both the Witch and the Spirit, as mentioned previously. In this case the poppet must be brought back after its work is done and the energy/spirit released with offerings and thanks. Again – nothing is got for nothing! Alternatively, other Spirits that inhabit the area may be persuaded to take up permanent residence in a poppet or artefact, but more of that anon.

Stronger manifestations of the Anima Loci are sometimes encountered and are often referred to in folklore as *White Ladies* or *White Goddesses.* In such cases they are often apparent to people other than Witches and may begin or be incorporated into a local cult of veneration; such has happened historically in such places as Walsingham in Norfolk and Knock in Eire, being incorporated as manifestations of the Virgin Mary. To the Witch, these may be viewed as appearances of the feminine Power of the Land, the Earth Mother, with whom many work deeply and intimately. Working in those areas of previous manifestation, the Witch may attempt to link in with such energies, to better empower and enhance their work. When collecting materials for spells, charms or medicines, particularly herbs of the Land, it is appropriate to petition the Anima Loci/White Lady of the area and such an appeal has been preserved and may suit modern Old Crafters in their work. This is a prayer from the 12th. Century, that was preserved in Latin in an English herbal, found in the Harleian Manuscripts in the British Library and translates thus;

> *"Earth, divine goddess, Mother Nature, who generateth all things bringing forth ever new the Sun which thou hast given to the Nations: guardian of sky and sea and all gods and powers...... Thou art named rightly Great Mother of the Gods, Victory is thy holy name. Thou art source of the strength of people and the gods: without thee nothing can be either born or perfected: thou art mighty, Queen of the Gods. Goddess, I adore thee as divine, I invoke thy name."*

Working thus with stronger manifestations of the Anima Loci, it is as well to remember that there are also occurrences of what are known as Black Ladies – or Black Mary's – as these may be encountered by the Witch in touch with the inner Life of the Land. These "Black" figures are not to be shunned, but represent and embody a different side to the normally expected verdant and life-giving properties of the feminine Power/s. Just as we have seen earlier in this book, the apparent duality in nature and ourselves is only an illusion and one that needs to be acknowledged, worked with and incorporated into the overall body of Knowledge and Wisdom gained by the Witch. The apparent "Black" manifestation is indicative of the decay and death that inherently and necessarily exists (with)in all Life; without it there would be no change, growth, learning or progress and all would ultimately stagnate. (This image is also indicative of further Mysteries that I will come on to in the next section). So too with the workings of the Witch; to embrace the dark or Black side of nature, is to gain in knowledge and understanding both of Nature and the Witch themselves. Any encounter with a Being of this kind is to be appreciated for what it is, acted upon appropriately and incorporated into the Witch's body of experience and learning.

Of obvious note in the landscape are Woods and Forests and the trees that they contain and these can be a major feature in certain areas, perhaps the majority of the terrain-type. I have spoken of working intimately with certain trees earlier in this book and all of those practices and methods apply to this current discussion. Indeed, having performed the Witchwalking technique and achieved heightened awareness and connection with the inner life of the Land, then the practice of any of them will only be enhanced for the Witch. However, there are a few more things that I would like to describe about working with the trees and their spirits themselves in this section.

Within certain sections of Traditional Craft, it is considered that some trees house the spirits or consciousness of departed humans. These are people who have worked intimately with the arboreal life in their area pre-mortem and have transitioned into this form of life post-mortem. Rather than going on to other things in the afterlife, they have chosen to merge with (a) tree/s and continue their existence in this form, until it is time for them to move on again. The aware Witch may find it possible to encounter, contact and work with such spirits as they Walk the Land and this can be of great benefit to both parties involved. The "transmigrated" human may still retain some form of understanding of the human condition, which will make it less difficult (not necessarily easier!), for the Witch to communicate and work with them. In this manner, knowledge may be exchanged, wood taken for various projects – wands, staffs, stangs, talismans, charms, etc. - with the full co-operation of the "tree" and the life inhabiting it. Let me just say that this is not a common occurrence and is rarely to be experienced by most Crafters, but it does occur and needs to be recognised for what it is. Most of the time, the Witch will encounter the innate spirit of the woods and individual trees themselves, in whatever forms they chose to present themselves.

Commonly referred to as Dryads, these spirits have a completely different spatial awareness to humans and may be encountered singularly, as individuals, or collectively as a group spirit. Unlike humans they are able to separate parts of themselves off into pieces of wood taken from the mother-tree and continue to inhabit it, which is known as livewood; this is what makes them so magically helpful and valuable to the Witch. I have spoken of this previously in Chapter One, but would like to speak more on the subject here. When taking a piece of wood for magical work, it is much better if it can be livewood and there are certain things to be observed before acquiring it. Obviously the Witch needs to have an intimate rapport with the Dryad and for it to be in agreement for the taking of the wood. It's a bit like taking a cutting for growing another tree; the spirit/life of the original tree remains in the cutting, to enable another tree to grow from it. Likewise the spirit/life of the tree remains in the wand, talisman, etc. once cut, but obviously doesn't grow into another tree; it stays in the wood and works co-operatively with the Witch or the subsequent owner of the piece. It is important that the "owner" of the tool takes the time to attune to and make friends with the Dryad once it comes into their possession, else the spirit will depart and all that is left is a piece of dry, dead wood; magically charged, yes, but not livewood. The Dryad will still retain a strong individual personality and, like any other friend, it takes work to get to know it and become attuned. Once the Witch has acquired the help and co-operation of the resident Dryad, then the spirit will be able to enhance any magic performed with the wand, etc. and add its own charge to the working, sometimes even guiding the Witch themselves. When carving any wand taken in this fashion, the Dryad often "takes over" and directs the form the carving may take, guiding the Witch's hands, producing beautiful and unique patterns in the finished item. It is best if wood for magical purposes is taken at either dawn or dusk, when the rays of the Sun strike the tree from the side, rather than from directly overhead. It is also preferable that the tree grows either along a line of force within the Land, or at a crossing of one or more; a crossroads within a wooded area is also a magically powerful place for the cutting of wood. Obviously this is not always possible, but is to be desired and sought after.

To some Old Craft Traditions, the ultimate and most prized livewood magical tool is a type of Keppen, or pocket wand, known as an *Elvenwand.* These, as the name may imply, are very small, palm-sized wands, capable of being carried in a pocket or hidden in the hand, without attracting attention in a group of people. They are considered to be extremely powerful tools, often used specifically for thought-form projection and communication with spirit-allies, as well as the usual casting of spells and charms. This type of wand is the physical manifestation of a particularly powerful

Dryad, whose mother-tree grew on hallowed ground, at the conjunction of two or more major force lines within the Land. The acquiring of this type of wand takes much practice and effort on the part of both the Witch and the Dryad involved and they must be in total accord for the wand to be of working use. This type of keppen may also be used as a pendulum in dowsing for answers to magical questions and in locating sites of power within the Land, the resident Dryad being intimately connected with the energies involved and able to pass this information onto its Witch partner. The whole practice of attuning, working with and taking wood in this manner is known as *tree-talking* in some Traditions and is a specific discipline in and of itself, taking years to master fully.

Whilst Walking in other areas of terrain, the Witch is naturally likely to encounter other types of Spirit and different forms of energy. To be found in all areas in East Anglia is the spirit known as a Hykey, Hyter or High Sprite, known elsewhere as Land Wights and their local equivalents. These Spirits are generally solitary beings and are seen to be essentially benevolent and well disposed towards human beings if treated with respect. They can generally be found in and associated with wooded and grown up areas, but may be encountered in fields, meadows and heathland also. If glimpsed out of the corner of the eye (which is usually the only way they can be seen), they appear to be long and gangly, somewhat twig-like and very swift. On occasion they can appear as shimmering lights in marshy or boggy areas. The Hykey Sprite will accept offerings such as a bowl of cream, or bread and milk and will create a calm and pleasant atmosphere for the humans in its vicinity. They are generally unwilling to aid the Witch but, as usual, if effort, time and respect is put into gaining their trust, then they can prove most helpful in most "earth-based" forms of magic. That aside, they generally ignore or leave humans alone and are rarely glimpsed these days. Much more badly disposed towards the Witch and humans in general are the spirits known as Yarthkins. These are also solitary creatures, but can be found almost anywhere, particularly on waste ground and uncultivated plots that have "gone off" or refuse to grow anything productive. The Yarthkin, in East Anglian lore, is particularly inimical to humans and cannot be placated with offerings, however well presented, these actually increasing their antagonism. They can, however, be trapped and removed or disposed of by various means, the particular art and practice of various types of Cunning Men in East Anglia. Using such items as red thread, various shaped staves and sticks, blown eggs, runic symbols and talismans, the Yarthkin can be safely disempowered and their influence contained. However this is time consuming and expends a lot of energy and the traps and wards must be renewed at intervals; it is much better to avoid a Yarthkin altogether. Places where the spirits of the Land, of all types, are absent or have been driven away by the folly, greed, intolerance, stupidity or just pure ignorance of humans are known in East Anglia as *Gast.* These are places where there is no life at all, where it feels psychically dead to the Witch and leaves a chill, barren feeling in the soul. All magic workers come across these from time to time – unfortunately – and they are best avoided. It *is* possible to remedy this situation, but the willing Witch needs to exert much time, effort and energy in its execution. I will speak more of this later in the section on Guardianship, but suffice it to say here that it involves attempting to encourage the spirits of the Land to return – which they will be very unwilling to do – with a combination of offerings, tending the Land both physically and energetically and other magical actions.

Caves and Subterranean sites

Caves and other underground places, such as tunnels – whether man-made or not – and dried-up water courses, are not found in all areas but, where they are, they hold a magic and mystery, a power and a numinosity all of their own for the aware Witch. As openings into the Land, they are necessarily entrances into the Underworld, and are valuable for the insights and knowledge that they may convey. As entrances to the Underworld, there are many tales that speak of beings from different realms emerging and interacting with humans from above; Elves, Fairies and other folk and one especial tale which comes from my home county of Suffolk. This particular story is unique – to my knowledge – in that it occurred within historically recorded time and is attested to by the people of that time. It is the story of the Green Children, long thought to be of the Faire Folk. This tale was vouched for by a contemporary historian, one William of Newburgh, and occurred some 800 years ago in the village of Woolpit. Some harvesters were gathering in their crop at St. Mary of the Wolfpits (as it was then known), when they beheld a young boy and girl, standing at the mouth of the wolf-hole or pit, from whence the village derived its name; these holes were always a mysterious sort of place and situated just below the field in which they were working. These children, who were of a normal size otherwise, struck the villagers with astonishment as their skin was tinged green all over. No one could understand their speech, nor could the children understand what was said to them. They were also clothed in some material of which even the oldest housewife in the village had never seen the like. They were taken to the house of Sir Richard de Caine, the local Lord, where white bread, honey and milk were set before them. But although plainly famished, the children would not touch this or any other food, until some fresh-cut beans were brought into the house. The green food delighted them and by signs they indicated that they must have some. When given some of the beans, they seized upon them with great delight and for a long time after would eat nothing else. The boy, who remained "languid and depressed", died shortly after his arrival in Woolpit, but the girl flourished and being highly intelligent, learned the common language. She also gradually came to have a liking for a normal diet and, with the change, gradually lost her green colouring. She was often asked about the place that she came from and how she and her brother had come to Woolpit. She used to tell her questioners that she came from a place called St. Martins Land, where the people, animals and all that could be seen were green. There was no sun there, only a soft light like that which shines after sunset or twilight, but beyond a broad river there lay a land of light. It was as they were following their green sheep that...

> *"they came to a certain cave, on entering which they heard a delightful sound of bells; ravished by whose sweetness they were for a long time wandering on through the cavern until they came to its mouth. When they came out of it they were struck senseless by the excessive light of the sun and the unusual temperature of the air; and thus they lay for a long time. Being terrified by the noise of those who came on them, they wished to fly, but they could not find the entrance of the cavern before they were caught."*

Of this strange tale, there has never been a "rational" explanation, other than that the two green children did, in fact, as they said, come from a Land under the earth. Strange indeed!

From the point of view of the Witch, it is only in caves that complete darkness may be found. Outside, even on the darkest night, there is some light from the sky, whether from clouds, Moon or Stars and the eye adapts to this light no matter how faint. In caves, however, the darkness is absolute. The only movement or sound, other than that produced by the Witch themselves, may be the sound of water dripping from the roof or a river running through. Add to this the natural echoes and reverberation within caves and it is understandable why the underground places have been sought out for delving into the deeper and darker Mysteries for millennia. It is an occult maxim that only in the Dark can the true Light be found and this is no less true in caves than in a metaphor. Such places have been sought out for performing rites of all natures, but especially those of the nature of personal or group vigils, divination and communication with the Underworld Powers. Such a place is Alderley Edge, a famous rock outcrop in Cheshire in north west England, where the western edge of the Peak District towers over the flat Cheshire Plain. The systems of caves and tunnels here are known to have long been used by local Witches, both groups and solitaries, for their workings and, as far as anyone is aware, still are today. It is said that a candidate for initiation into one of the local groups would be blindfold and bound, ferried underground on one of the waterways and left overnight on their own in the complete darkness, being collected the next day. In the properly prepared and aware candidate, this could bring about certain realisations that would make them suitable for subsequent admission into the group. (Interesting parallels concerning vigils in caves exist with other belief systems also. In 1214 C.E., the founder of the Catholic Dominican Order, Dominico de Guzman – St. Dominic – entered a cave near a wood in Toulouse, France, with the aim of a spiritual retreat and vigil. After meditating, praying and fasting for three days in the darkness of his retreat, he received a visitation from "Our Lady", who had fifty eldritch women attending Her. During this visitation he was given the technique of the Rosary, which he later strongly promulgated and which is now a major form of devotion and spirituality within the Catholic faith system).

Similar cave systems to Alderley Edge exist on the Lizard peninsula in Cornwall and are also used for arcane rites. The researcher Robin Ellis, writing in the Cornish Earth Mysteries and folklore magazine, *Meyn Mamvro* (issue 22, Autumn 1993), has described the "Kachinas", members of the local Pellar cult, who work with the dark Serpent Goddess. They believe that it is She who is the guardian of the secrets of the Serpent or Lizard power, which flows through the Land there and they have a specific rite for conjuring Her. Ellis states that it requires a rock-pool, or "rock-chalice" to carry it out properly; one within a sea-cave inside the earth is best of all. The intention is to communicate with this entity, by seeing pictures, either in the pool, or in your mind. This can supposedly be achieved by intoning aloud the following invocation, which can be repeated as often as you like, until you feel that contact has been established.

"To Summon the Serpent of the Lizard
Treasures that no mind can comprehend,
That no man can harm.
Dream on with tripled powers.
Shining One, your strength is in the stars.
Great is the Moon Glow,
And the Moon's Powers!

Keepers of the ancient Dream,
Come, Dream in here with us.
If I cry, CAR-AW! CAR-AW!
Show thy self!
If I cry, CAR-AW! CAR-AW!
Take it to Yourself!

From the Ancient Dreaming,
The Wise Goddess speaks.

(Meditate for a while).

Oh, Mother of Light and Dark.
You who know mercy.
May your moon visions be with us,
As with our ancestors of Horrendous Powers.
Take us now to the Threshold,
Of the Otherworld.
But do not leave us there!

(Meditate)."

It can clearly be seen that the Power being worked with here is considered to be of both orders, both Dark and Light, but that She holds the keys to certain energies and mysteries occurring in that specific area. Working with Her in the darkness of a sea cave could certainly bring about profound realisations and discoveries, but not all Witches have access to the Lizard and this particular incantation is specifically meant to be used there.

A slightly different rite may be used in any cave or underground space, with the intent of bringing about contact and communication with the Dark Goddess. In this case the rite is meant to give insight into the workings of the Fate or Wyrd of the Witch and to aid in making decisions about their personal future path and Way of working. It is the Dark Goddess who is seen to have these things in Her charge and keep and may bestow knowledge and understanding of them as She will. Hers is not just the responsibility for dissolution and decay, but of the promise of future Life that arises from these things; all Life is cyclical and there is no end to the eternal cycle of Black and White, Light and Dark. It is therefore to the Black form of deity that the wise Witch goes when seeking the details of Life in the future. This working can be seen as a type of "Sitting **In**" rite, as opposed to the "Sitting **Out**" described previously in the chapter on Moon working.

This form is best undertaken at the Dark of the Moon, but any time during the Waning phase will suffice. To be performed alone, inside your chosen cave or subterranean space. Have a large chalice or bowl in the centre of your working space and a lit candle within it; just a small one, or a votive candle in a glass container. No other light at all. Keep all other paraphernalia to an absolute minimum.

Hallow your compass in your usual manner, paying particular attention to personal balancing and centring. Face north, over the bowl and state the following, or similar;

"Deep One of Mystery and Night,
Uncover the Well of Knowledge.
Lift the Cover over the darkness
And let me see the Truth beyond."

Stand silently and let the atmosphere build around you. Feel the directions and the centre where you stand. When you feel the virtue swirling about you, bow to the north and begin to pace the round, using the following, or similar, chant, whilst focussing on the light within the bowl.

"Ancient One beneath the Land,
Keeper of the Silent Cup,
Let the secret waters flow,
From the deeps I wish to sup.
To worlds below I send my Call,
By virtue's honest prayer,
Awaken here the inner Sight,
On breath of Serpent's lair."

Continue the pacing until you feel the virtue peak, then swiftly kneel before the bowl and blow out the candle. Gaze deep into the depths before you and open yourself to what may unfold. Do not look around you, whatever you may feel, but continue to focus on the bowl until the energies die back and you feel the connections have broken or dissipated naturally. Sit back for a moment and collect yourself before relighting the candle in the bowl. Bless some, dark, wine in the name of the Black Goddess and take a sip yourself – but only a sip! Pour the rest out on the ground beside the bowl, in Her honour. Stand and pace the round in the opposite direction, chanting;

"From the deepest depths return,
Serpent's lair depart,
Light regain and Land attain,
Knowledge for the heart."

Rebalance yourself carefully and clear away in your normal fashion, leaving nothing but your footprints behind you.

Not every Witch may wish, or be able, to perform the above, for whatever reason and so I offer an alternative here. This "rite" is known to some Traditions as "Riding the Serpent's Breath" and relies on the ability of the Witch to attune themselves to the virtue arising from under the Land. In certain places the Witch may encounter caves or tunnels from which issue winds or gusts of air, either continuously or at certain times. Traditional lore knows these phenomena as the Breath of the Serpent, the energies of the Land itself, emerging above ground in aerial form. The Serpent, Wyrm or Dragon has long been a personification or representation of the winding and undulating energies felt by many to exist within the living body of the Earth and these winds are traditionally said to be the exhalation of the chthonic beast. In some locations this wind is felt – and heard – to be the hammering of Underworld smiths, the rumbling of drums, eldritch fiddling, or the drone of bagpipes, all depending upon the culture of the area. Yet all agree that at the root is the rumbling of the very Earth Serpent itself. For the Old Craft Witch, this exhalation of virtuous breath may be utilised for their own ends and purposes, mainly and usually of a divinatory nature.

Having found a suitable site where winds and gusts reliably come forth, the Witch sits and composes themself with the drafts at their back, from whence it issues from the Earth. This may be done either at night or by the light of day but, in this instance, daytime is better as you will see. The Witch *closes their eyes* and enters a light trance, if not already induced by their Walking to arrive at the site and opens themselves to the Breath arising from the Underworld entrance. The Witch breathes in deeply, taking the Underworldly essence deep into the lungs and, thence, circulates it around the rest of the body. It is a steady rhythmic breath, tuned to the Witch's own natural, bodily flows; one in-breath and one out-breath completing one cycle – no holding the breath in-between. Slowly, so as not to hyperventilate, the body is infused with the Serpent's Breath. Once in a suitable state, the technique used is to "rise" up, whilst still in the body, and mentally ride the stream of air at their back. Picture a hawk, or similar, balancing on an updraught of air, remaining stationary and hovering whilst the wind is blowing around them and you will understand what I am trying to convey. Like all techniques, this cannot be expected to be mastered at the first attempt, but perseverance will bring significant results. Having achieved this state and allowed the eldritch influence of the Breath to course through them, the Witch must hold the question or situation to which they need an answer firmly in mind – not to be dwelt upon, just held in mind. Then *open the eyes* and look out upon the Land around. The first thing to be seen will be the answer to the question and it should hit the Witch with the force of a hammer blow as, being linked to the Land in an intimate manner, the answer will be immediately obvious. The Witch may see a flight of birds in a certain arrangement; a pattern of tree branches against the backdrop of the sky; a formation of clouds; an alignment of field boundaries, or a herd of deer running in a specific direction. Anything may appear and be instantly significant. These signs are known as "*Ostenta*", or portents and, unlike omens, give an immediate answer to a question, rather than something to be worked out or manifested at a later time. I shall go further into these signs in the next chapter, but here it is sufficient to know that they will occur and be immediately obvious, should the exercise have been successfully accomplished.

Having gained the answer to their question, the Witch slowly and gently lowers their senses and releases their hold on the Serpent's Breath, coming softly down to Earth again, so to speak. Some time is then given to readjusting the perception to everyday reality, before departing the site and returning home.

This technique, whilst tricky to master initially, can be quite versatile in its usage. Having achieved the required state, the Witch may choose not to take note of Ostenta for their divination, but to utilise other, equally valid, techniques. Whilst using such things as tarot cards and pendulums may not be the best idea with a wind blowing at their back (depending on its strength), such methods as casting the runes, bones or other forms of lots is ideal, particularly if seated on a sandy area where these may fall easily. An excellent method in this situation is the Art of Geomancy, linked to the Earth as it is. This is not the technique of discovering the flow of energies within the Land, but of the ancient Way of divining using the fall of marked sticks, or other indicators, and making figures in/on the Land, depending on the way they fall, then making the divination from the resulting figures. I do not have room here to describe this technique sufficiently, but will go into it in more detail in the next chapter.

Holy Wells and Springs

Walking back out into the landscape, the Witch may become aware of another type of numinous water, that of the still pools of Holy Wells, often fed by Springs from underground sources. These, thus, partake of the same essence and virtue as we have already encountered in other natural features of the Land. However, being of a more static type, Wells, Springs and Pools, exhibit different types of virtue, manifest different energies than the flowing waters of rivers and streams. Theirs is the energy of stillness, of quietude and a focussing of virtue in one place, which results in quite different reactions from humans in general and Witches in particular. Like Caves and Tunnels, Wells are also seen as entrances to the Underworld, hence also linking into the powers of the Land, the Spirits and the Beings that inhabit it. They often inspire a sense of reverence, hush and devotional reflection, not generally associated with the more rushing waters of Rivers and Streams. Some Wells have become world-famous for their history and attributes and such as these are found at Walsingham in Norfolk. This is the most visited holy wells site in the U.K. and a place revered by both Catholic and Protestant Christians alike, but its origins go back much further.

In 1061 the young widow, Richeldis de Favarches, Lady of the Manor of Little Walsingham, prayed that she might undertake some special work in honour of the Virgin Mary. In response to her petition, the Blessed Virgin took her in spirit form, whilst asleep, and showed her a vision of the Holy House in Nazareth, scene of the Annunciation. Bidding her to mark well the measurements of the house, the Virgin commanded Richeldis to build an exact counterpart of it at Walsingham. When she awoke, craftsmen were at once called in to produce a replica of the Holy House. But when the wooden building was completed, she was at a loss as to where to have it placed. While she prayed for guidance, a heavy dew fell one night on a nearby meadow, leaving two small areas quite dry over two wells. This occurrence Richeldis took to be a sign from the Virgin Mary that the replica of the house should be placed on one of them. But naturally she did not know which one. Eventually, when she did reach a decision, it proved to be the wrong one, for although all measurements for the house had been carefully adhered to, the craftsmen were unable to fit it to the foundations prepared for it. However, the next morning they discovered that, during the night, the little wooden structure had been moved to the other site, not haphazardly by wind or weather, but presumably by supernatural hands, as it was firmly fixed, each part of the building joined together better than they themselves could have done it. This, then, Richeldis decided, was the chosen site. She had the little house enclosed in a stone chapel, while in later years, her son Geoffrey endowed it with money and lands and a priory was founded there. During the Reformation, the Priory and much of the site was mostly destroyed, the shrine being desecrated and pulled down. All that remained was the site of the two wells, which became sadly neglected by many.

However, several centuries later, the Rev. Robert Forby, writing in "*The Vocabulary of East Anglia*" (pub. 1830), had this to say concerning the wells at Walsingham;

> *"Amongst the slender remains of this once celebrated seat of superstitious devotion, are two small circular basons of stone, a little to the north-east of the site of the conventual church, (exactly in the place described by Erasmus in his "Peregrinatio religionis ergo"), and connected with the chapel of the Virgin, which was on the north side of the choir. The water of these wells had at that time a miraculous efficacy in curing disorders of the head and stomach, the special gift, no doubt, of the Holy Virgin: who has probably since that time resumed it, for the waters have no such quality now. She has substituted, however, another of far more comprehensive virtue. This is nothing less than the power of accomplishing all human wishes, which miraculous property the water is still believed to possess. In order to attain this desirable end, the votary, with a due qualification of faith and pious awe, must apply the right knee, bare, to a stone placed for that purpose between the wells. He must then plunge to the wrist each hand, bare also, into the water of the wells, which are near enough to admit of this immersion. A wish must then be formed, but not uttered with the lips, either at the time or afterwards, even in confidential communication to the dearest friend. The hands are then to be withdrawn, and as much of the water as can be contained in the hollow of each is to be swallowed. Formerly the object of desire was most probably expressed in a prayer to the Virgin. It is now only a silent wish: which will certainly be accomplished within twelve months, if the efficacy of the solemn rite be not frustrated by the incredulity or some other fault of the votary."*

The excavations that took place at Walsingham in 1961 showed that where Richeldis built her Holy House, an early Anglo-Saxon shrine had once existed; the choice of its site being governed, no doubt, by the presence of the already sacred wells nearby, long before they later received their Christian "hallowing". However, it is here that the Virgin Mary chose to make Her presence felt and it is still a sacred, powerful and holy site to many. The waters are still used for many healing rituals and not a few Witches and Cunning-folk have been known to bend the knee there, the site being revered for its appearance of the Divine Feminine, under whatever guise.

I would like to give another example, which is quite lengthy, but gives a very well-rounded image of another, typical use of a holy well. I will begin with a quote from Janet & Colin Bord's book, "*Earth Rites*" (see Bibliography) and then give some fuller details.

> "In the late 1860's, two men were by chance able secretly to watch a fertility ritual being practised at a holy well, the well of Melschach in the parish of Kennethmont in Grampian, and this account of the event is by J.M. McPherson.
>
> *On the first Sunday of May, a keeper, accompanied by an expert from Aberdeen, set out for the moors to investigate grouse disease then prevalent. From a distance, they spied a group of women round the well. With the aid of a field-glass, the men watched their movements. The women, with garments fastened up under their arms and with hands joined, were dancing in a circle round the well. An aged crone sat in their midst, and dipping a small vessel in the water, kept sprinkling them. They were married women who had proved childless and had come to the well to experience its fertilising virtues. No doubt words had been repeated, but the two observers were too far off to hear. There are many marks here of a primitive rite. The Convention took place on the first Sunday of May. The women were formed in a circle with their skirts kilted up, and the old woman, the presiding priestess of the well, administered its waters by sprinkling. Sprinkling was one of the methods employed at the ancient fertility wells. But so little is known of the ritual at these wells when the object was to cure sterility,*

that the account of this ceremonial at Melshach receives an added importance. The remarkable thing is that the custom lingered so late."

There is also this information recorded of the well in the local archives, dated to 1793;

"Melshach Well - They use it both internally and externally in the summer season, particularly in the month of May. Its sanative qualities are not confined to man, they are supposed to extend even to brutes. As this spring probably obtained vogue at first in days of ignorance and superstition, it would appear that it became customary to leave at the well part of the clothes of the sick and diseased, and harness of the cattle, as an offering of gratitude to the divinity who bestowed healing virtues on its waters. And now, even though the superstitious principle no longer exists, the accustomed offerings are still presented"

(http://www.kinnethmont.co.uk/local-news/statistical_account_1793.htm).

F. Marian McNeill in her fascinating book, "*The Silver Bough*" (see Bibliography), gives a rather more full account of a fertility ritual recorded at an unnamed well at a place in Scotland named "Willie's Muir". This well was visited by childless women, led by an older woman, during Midsummer's week. Whilst at a different time and place to the above, I feel the ritual is virtually identical, but with much more detail and so I reproduce it here in full.

The women had to take off their boots and kneel by the water and:

"rolled up their skirts and petticoats till their wames were bare. The auld wife gave them the sign to step around her and away they went, one after the other, wi' the sun, round the spring, each one holding up her coats like she was holding herself to the sun. As each one came anent her, the auld wife took up the water in her hands and threw it on their wames. Never a one cried out at the cold o' the water and never a word was spoken. Three

> *times round they went. The auld wife made a sign to them. They dropped their coats to their feet again, synt (then) they opend their dress frae the neck and skipped it off their shoulders so that their paps sprang out. The auld wife gave them another sign. They doun on their knees afore her, across the spring; and she took up the water in her hands, skirpit (splashed it) on their paps, three times three. Then the auld wife rose and the three barren women rose. The put on their claes again and drew their shawls about their faces and left the hollow without a word spoken and scattered across the muir for hame."*

These two accounts give very good examples of some of the ways in which wells and springs have been used over time – and it is a long time. These pools of still water have been recognised as having eldritch properties from time immemorial and have been treated as such. Originally coming under the auspices of a local Spirit, Fairy or Deity, many wells were later "Christianised" under the name of a Saint. These names of saints, although in general quite historically valid, were often in many places simply the name of the local deity/spirit under a different guise. The actions that the local populace and magic workers were used to practising at the wells continued openly, mostly unchanged until the Reformation, when they simply went underground and were continued in secret. The rituals of healing and pilgrimage, also, once safely taken under the wing of the Church, seem to have been allowed to continue without serious interference until the Reformation in the 16th Century. It is not known exactly how old the rituals which are performed at many wells and springs may be. However, many pre-Christian elements may well have been passed down orally for over a thousand years – judging by the number of sites which require a visit or pilgrimage to be carried out on May Day, at Midsummer or Lammas, at or before sunrise and for the visitor or pilgrim to circle the well three times sunwise. It is generally considered that travelling would be too difficult and the weather too inclement in other seasons, which is why Candlemas and Hallowmas, although major and notable dates, are rarely if ever mentioned in the known records of activities at holy wells and springs.

Many, many rites were and are carried out at wells, for all sorts of reasons. We have seen above how devotion or veneration and matters of fertility were obviously of importance. Alongside these, healing, cursing, un-cursing, love spells, the binding and banishing of enemies and evil spirits, weather magic and divination were all practised alongside the waters of holy wells. Not all wells could be used for all types of magic; some were used strictly for only one type or another. Some were able to be used by animals – i.e. to be washed in the waters or able to drink them – whilst at others it was strictly taboo and dire results would issue should the ban be broken. At some wells there were – and, again, still are – guardians, often of a hereditary nature. These people would perform the required ritual for the petitioner, or guide them in the actions they were meant to perform themselves. These would often include circumambulating the well a given number of times (usually multiples of 3), normally in a clockwise manner, but sometimes not, depending on the rite. In the case of healing, it was usual for a piece of the patient's clothing to be *ripped* off – the closer to the site of the problem the better – dipped in the waters and hung on a nearby bush or tree. As the natural fibres of the cloth rotted away, so would the disease or complaint of the patient wane and disappear. These pieces of cloth are known as *clouties* and can still be seen in their myriads beside wells today, as it has become very popular to leave these as "offerings" or "wishes", instead of what they were originally meant for. Unfortunately, not all are of natural materials and so instead of rotting away naturally, are a cause of much pollution and damage to the local flora and fauna.(Personally, I have encountered such hideous and inappropriate things as empty crisp packets, rubber bra straps, plastic dolls and animals and glitter canes left at supposedly holy sites). Another item that was/is much used is the pin.

Often inserted into a votive offering and hung by the well, many pins are bent and thrown into the waters, for various reasons. The bending of the pin takes it out of everyday use in this world and dedicates it for the use of those in others. Coins, also, are often dedicated in this manner, by being bent, and offered into the waters as gifts to the spirits or saint that watches over the place, in an effort to gain their favour. In some places, coins are also traditionally pushed or hammered into the bark of the trees around the well, or one tree in particular, also as offerings. Unfortunately, due to the increased popularity of this practise at many sites, a lot of trees have been killed due to ignorance and the site has thereby lost much of its sanctity and virtue. For much more detail and information on traditional practices at well sites than I have room for here, I can, again, do no better than to recommend Gemma Gary's book, "*Wisht Waters*".

Interestingly enough for the purposes of this present work, the trees – or lone tree – that are most often found growing by a well or spring and that are linked to it by custom and practice, are the Thorns, both Black and White. This is often explained by saying that they are deliberately grown there, or allowed to grow, because the thorns or spikes are used in the magical practices associated with the well or spring. This may very well be the case in many places, but the Old Craft Witch knows that there are deeper reasons for this than are immediately apparent. We have seen throughout this work how both the Blackthorn and Whitethorn may stand as exemplars of both the Witch and their "crossed" nature, neither dark nor bright, but a combination of both. We have also seen how these trees are both gateways into the realms that are known as "Other" to non-witches, but are very much part of the Witches own experiential worlds. It is this oft-overlooked aspect of well-lore that I would now like to turn to.

All the traditional usages of wells and springs mentioned above are part of the Witches working practices, along with other such rites as scrying in the waters, taking and using the waters for various magical and healing rites and for use in potions, etc. I would here like to mention two uses of wells and springs that normally are not covered and are little known, namely the use of them for spirit flight and for practical, magical work; this is for uses other than those mentioned above that the general public practises. For a Witch immersed in the life of the Land in their locale, wells – as numinous and connective locii - are exceedingly useful sites for these two activities. Both of the activities mentioned require the active co-operation of the Spirit of the well or spring and also of the Tree – be it Blackthorn or Whitethorn – although these are often the same, or at least connected, as may be seen.

For practical, magical operations – and these can be of any kind that the Witch needs to do – a close connection and working relationship needs to be developed with the presiding Spirit. Again, this takes time and effort, but that is only to be expected in any genuine magical work. The Witch needs to gain the favour of the Spirit by offerings, but also by practical measures, such as cleaning up and tending the site and removing any litter or unwanted material there. In my experience this goes a long way towards gaining favour, as these things can cause quite a lot of damage and clearing them away is something that the Spirit just can't, physically, do. Meditate by the well/under the tree and come to know them both, bearing in mind all that I have written previously about Spirit and Tree contact. (It is unlikely that the tree by the well will also be your kin tree but, if it is, then you have an added advantage and head start with the Spirit of the well). Once you feel that you have created a genuine and valid bond with the resident Well Spirit, you can begin your magical work there.

Create your charm, poppet, pouch or sigil for the work that you have in mind – or whatever other physical basis suits the work. Whatever form it takes, it **must** be made from natural materials; cotton, linen, jute, string, paper, clay, wood, etc. as long as it will degrade naturally. Once made, it must be taken to the site of the well and the tree and impaled upon a thorn or spike of the tree. The aim of the spell or working must be stated out loud (but quietly), three times, clearly and the physical materia left overnight on the thorn (better if it can safely be left for 3 nights). After this time, carefully detach the spike holding the charm from the tree, doing as little damage as possible, so that the charm is still pierced by the thorn. The tree that grows by the well has the power of the water in its body - the thorns taken from it are thorns of that well and the spirits of that well are in the thorns. Take a piece of bread and lay the charm upon it; do not remove the thorn. Circle the well three times in an appropriate direction for the work. Place the bread upon the surface of the waters in the well, saying as you do so;

> *"In the well, long before me,*
> *Spirit grow, beneath the tree.*
> *Take my gift, given free,*
> *A help for me if it may be."*

Gently repeat this as you watch the bread absorb the water from the well and begin to sink into the depths, taking the charm that lies upon it with it. When all has sunk below the surface, make a libation of one drop of your own blood into the water. Stand up, turn around and walk away, without looking back. Manifestation will take place in due time.

As major features in the Landscape and foci of numinous power, developed over centuries, if not thousands of years, Wells have a strong link with the Ancestors in the Land and may be utilised as a contact point for them. I have spoken earlier in Chapter 4 of conversing with the Dead and here is another Way of making contact, directly through a gateway in the Land itself. The Dead and the Ancestors have been closely associated with Wells and Springs from time immemorial, many sites having tales of how the original waters gushed from the ground after a saint/hero/king/queen, etc. had been beheaded or otherwise slain on the spot.

Some of these remained to become the Guardian Spirits of the site in perpetuity, or handed on the responsibility to another after a set number of years. (Other, smaller, less well known sites often have no name, but still have an active guardian spirit. These are usually much better for the Witch to work at as there is less disturbance from others and they are more out of the way. The exception to this is if the area and/or Well itself is *gast*, in which case it is to be avoided and not worked with at all).

There is a tale about a *Ffynnon Dewi* (St David's Well) near to Henfynyw Church in Cardiganshire of which it was once said:

> *"An old man visited this well one Christmas Eve. He heard cries for help issuing from the well; a hand then rose and a voice asked the man to hold on tightly. He did so, but relaxed his hold. The hand then vanished into the well and the voice cried "I am bound for another fifty years."*

The binding of this spirit to the well appears not to have been voluntary in this case but is not too far in essence from many other tales told about wells all across the country. Many include the motif of a reaching hand or arm, the Guardian seeking for help or relief in many cases, but shunned by ordinary mortals. The Witch may safely engage with the Spirit of the Well, once a working relationship has been developed. In addition to whomever may be acting as Guardian, people have been visiting these sites for many, many years, pouring out their heartfelt prayers and desires, asking and giving thanks for wishes granted and deeds done on their behalf. All of this energy has accumulated over the years and adds to the virtue available to be tapped and used by the Witch in their work. It is by contacting and developing a connection with the Virtue, Guardian or Spirit of the well, that the Witch may use the waters as a gateway or portal to journey in spirit flight within and encounter these ancient people in the Land, or ask that they be guided to others that may help them in their quest for answers, knowledge or other appropriate wisdom. The technique is simple but, as ever, requires practice and effort and a strong spiritual connection.

Unless the Witch has access to a Well on their own, or other, private Land, all these rites will necessarily be performed at public sites where they will either have to wait until everyone is gone for the day, or otherwise utilise a less well-known site in secret. Therefore, hallowing a full compass in the situation would probably be very difficult, but in this situation it is not absolutely necessary. The Well acts as a gateway into the Land, just as any direction in a compass can; what the Witch needs to do is retain a hold in this reality whilst journeying elsewhere and this may be achieved by the use of the Witch's cord. I have explained the manufacture and use of this type of cord already in Chapter 3 and this will be perfectly suitable for this working. Having said this, certain balancing procedures are advised and I would suggest the Witch begin this working, at the site, with the Circle Cross technique (see *Treading the Mill*), adapted for this situation, or something similar within the Witch's own working practise.

Stand facing the Well.

Close your eyes, take a few, deep breaths and visualise. Raise your dominant hand and touch your brow. Say;

"From Stars Above".

See a source of shining, astral light high above your head, sending down a stream of energy to connect with your brow area. Trace a line of light down from your brow and touch your navel. Say;

"To Earth Below".

See the line of light continuing down and penetrating the earth at your feet.

Touch your left shoulder. Say;

"By the Blackthorn".

See a source of light coming from your infinite left and connecting with your left shoulder.

Trace a line of light across to your right shoulder. Say;

"And the Whitethorn".

See the line of light continuing off to your infinite right.

You now have an equal armed cross emblazoned on the front of your body, stretching to infinity and linking you to the four quarters of the universe, in whatever direction they may be.

Cross your palms over the centre of your chest where the lines meet. Visualise a circle of light whose circumference touches your left and right shoulders, your brow and navel. Say;

"Around me forms the Landward".

Now, breathe in and visualise the cross; breathe out and visualise the circle surrounding it. Repeat twice more (three times in all). Continue with your work and maintain at least a minimal awareness of the circle-cross held before you.

Circumambulate the Well 3 times sunwise, intoning the following, or similar;

"I step about the shining Well,
silent Pool of landborn might,
The eldritch Thorn stands ever nigh,
sustains the ever-watching Wight.
Spirits underneath I Call
Open up that Gate below,

Allow my passage unopposed,
That I the inner Way may know".

Tie one end of your cord around your waist (or wrist, depending on its length) and the other end to your kin-tree or the closest Thorn. If this is too far from the well, tie the other end to a nearby rock, tree stump or other solid object (well cover-support?).

Sit down comfortably and as closely to the Well as you can, whilst remaining safe and making sure that you will not fall in during the work. Compose yourself and begin to enter/ deepen trance whilst chanting the following, or similar;

"To the depths, down below,
Spirit guard me, Spirit guide me.
To the depths, down I go,
Spirit guard me Spirit guide me".

Continue chanting for as long as you feel the need to.

Whilst you are doing this, place your hand gently and slowly into the water. Follow your hand (and arm?), down and down through the still waters of the Well, as you gently project your spirit along with it. As you go, if you have achieved a good communication and working bond with the Guardian Spirit of the Well, you may find that a hand rises from the depths to greet you and take yours. If this is the case, allow yourself to be guided and led further down and to continue your journey. If you are not greeted in this manner, continue as far as you are able with your journey by yourself.

Where you go and what you do is either a joint venture with the Guardian of the Well, or entirely up to you and your own abilities. Wells and springs are almost always linked to others by underground water courses and also by the energy lines and Spirit Ways within the Land; these can lead to other foci elsewhere. These could be other Wells and Springs, Rivers, ancient Trees, Standing Stones or Circles or any number of other numinous sites. It is up to the Witch to explore and discover what they will – this is, after all, the whole point of the exercise. If you find that you are being led by the Guardian – and also if you achieve your goal of meeting the Ancestors within the Land - feel free to ask appropriate questions, but always remember politeness, honour and respect!

When you feel that it is time to return (or in the unlikely situation that you find yourself in trouble), simply disengage – politely – with whatever/whoever you are with and retrace the length of your cord to your body by the Well. (This is the benefit of using the Witch's cord for this working. A well and properly made cord will have its astral/etheric counterpart and will remain tied to your spirit body however far away you are. Simply return along its length). When you have regained your body and normal, waking senses, it is obviously appropriate to hallow some offerings and make libations in thanks at the Well. Again, a single drop of your blood would also be an acceptable gift. Once you have finished, it is a good idea to again perform the Circle-Cross to re-balance yourself, before clearing all away and departing, leaving no trace of your presence or actions.

Guardianship

Working with the Land for an appreciable length of time at a deep energetic and spiritual level can change a person. This is all to the good and is, after all, what part of a Witch's work is all about; some would say perhaps even the main part. After some time, there may develop a connection at a visceral level, such that if there is occasion to be absent from the place in the Land of the connection for an appreciable period of time, then there is felt to be a sense of disquietude, of painful separation that only returning to that place will alleviate. This normally develops only after a significant number of years of working with a place but, once developed, cannot be mistaken. This may happen after working and developing a relationship with an area of Land in general, a specific Tree, a Well, Cave, Circle of Stones, or any number of other sites, but cannot be denied once brought into being. There becomes a bond between the Witch and their place that goes beyond words and is simply "felt". It betokens an acceptance and a trust on the part of the non-physical Guardian of the area or site, which is rarely given at all. Conversely, in places where the human is not welcome, or not wanted at all, the Genius Loci will let them know in no uncertain terms. This is when the individual feels at least a sense of discomfort which, if left unacknowledged and not acted upon, can mount to panic and sheer terror – the presence of Pan in the true sense of the word. Many is the wanderer who has entered a grove, a cave or climbed a hill or a mountain and has turned, running in sheer horror at the feelings provoked by their presence, only to have them disappear completely after passing an unseen or unacknowledged boundary. The feeling dissipates totally after crossing a bridge, leaving the wood, coming off the hill etc. and all returns to normal, making the individual wonder what on earth just happened – they were warned off by the place Guardian in no uncertain terms!

In my own case, as I mentioned earlier in the Introduction, I have been working magically at a particular place for over 40 years, on and off. It has neither a Holy Well nor a Standing Stone. It doesn't contain a Cave or a flowing River, but it does have a special Tree that is particularly dear to me and whom I watched grow into the spectacular height it now is. This place is situated on heathland, near woodland, not far from the sea on the coast of East Anglia and, quite simply, I love it. I do not live there, but some 40 miles away and I feel an aching loss in my guts when I'm not there. I have no desire to go anywhere else for a break or holiday and the thought of not visiting and experiencing that site at least three or four times a year fills me with a kind of panic and loss. It is this kind of physical, energetic and spiritual attachment that I am trying to convey. It doesn't always happen and, indeed, is quite rare in this day and age, but it is at this point that the question of Guardianship may occur.

By using the word "Guardianship", I do not mean the term as it is generally applied these days. It is often the word that is used when a person or group "adopts" an area for a ritual working site, or people get together to look after somewhere like a local Holy Well, Spring, stretch of River-course or other natural site or feature. The place is cleaned, cared for, watched for vandalism, fires and other senseless acts carried out by mindless humans and generally protected from accidental or deliberate damage. No, worthy as these acts are and they are greatly to be lauded, it is not this. The act of magical Guardianship goes much deeper and further. It is a deliberate bonding of the energies of the Witch with the site, such that each becomes part of the other and partakes of a kind of shared life, a union; a sort of marriage. Many readers will be aware of the rite of Sacred Marriage, conducted between the Kings of certain pre-literate, Iron Age peoples, particularly known in the British Isles, and continuing through into historical periods, later being recorded by monkish scribes. Some readers may also be aware of the beings variously known as Burial Kings or Chiefs, those spirits bonded to ancient, sacred sites in pre-history, who still exist in a sort of "timeless now", continuing to watch and ward over their especial places in perpetuity. These are a few examples of what I mean by the specific term of Guardianship. When a living individual or group is granted the right of Guardianship over a particular site, it happens in effect because the Genius Loci, the Spirit Guardian, has entrusted to them part of its own responsibilities for protecting the place in question. Such trust is not given lightly. It must be earned and can be taken back at any time. Human Guardianship is for a lifetime – and possibly beyond - unless that trust is withdrawn. The responsibilities and activities involved in it cannot be simply walked away from just because a better job is available elsewhere and the Witch expects to find a more convenient working site. Bluntly put, it is an honoured burden and a privilege, which makes demands on those on whom the Genius Loci choses to bestow it, which partly explains why it is not simply given to anyone who just "adopts" a site. It is a huge responsibility and should be carefully considered, should the situation ever arise and the offer made.

This is not to say that if a Witch becomes the human Guardian of a site that they must live in the place or stay there all the time. Journeys and holidays away are certainly possible and acceptable – if desired - as there is always the return afterwards. Even moving away from the site is possible in some unavoidable situations. However, where that does occur, the split is purely geographical – the burden and responsibility remains. The essence of human Guardianship is in the *long-term nature* of the responsibility and resulting actions voluntarily accepted and taken on. This is not an exercise which should be contemplated because you expect to be living in an area for a few years, as this leaves scant time for the necessary and required relationship with the non-human Guardian to develop.

At the end of the life of the Witch Guardian there comes the time when it is possible, as I have mentioned above, that they may wish to fully merge with the Land in spirit, and take on the responsibilities of a Spirit Guardian, post-mortem. That this does, indeed, occur can be seen not only from those examples given above and oral tradition in Old Craft lore, but in the very many folktales handed down over the centuries. Humans have been experienced within Wells (as described above) after passing; they have been seen numbered amongst the Faire and Elven kind in accounts stretching back millennia; and human Spirits have been encountered at the sites of ancient Trees and also at megalithic sites, closely associated and bound into the very stones themselves. This is only ever a choice that the Witch can make for themselves at the point of death, and one that has profound importance for their future spiritual development. It is not a choice given to many, or even a few, but that it does exist as an opportunity cannot be ignored or denied.

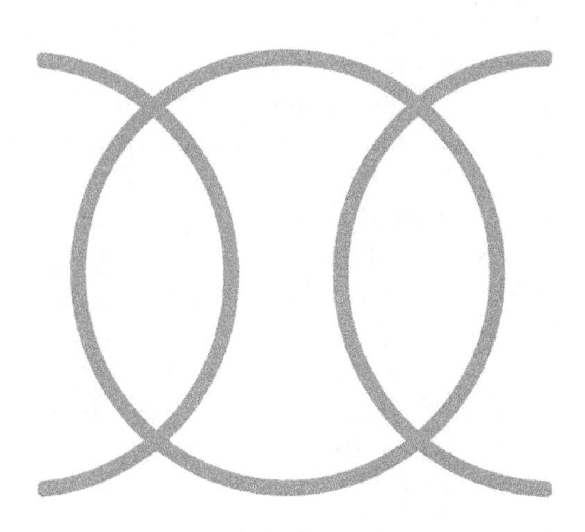

Divining the Ways.

"To the aware Witch, time is not a continuous ribbon passing under the keys of some celestial typewriter, but rather a complex field extending into many different directions and dimensions."
Paul Huson - "Mastering Witchcraft".

Within the working practise of the Old Craft Witch, divination necessarily plays a large part. Before undertaking any magical action, or to understand a certain situation better, or simply to find out hidden information, the art of divination comes into play. For the Witch, it is not a question of "seeing into the future"; it is a question of determining the likely outcome of events, if the current situation remains unchanged. Having received foreknowledge of the likely events, the Witch may then decide if, or how, to change the current situation, to bring about the desired future situation. In the case of seeking hidden knowledge or information, it is a question of looking into areas hitherto unsearched, using methods otherwise overlooked. Working with an awareness of the forces of the natural world, and the Powers and Spirits that inhabit it, the Witch would inherently do nothing other than call upon their allies, guides and helpers in such situations and seek to work with them in discovering those things that they wish, or need, to know. This is not to say that *all* forms of divination rely on input from spiritual beings but, even in those forms that don't, the Witch would naturally call upon their aid in helping to understand the knowledge and information revealed. This also necessarily means that the Witch needs to examine themselves and the situation that they are currently in. To divine accurately, with insight and wisdom, the Witch must be in the correct state of mind. This means that they must be both open to information that may conflict with what they *wish* to receive and also be honest enough within themselves to see and accept it. To divine with dishonesty is a waste of time and is purely an act of wish-fulfilment! "Know Thyself" is a core tenet of the Mysteries and is just as appropriate in divination as anywhere else.

There are very many forms of divination available to the Witch – both well-known and some more arcane forms – but all involve a certain facility with entering into a certain state of mind, or being, whereby information may be apprehended, received and understood. This necessarily involves having at least a foot in those realms where the information is more available and in bringing it back intact. This is another example of the ways in which the magical practitioner is changed by their practice and takes what is generally known as the "other" in their stride – it is a part of them, not apart from them.

Whilst delving into regions not normally accessed by most people, the Witch comes into direct contact with those forces known by various names, such as Wyrd, Fate or Destiny, particularly if they intend to change or alter situations with the knowledge they have uncovered. So, how does the Traditional Witch view these forces and/or interact with them? The answer to this question will be as variable as the number of Witches replying but, in general, some attitudes can be said to be held in common. The Witch does not consider that *all* events are fixed and immutable, unable to be changed in any way – far from it. Certainly there are those events that are common to all and must happen – we are all born at some point in time and we will all die at some point. It can be said that it is likely that *most* people will get married, or form long-term or life partnerships, generally producing children along the way. However, apart from these things, everything else is pretty much unwritten and depends on our own actions. Each thing that we do sets in train a sequence of events, that results in other things happening, which in turn set off others. If we change what we do, think, or how we act in any given situation, then subsequent events will change, either for the better or the worse. We create our own destiny by the actions that we take. However, all these actions and counter actions are all part of the larger scheme of Life – those actions made by other people that interact with ours, as ours do with them – and together they form what is generally considered to be a vast tapestry, if you like. All the actions of the people are like the threads in the tapestry, the warp and weft, and all are interconnected. Pulling on one thread affects all the others and can alter things immeasurably distant from the initial action.

The attitude of the Witch is generally that the more information, the more knowledge, that they have, the better they may perceive the outcome of any given situation and the more likely they will be to be able to change it for the better - if required - either for themselves or for another. The key word here is *change*, as it is deemed totally possible to deliberately change events; this is the basis of magic after all. The mere fact that the Witch has performed a divination, looked into the "future" and seen the outcome or event, has necessarily incurred a change, thereby denying the fixed nature of Life. It can, of course, be argued that this was also part of the fixed nature of life and that the Witch was predestined to see the outcome, but that is pure sophistry and running in circles. The fact that an event has been foreseen means that it is now able to be changed, in however small a way. This involves the Witch in taking responsibility for their actions - an exceedingly important part of magical work and one that a lot of more modern practitioners seem unwilling to do these days. If one deliberately and with forethought changes an event, then the resulting repercussion/s of that change becomes the responsibility of the Witch involved and they need to be prepared to take the consequences. An

Old Craft Witch knows this, as part of their training and learning, and is prepared for this. It makes for a stronger base for practising their Craft, if this is accepted in advance. A Witch of this nature doesn't, therefore, "dabble"; they change events with foreknowledge and responsibility, based on having weighed up the likely consequences beforehand, as far as is humanly possible. Of course, if performing any actions on behalf of a client, then the client also bears some of the responsibility, but it is the Witch that actually performs the magic to make the change and will bear this in mind before taking on the client and working the magic. Naturally, it is impossible to see the outcome of every single action or changed event, but this is where the skill in the arts of divination come in. The more overall knowledge that the Witch may obtain, the better decisions they can make and the more likely their actions are to be able to bring about the desired result. Each Witch will have their own favoured form of divination, the one they are best suited to or skilled at and these will vary widely from one individual to another. I have already detailed some techniques of searching into the unknown in previous chapters, but I would like here to look at a few techniques that are not widely or generally discussed, some simple, some more technical, but all able to bring the aware Witch the knowledge and understanding that they desire, when applied in a wise manner.

The Art of Geomancy

The term "Geomancy", as used here, is derived from the Latin "*geo-mantia*," which in turn is derived from the Greek for "*divination by earth*." It originated in the Middle-East, as far as is known, the Arabic name for the technique being "*'ilm al-raml*," which means "*the science of the sand*." It has no connection to Chinese *Feng Shui*, or other currently fashionable "earth mysteries" methods. In its original form, the geomantic figure was created by making lines of random numbers of dots in the sand or earth, hence the name. It was brought to Europe during the mediaeval or Renaissance period, when it proved exceedingly popular amongst esoteric practitioners. It was at this time that writers decided that it was also acceptable to draw the dots on parchment or paper and the more modern methods were born. This technique has been used up until the present time, although it has fallen somewhat out of favour in recent years and is now little known or used; this is a pity, as it is a versatile and accurate technique and one that many would derive benefit from.

The technique is very simple; having created the random dots or points, by varying methods, the Witch derives a series of figures which are arranged into traditional patterns. There are sixteen possible figures consisting of single, or pairs of, dots. Each figure has a name, associations with the elements, planets, etc., and good or bad qualities. It is possible to obtain a simple "Yes" or "No" answer to a question or problem, fuller answers by consulting the meanings of the individual figures, or to obtain a much more detailed response depending on the meanings of the figures when placed in particular locations on an astrological horary chart. This owes a great deal to the practice of medieval astrology and I will not go into this more technical aspect here. Unlike astrology, however, geomancy requires no instruments or complex calculations. (Readers interested in a deeper understanding of this method are advised to consult, "*Ars Geomantica*", by Gary Nottingham – see Bibliography).

As mentioned, the geomantic figures were originally derived by making random dots in the sand or earth – which is ideal if you are sitting out in the Land - but there are other ways of doing this too. In this explanation I shall utilise the dualities of the Blackthorn and the Whitethorn, ideally suited for this purpose. You will need to obtain 2 short lengths of wood from each of your Blackthorn and Whitethorn kin-trees, so 4 in total (or other trees, if you have not yet made a bond), each about 6" in length, using the techniques previously given in this book. Strip the bark from each stick and sand or shave it flat on each side. Alternatively, if also obtaining a length of wood for other purposes from your tree/s, cut a disc about 2" in diameter and 1/2" thick, from each Thorn (2 from the Black, 2 from the White), like thick coins and use these instead. Whichever method you are using, on one side of the stick/coin mark a single, black dot; on the other side, mark two dots. Once you have created these items to your satisfaction, hallow them in your usual manner and keep them wrapped in a special cloth, used only for this purpose. Something like a square of black silk, linen or cotton would be ideal.

The initial part of this form of divination is to create 4 figures, which are known as the *Mothers* or *Matres*. This is the only part of this technique where intuition/spirit guidance/ Wyrd or Fate comes in – everything after this is derived from these initial 4 figures and, hence, they are exceedingly important. Unwrap your wooden tools and lay the cloth on the ground, thus making it your working surface. (In my opinion it is essential that you do this on the ground, not on your altar or a table, so that you retain the link with the original Land/Earth-based origin of the system). Take your sticks, one at a time and spin or flip them lightly in your hands, then let them fall as they will on the cloth. Whilst doing this you should be focussing on your question and also calling on whatever spirit allies you wish to aid you. This may be the spirits of the Black & White Thorns themselves (which would be most appropriate), your familiars or whatever other Powers that you work with. The main point is that it is at this juncture that the actual foresight/divination is made, so the spirit input is most important for the Witch. It is here that the effects of Wyrd/Destiny/Fortune are brought to bear explicitly and intrinsically and all else follows through from this point. Once the stick has landed it will have either one or two dots uppermost. Mark whichever this is, either on a piece of paper or, if you are outside and wish to be very traditional, in the earth or sand. Do this again with the next stick, marking either the one or two dots obtained **underneath** the first one you have marked. Do this again with the third and fourth sticks, until you have a figure of four lines, with either one or two dots to a line. Repeat this procedure another three times, until you have created four figures in all. At this point, give thanks to those spirits and/ or Powers you have invoked for aid, re-wrap your sticks and put them away safely. (If outside it would be nice to pour a little libation out in thanksgiving, directly onto the ground).

As an example, the resultant divinatory figures may look something like this, but obviously yours will be different;

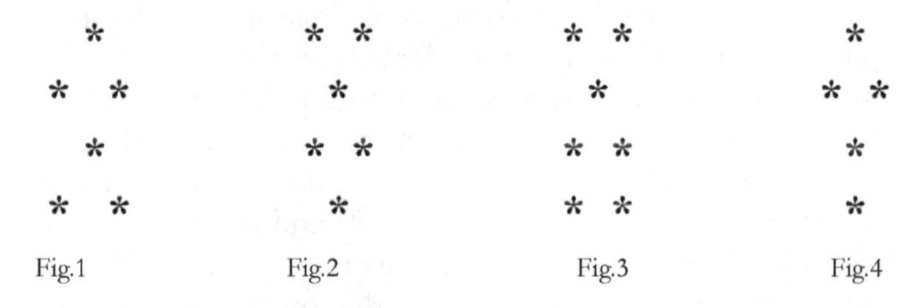

Fig.1 Fig.2 Fig.3 Fig.4

These, then, are your Mother figures and will "give birth" to all subsequent configurations. These are the fount and origin of the whole divination and are, therefore, of supreme importance in their creation. From the Mothers you will derive the four *Daughters*, or *Filiae*, next the four *Nieces* or *Neptes*, then the two *Witnesses* or *Testes*, then finally the *Judge*, or *Iudex*. The Witnesses will tell you of the factors surrounding your enquiry and the Judge will give you your final Yes or No answer. This all sounds very complex and difficult, but is actually quite simple and is merely a process of "adding" together the lines from the Mothers to make the next two sets of four figures; the Witnesses are derived from those and the Judge from the Witnesses. Along the way, you will be able to derive increased understanding of the situation, based on the meanings of the individual figures (which I will describe anon).

To create the Daughters; take the first line of Fig. 1 to be the first line of Fig. 5. The first line of Fig. 2 becomes the second line of Fig. 5, the first line of Fig. 3 becomes the third line of Fig. 5 and the first line of Fig. 4 becomes the fourth line of Fig. 5. Repeat this for lines 2, 3 and 4 of all the figures until you have created the next 4 figures, the Daughters – thus (using the examples given above);

*	* *	*	* *
* *	*	* *	*
* *	*	* *	* *
*	* *	*	*
Fig.5	Fig.6	Fig.7	Fig.8

Next you need to create the Nieces. Add together the first lines from Fig 1 and Fig 2, to create the first line of Fig. 9. (i.e. if the result of the addition is an odd number, place one dot. If the result is an even number, place 2 dots). Then add the second lines of Figs 1 & 2 to create line 2 of Fig. 9. Add the third lines of Figs 1 & 2 to create line 3 of Fig. 9 and finally add the fourth lines of Figs 1 & 2 to create line 4 of Fig. 9. To create Fig. 10. add Figs 3 & 4 together in the same manner. To create Fig. 11. add Figs 5 & 6, together and to create Fig 12. add Figs 7 & 8 together in like wise. Using the examples above, this will produce the following Nieces – thus;

*	*	*	*
*	*	*	*
*	*	*	* *
*	*	*	* *
Fig.9	Fig.10	Fig.11	Fig.12

Now you need to derive the two Witnesses from the four Nieces. Add together Figs 9 and 10, as previously, to produce the First Witness. Write/draw this to the **right** of your working space; this will give you an indication of the events in the past that have had an influence on your enquiry. (The first Witness is written to the right, in keeping with the Arabic origins of the system, the Arabic script being written from the right to the left – the opposite of the Latin method of writing). Add together Figs 11 and 12 to produce the Second Witness and place this to the left of your area; this figure will indicate the future of your enquiry.

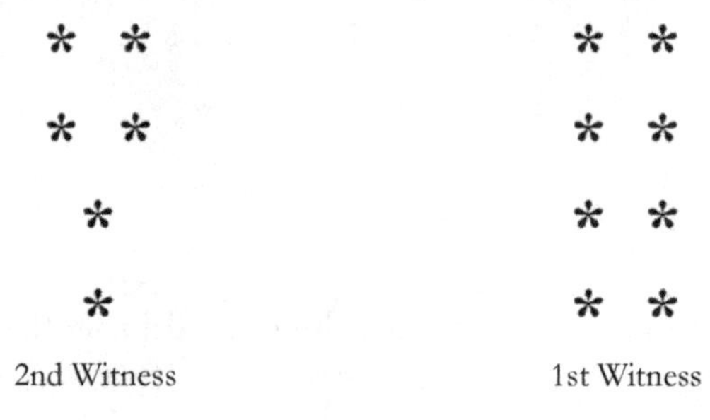

To complete the divination, add together the First and Second Witnesses as above, to create the Judge and the final Yes or No response to your question. If it is a beneficial figure, then the answer is Yes; if it is a negative figure then the answer is No. The Judge in this situation is;

Judge

In this situation, despite the strange seeming figures produced earlier, the Judge arrived at here is Fortuna Major and is exceedingly favourable; so a positive Yes in this instance. In general, you may see the Judge in the following manner. If it is a beneficial figure then the answer is a Yes; if it is a negative figure, then the answer is a No. A negative Judge that is produced from two negative figures is a definite

No and you would be well advised to heed this advice. If the Judge is positive and comes from one positive and one negative figure, then the situation will deteriorate from good to bad. If the Judge is negative and is derived from two beneficial figures, the response is still negative, but won't be too bad in effect. A positive Judge derived from two positive figures is definitely to be considered a Yes and a good omen. If the Judge is positive but comes from two negative figures, then the response is still Yes, but there will be difficulties surround the result. A Judge derived from one positive and one negative figure will be a Yes, but the result will not be terribly good.

In the example above we can see that the Judge is Fortuna Major, which is a Yes answer to the question. It is derived from the first Witness, Populus, in the right-hand position of the past, which is generally neutral, but positive with a positive figure. The second Witness is, itself, Fortuna Major and betokens a positive result, so all round a very good answer. (To be honest, I was a bit concerned when working out this example, because of the – seemingly – strange Nieces I was getting, i.e. three Via figures, despite the favourable outcome. I checked and re-checked the "calculations" from the original Mothers and all seemed correct. It was only later that I spotted a possible reason for this. I was not particularly thinking of anything when I created the Mothers, as they were simply being used as an example, but obviously my mind was on the creation/ writing of this book at the time. It occurred to me later that the preponderance of "Vias" was appropriate as the subtitle and meaning of this work involves the Ways of Witchery! And hopefully the fortunate outcome bodes well for the success/popularity of the book. In this manner it can be seen that all stages of the working out of the question can have insightful meanings on the final result).

Here then, are the Sixteen Geomantic Figures and their traditional meanings, along with their planetary and elemental associations.

*	* *	* *	*	* *	*
*	* *	*	* *	*	*
*	* *	*	* *	*	*
*	* *	* *	*	*	* *
Via	Populus	Conjuncto	Carcer	Caput Draconis	Cauda Draconis

*	*	* *	*	* *	* *
* *	*	* *	*	*	* *
*	* *	*	* *	* *	*
*	*	*	* *	* *	* *
Puella	Puer	Fortuna Major	Fortuna Minor	Rubeus	Albus

* *	*	* *	*
*	* *	* *	* *
* *	*	* *	* *
*	* *	*	* *
Acquisitio	Amissio	Tristitia	Laetitia

Via (The Way). This figure is generally unfavourable but good for journeys and travelling. It symbolises alternating change between good and bad, both in fortune and in character. Dislikes static situations and likes to be in motion. It is assigned the Moon (waning), the element of Water and the sign of Cancer. Its scent is Camphor.

Populus (People). This figure is considered to be neutral; beneficial with positive figures and bad with negative ones. It is a symbol of crowds and gatherings of people and of individuals who like to be on the move, disliking staying in one place too long. It is assigned to the Moon (waxing), the element of Water and the sign of Cancer. Its scent is Jasmine.

Conjunctio (Conjunction). A figure which is neutral; it promotes good with beneficial figures and bad with negative ones. Aids in the discovery of missing or hidden things. It denotes a person of intelligence with the gift of eloquence, but tending to dishonesty and overspending. Its planet is Mercury (retrograde), the element of Earth and the sign of Virgo. Its scents are all those of a Mercurial nature.

Carcer (Prison). A generally unfavourable figure, being concerned with binding, delays, imprisonment and restraint. However, it is beneficial for buildings, stability and security. It denotes a fierce and passionate character and one who may be generous of nature. It is assigned the planet Saturn, the element of Earth and the sign of Capricorn. Myrrh is its fragrance.

Caput Draconis (Head of the Dragon). This is favourable figure and good for beginnings and for making profit. It has a good, honest and faithful character, although it may turn negative with bad figures. Its planet is the north node of the Moon and its element Earth. The scent is made of a combination of Rose and Cedar.

Cauda Draconis (Dragon's Tail). An unfavourable figure, that brings loss. It conveys good with evil and evil with good, being of a corrupt and dangerous nature. It betokens the endings of things. Its planet is the south node of the Moon, its element Fire and its scent a blend of Myrrh and Dragon's Blood resin.

Puella (Girl). A beneficial figure of happiness and harmony, but with a tendency towards fickleness. It denotes passion and the emotions, easily falling in and out of love and a noted awareness of appearances over substance. Its planet is Venus, the element being Air and the sign Libra. Its scent is Musk and all Venusian perfumes.

Puer (Boy). An unfavourable figure, denoting, violence, rashness, destruction and war. Bad in all situations except love and war, producing a large amount of energy. Its character is excitable, troublesome and passionate, pursuing sexual pleasure to the detriment of all else. Quarrelsome.

Its planet is Mars and the element of Fire, its sign Aries. Its perfume is Dragon's Blood resin.

Fortuna Major (Greater Fortune). This figure is one of positivity in any event, particularly at the beginning of any situation. An indication of good fortune and favour, bestowing power and success. Although possibly frivolous financially, it denotes honesty, generosity and ambition. Its planet is the Sun (direct), its element being Fire and its sign Leo. Frankincense is its scent.

Fortuna Minor (Lesser Fortune). Although a figure of good fortune, it denotes change and instability and promotes things that need to be done rapidly. It has an honest and generous nature, but can be presumptuous and somewhat bold in character. Its planet is the Sun (retrograde) and its sign is Leo. The element is Air and all solar incenses, such as Olibanum, are its scents.

Rubeus (Red). An unfavourable figure of vice, violence and passion. It delivers good for evil and evil for good. It promotes trouble and determination in a negative connotation and this may not be the right time for an answer to the question asked. Its planet is Mars (direct), its element being Water. Its sign is Scorpio and Opopanax or Dragon's Blood are appropriate perfumes.

Albus (White). This is generally a favourable figure, promoting wisdom, peace and purity, but can be weak in activity in many situations. It is beneficial in profit and beginnings of all kinds and is peaceful and honest. Shy in nature, the character is charitable which may lead to spending extravagantly. Mercury (direct), is this figures assigned planet and its element is Air. Its sign is Gemini and all mercurial scents, such as Mace and Lavender are its perfumes.

Acquisitio (Gain). A positive and beneficial figure for all material endeavours. It promotes success, good fortune and gain in all manner of enterprises. The character is stubborn and concerned with appearances. The planet is Jupiter (direct) and the element Fire. Sagittarius is the sign associated with this figure and Cedar the scent.

Amissio (Loss). This is generally a negative figure, denoting loss, but it is good in matters of love. It denotes a thing or situation just outside of one's reach and, hence, unfavourable for gain. Its character is much concerned with honour, but is easily angered, possibly blunt and also tactless. Will stretch a point in their favour if possible. The planet is Venus (retrograde) and the element is Earth. Taurus is the associated sign and the perfume, Rose.

Tristitia (Sorrow). This is an unfavourable figure, representing illness, sufferings and sorrows. However, it is good for questions relating to buildings or the Earth. Its character is slow to laugh, dishonest and quick to anger; they do not forgive and forget. Its planet is Saturn (retrograde) and its element, Air. The sign associated is Aquarius and the scents Myrrh or Civet.

Laetitia (Joy). A figure of health and happiness, being favourable in all questions and situations. Its character is good natured, honest and intelligent and frequently religious in temperament. Its planet is Jupiter (retrograde) and its element is Water. The sign associated is Pisces and the perfume is Cedar.

I hope it will now be clear from the foregoing descriptions of the Figures how versatile and adaptable this system of divination may be. It is quite simple and easy to use once mastered and may be put into action anywhere you happen to be; all that is needed is a pen and paper. Not even that if outdoors and you clear a piece of earth to place the dots on. As with any formulaic system, although the Figures are given traditional meanings, it is in their application to the question and the situation that the true skill lies and here the intuition of the Old Craft Witch comes into operation; they may make it their own, with a little help from their Spirits.

Having received a, hopefully, favourable answer to their enquiry, the Witch may then incorporate the Geomantic Figures into any resulting magical working, if they so wish. The Figure (Judge or Witnesses as well if favourable), may be drawn or painted onto any talisman, charm or physical object used in the subsequent working, the element/s associated may be called upon or used in various manners and incense/s may be concocted from the associated scents of the Figures. All of this added together by the versatile Witch results in a very powerful working practice.

Casting the Brass

I have mentioned the subject of Horse Brasses in my previous work, *The Devil's Plantation*, but I feel it is worth repeating here in the present context. Having undergone the Witchwalk and being in a betwixt state, this is an ideal condition to perform a divination of this kind. Of particular import in this situation, is the sound that the brasses make when they fall and the feelings, emotions, images that arise when hearing the sound. Being in a heightened state, these are likely to be one of the main factors in determining the outcome of the divination attempt, the Witch relying heavily on their own, inner senses to understand the likely outcome of their query. Also to bear in mind, of particular note, will be the forms of shadows, of light and shade on the cast, this giving an additional nuance of meaning whilst in the Witchwalk condition. I quote from my own work here, the original explanation still being apposite in this instance.

> *'East Anglian witches made use of many everyday objects to make divinations and not just for lost or stolen goods, but perhaps the most locally relevant were horse brasses. This is a technique relatively unknown these days and mostly fallen into disuse. As a rural area, East Anglia had a large number of working horses (now, sadly, almost vanished), the most famous of breeds being the Suffolk Punch. Horses brought by the Normans may have been the ancestors of this breed, but the first mention of it dates from the 16th. Century and they were specifically bred to work on the heavy, clay uplands of East Anglian agricultural land. The brasses used to decorate the horse trappings originate thousands of years ago in amulets designed to ward off evil influences and protect the bearer from all forms of negativity. Designs such as*

the Sun, Moon, Stars, Equal-armed Cross and Circle have been found on amulets dating from the Iron Age period in Britain and still appear on brasses today. Other designs have been added over the centuries, such as sheaves of wheat, animals, bells, geometric designs, hearts, heraldic crests, farming implements, acorns and, of course, the horse and horse shoe designs. All of these have a meaning and are useful in divination, but the witch would not stick slavishly to one set, definition only; like all good diviners, the witch would have their own meaning attached to the individual brasses and this would be tempered and the meaning vary, depending on subtle factors felt during the casting. The technique was (and is), simple, but can be as deep in meaning as the caster is able to go. Firstly, a light trance state is entered into, whilst the subject of the divination is held in the mind. The brasses are then cast onto a specially prepared cloth on the ground and the divination is made. Factors affecting the result would be; the noise the brasses made whilst falling onto the cloth, what that makes the caster think of, whether it is a positive or a negative sound. Next, the positioning of the brasses would be examined; what was lying where, who was next to what, what was covering, or being covered by, what. Depending on the foregoing, some of the standard meanings of the actual brasses might be altered slightly or greatly, depending on how the witch felt. Light falling onto the brasses and making one shine whilst another was in shadow could affect the meaning, as well as where they had actually fallen on the cloth. Were they all bunched together, or were some off apart from the rest, maybe there was a pattern of small groups. All these factors and others unmentioned can affect the eventual outcome of the cast. The witch will make their decision and pronouncement based on feelings and intuitions developed over long periods of study of the brasses and of their own internal guidance."

(*The Devil's Plantation* – see Bibliography).

Depending on the Pendulum

Possibly the most simple divining tool ever invented is the Pendulum. This is purely a weight on the end of a length of cord/hair/chain that will swing freely backwards and forwards. However, it is capable of producing some of the most enlightening and remarkable results and is a valuable and versatile tool to the Witch. As with any form of divination, anyone can get a result with practise, but those that have an affinity with this method can get extremely detailed results. This also applies to the divining Rod, a somewhat different technique and one that many people are wary of, because of the mystery surrounding it. These days, the magical side of the process is generally played-down by practitioners and the scientific and so-called "rational" side is emphasised; it is, however at heart a magical technique. Nigel Pennick quotes from the 18th C. almanac "*The Shepherd's Calendar*" in his "*Secrets of East Anglian Magic*", giving the necessary, magical procedures for taking and using an effective divining Rod.

> *"Cut a hazel wand forked at the upper end like a Y. Peel off the rind and dry it in a moderate heat: then steep it in the juice of Wake-Robin or Night-Shade, and cut the single lower end sharp, and where you suppose any rich mine or treasure is near, place a piece of the same metal you conceive is hid in the earth to the top of one of the forks by a hair or very fine silk or a thread, and do the like to the other end. Pitch the sharp single end lightly to the ground at the going down of the sun, the moon being on the increase, and in the morning at sunrise, by natural sympathy you will find the metal inclining, as it were, pointing to the place where the other is hid."*

In East Anglia, the tradition is to cut the wand from Hazel at the time of the full moon, with a single stroke of the knife, in the hour of Mercury, on a Wednesday. The lore of dowsing in this area describes seven different types of dowsing rod, all with their own separate abilities and uses; these are the Divine Rod, the Shining Rod, the Leaping Rod, the Transcendent Rod, the Trembling Rod, the Dipping Rod and the Superior Rod. If requiring a rod for finding water or minerals hidden in the earth, then it should be made of

Hazel, used after sunset and before sunrise, and only on the following nights; the first night of a New Moon or the one before it, Epiphany, Shrove Tuesday, Good Friday and St. John's Day (an excellent day for all types of divining). However, if you need to find lost property, then Hazel will not do and you will need to make one from Yew wood, following the same methods and procedures. As with all magical artes, the Rod should only be employed when needed and not purely for fun or show.

However, to return to the Pendulum now. This is an ancient tool and it can easily be imagined that the builders of structures such as Stonehenge, the Pyramids, Newgrange and other venerable "temples" first noticed the effectiveness of a weight on a cord many millennia ago, for things other than getting a stone to stand upright. The weight at the end of the cord is normally known as the "bob" and can be made of many different materials and comes in many different shapes and sizes. To my mind, a teardrop-shaped bob, about one to one-and-a-half inches long with a pointed end is probably the most effective; it gives a good swing and the pointed end gives a better indication of the answer. The bob can be made of metal, crystal, wood, glass, stone, or anything else that gives a good weight to it; lighter materials just don't work as well. Sometimes the interior of the bob is hollowed out (this type tends to be made of metal and screws apart into two halves), into which a sample of the subject of the question is inserted whilst performing the divination. This sample is known as a "witness" and is exceedingly useful when dowsing for a particular object, natural or man-made. For example, if the Witch is searching for something lost, then a piece of the material of the item, a small picture or description may be inserted into the bob, whilst the operation is going on. In keeping with the theme of this book, the obvious choice for the Old Craft Witch, would be a bob fashioned of either Black or White Thorn, taken from their kin-tree and carved by themselves into a suitable shape; preferably with guidance from the tree. This has obvious advantages over other kinds and I will go into this later on. Other trees obviously all have their own, associated meanings and attributes, such as Hazel for knowledge and wisdom and is very traditional for a divination tool. The main point is that the Witch should feel comfortable and in tune with their pendulum; in time and after use, this tool can become a close ally and friend and many Witches treat their pendulums with great care and respect.

The cord to which the bob is attached needs to be light and loose and able to swing freely. As mentioned, many materials have been used; cotton, linen, wool, fine chains or even hair have been utilised to great effect. The main point is that the cord should not be either rigid or too heavy in itself. The colour of the cord also, like the material of the bob, should also be taken into consideration when making or buying a pendulum. There are obviously the traditional meanings of the colour correspondences but, over and above that, the Witch needs to feel completely comfortable with both the look, feel, colour and overall aesthetic of their pendulum; this is a very subtle art and little things that don't feel right can throw a working completely awry.

To use the pendulum, the Witch first needs to determine the basics, i.e. which way it will swing to denote "Yes"/ positive and which way for "No"/negative, *for the particular individual.* There is no, one, universal direction for everyone and this is a very important first step. Hold the cord of the pendulum at a suitable length for you, such that it swings freely, in the fingers of one hand. Hold it steady so that it comes to a complete standstill and is not swaying in any direction. At this point, ask a question, that you know the answer to, that has a yes or no answer, such as, "Is my name Julie"? Gently at first, the pendulum will begin to swing. For some people it will swing in a clockwise direction for yes and anti-clockwise for no. For others, it will be the opposite directions. Alternatively, it may swing up and down for yes and side to side (left to right), for no, or the opposite. None of these is right or wrong, they are just how it works for the individual. Once you have a direction for a positive answer, check this by asking a question that you know has a negative answer and making sure the pendulum swings in the opposite direction. If it doesn't, or you get a confusing result, put it away and ask again later. As mentioned, this is a subtle technique and you may just be having an off day; this will definitely affect your results. Once you have established these base lines for yourself, be aware that on occasion you may still get an ambiguous answer, i.e. the pendulum may not move, or just judder a bit or other non-definitive responses. In my experience and those of others, this generally means that the answer is either not known, or there is no information available at this time. In this instance, again, put the pendulum away and ask again at a later date. Remember though, in all situations, keep the questions clear and simple and keep the mind focussed on one thing at once.

There is a slightly alternative technique that can be used for a positive or negative response to the above, when working outside and there is a medium to strong wind. In this situation, the wind can sometimes "blow" the pendulum off course if starting in the hanging still position and you can get misleading or ambiguous results – or none at all. Here it is best if you start the pendulum swinging yourself, by "twirling" it, or swinging it in a gentle circle to start with, asking your question and letting it come to a rest, either swinging up and down, or from side to side. This can take a little adjusting to if you are used to doing it a different way, but the results can come out much more reliably with this method. Just explain to your pendulum what you are doing, and ask it to make the adjustment and you should find that it works fine. Don't forget to test for which way is Yes and No, for you, beforehand though.

For those who find that they have a definite affinity for pendulum working, there is little limit to what may be discovered. Once the Witch has formed a strong, working bond with their pendulum, they really do take on a strong character of their own. Some will quiver when facing a difficult question and some will sulk and refuse to answer if asked to work for too long, so be nice!

Obtaining full benefits from pendulum dowsing can call for a certain amount of practical study. For example, the length of the cord (or the length at which you hold it), may need to vary depending on the materials/object that you are trying to find. As mentioned above, even the colour of the cord or string may alter the pendulum's results or reactions in certain situations. Here we enter the realms of personal experimentation, but there are guides to help the budding pendulum operator. The works of the noted dowser Tom Graves and, in particular, the archaeologist T.C. Lethbridge are well worth studying; it was Lethbridge who uncovered the – sadly much disputed and now invisible once more – chalk figures of Gog and Magog in the Cambridgeshire Hills through the use of dowsing techniques. Lethbridge did much research on the use of the pendulum and came up with very interesting results. He found that when the length of the cord of the pendulum was up to 40", it reacts to materials and questions relative to the physical world. Beyond the length of 40", the pendulum appeared to react to the realm of death, or what some call the Otherworld. The pendulum will still react to the same substances, but will only work when held slightly offside them. He devised a basic list of cord lengths for different substances, which most people have found to be accurate and effective.

Cord Length	Substance Dowsed
7"	Sulphur
10"	Graphite
12"	Carbon
13"	Slate/Concrete
14"	Glass/Porcelain
15"	Quartzite/Flint

20"	All animals/Plants/ Wood/Rubber/Coal/Paper
22"	Silver/Lead/Salt
23"	Vegetable Oil/Amber
24"	Masculinity/Diamond
25"	Alcohol
26"	Running Water
29"	Femininity
30"	Copper/Brass/Tin
32"	Iron
40"	Death

If the cord is used at longer than 40", the entire pattern appears to repeat again, only the reactions are just off to one side, as stated. In this area, the pendulum does not seem able to work with the concept of time as we currently understand it. If wishing to use this method, a long cord with knots (a traditional Witch technique!), tied marking the different lengths noted is useful. Allow plenty of cord beforehand as the knots will shorten the cord considerably and measure lengths before tying each knot – do not mark the lengths out on the cord beforehand. If using a long cord, then the bob needs to be of a suitable weight also, so you may need to change your usual one.

To some readers, it may seem that I am teaching Granny to suck eggs here, however, there is a point to my somewhat meticulous descriptions. Firstly, if you don't know how to go about using a tool, how can you expect it to work effectively, or you with it? And, secondly, in my experience, even fairly long-standing practitioners of dowsing still don't understand the basics and, hence, often get unusual or widely varying results in their operations. I am here endeavouring to give a sound basis for dowsing work, for both beginner and experienced practitioner alike. We all need a little help sometimes, no matter how far we think we've come – and everyone has to start somewhere!

There are various ideas as to actually *how* this particular technique works and everyone has their own favourite. In general, the pendulum is deemed to act as an amplifier for very subtle types of energy – or energy fields – that are normally too subtle for humans to be able to notice consciously. The human mind/body/spirit complex is actually able to perceive these types of forces, but they are either so small or indistinct that they normally don't impinge on our conscious awareness. The pendulum would appear to react to minute movements in the arm, hand or fingers and magnifies these into observable results. It is actually the Witch that is making the pendulum move, but as a result of outside forces too small for them to normally be aware of. For some people, this magnifies "psychic" abilities that are already inherent; for others it appears to bestow these abilities upon them. However it is viewed, it is safe to say that the pendulum is a tool – like any other, magical or otherwise – that the Witch may make use of in their workings. Dowsing is a totally natural ability and many animals seem able to practise it without thinking. There are many stories and folk/origin tales of either Saints or Heroes following cows, deer, foxes or other wild kin on journeys, until they settle in certain places, only to miraculously have springs of water suddenly emerge where they've stopped, which go on to become holy or healing springs/wells. Else-wise, holy wells are discovered by watching the actions of animals and noting where they go, or even certain types of plant that are safer to eat than others. Dog owners will know well that their canine friends will search out one spot amongst all others to curl up in and have a nap, that is imperceptibly different from any other, to us. If this is dowsed, it will give a different reaction to the spaces around it. I have tested this myself with quite spectacular results. I once followed one of my dogs into some woodland, that I was unfamiliar with, and watched as he led me a merry dance in and out of the undergrowth. At one point, he stopped, looked back over his shoulder at me, lay down and curled up, still staring at me. Not being one to ignore a hint obviously given, I got out my pendulum and began to dowse the site. To begin with, I seemed to get no reaction at all; however, after a while, something strange began to happen. The pendulum, instead of hanging straight (I wasn't using the "twirling" technique), began to "hang" at a slight angle; the nearer I got to a certain place, the greater the angle became and it seemed like the actual bob was being pulled by some "magnetic" force. Naturally I walked in the direction of the pull and very shortly, behind some trees that were obscuring my vision, I found a small pool of water, fed by a natural spring! I wasn't familiar with this particular area and didn't know about the spring but, on my return home I looked up the location and found out that it was a quite well-known holy spring that was regularly cleared and kept clean by local volunteers. Never let anyone tell you that dowsing doesn't work!

Having described the, generally accepted, way in which the pendulum actually functions, the point to examine is; what are these energies that the Witch is tapping into and getting answers from or about? This is a vast field, ranging from theories concerning Universal Knowledge stores, sometimes known as the Akashic Records, to Ley Lines and Earth Energies, to the use of the pendulum for diagnosing and treating illness, known as Radiesthesia, and everything in between. Whilst all of these areas are of interest to the Witch and research into them may prove very rewarding for individual discovery, it is another area that I would like to focus on here and that is the contact and communication with Spirits. I feel that this area has been somewhat overlooked in the urge to make dowsing a valid, "scientific" discipline and that the origins and one of the original uses of the Arte have been ignored. This is a technique employed by Witches for centuries – if not longer – and we have been happily using it to communicate with our spirit allies and friends in different realms, without feeling the need to justify it to scientific rationale. So too now.

As mentioned previously in Chapter 4, it is possible to use this technique to make contact with and communicate with the spirit realms, both of the Dead and those of other Spiritual forms. A good place to begin one's research, is in making the bob of the pendulum from one of the exemplar trees, as suggested, and getting to know your kin-tree, or their realm, in more detail. Initially this would necessarily involve asking yes/no questions, to build up a store of knowledge and information on the tree, its spirit or character and whether/how it wishes to communicate. Once these things have been established, it is possible to move on to more detailed "conversations" and to derive more complicated answers. In this case, a yes/no answer system doesn't work as well or as flexibly as could be desired and so a different system needs to be put into place. This is where the use of more detailed dowsing charts come into play, as previously mentioned.

To give an example. You may have got to the stage with your kin tree where you are fairly familiar and comfortable with the basic concepts concerning its type, but would like to learn more about lost lore surrounding it. First, determine if it is willing to co-operate, with a yes/no question. Assuming the answer is positive, you next need to determine the area or type of information it is willing to give, so you need to devise a chart with different areas of knowledge on which it is willing to "speak". Below is an example of what I suggest you could start with. (I have given this chart seven sections, but obviously it is up to you how many you have; however, I would suggest no more than ten or perhaps twelve, at least to begin with. It can be confusing for the Spirit/ Pendulum/Witch to have too many alternatives to cope with and can lead to confusing or misleading responses. Remember, this is a very subtle Arte and needs to be kept as simple as possible). With this technique, the Witch holds the pendulum stationary over the central arc at the bottom of the chart, composes themselves and asks the question. In this particular instance it would be something along the lines of; *what area of knowledge would you be willing to give me some information on at this time?* The pendulum will usually remain still for a moment, then begin to swing backwards and forwards, along the angle of one of the answers on the chart. If it is not a strong swing, you may stop and ask again to clarify the answer. Also, even if you get a strong response, you may like to ask again, to see if there are other areas that the spirit is willing to "speak" on. However, again, don't ask too much as this may not be appreciated. As ever, feel your way through this and see how it goes.

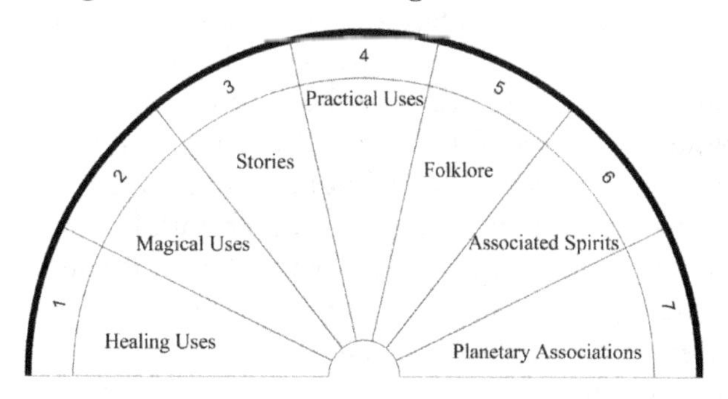

Once you have received a response for the area that the spirit will communicate on, you can change the titles in the sections and carry on. For example, if you get a reply that the spirit is willing to talk about Magical Uses, you could change the numbered sections to something like;

1 – Protection;
2 – Defence;
3 – Energy-gathering;
4 – Hexing;
5 – Image-magic;
6 – Cleansing;
7 – Hedge-riding.

Again, check how many areas the spirit is willing to give information on – carefully and politely – and then further refine your chart/questions to gather the information. It is a good idea in later requests to include a section that says, Not Known or Not Able To Say, or something of the sort. The spirit is not always able – or willing – to answer all questions and it is a good practice to give them an opportunity to say this. Trying to force an answer out of an unwilling spirit – either through persistence or misunderstanding – is never a good idea!

Having given a basic understanding of the Arte of dowsing with a pendulum, I hope it can be seen how versatile a technique this actually is. For those unable to adequately use other forms of divination, such as the tarot, runes, etc. this is an extremely simple and versatile alternative. It can also be used as an addition to these other, more common, techniques to check responses and maybe acquire different answers. To my mind the pendulum is as much a magical tool as a knife, a cup or a stang and should be considered as such. In its more advanced forms of use, it can be used to question many types of Spirits, Ancestors or Faere Folk for information and is a valuable tool also of self-discovery; this is, after all, one of the main reasons for practising the magical arts. Its use is only limited by the ingenuity and inventiveness of the Witch and their magical allies and can reveal much of both an internal and external nature.

Searching the Stars

Divination may be defined as the practice of attempting to foretell events or discover hidden knowledge by occult or supernatural means. One method of attempting to uncover hidden knowledge has, for many millennia, been to observe the stars. These astral luminaries are considered to have a direct, if insubstantial, effect on peoples' lives and to conceal wisdom that may be revealed only to those with the abilities and knowledge to uncover it. For the Ancients, the celestial cycles provided a pattern for the world below. Even in cultures where the heavens might be denied a deciding role – such as the monotheistic faiths – the stars were nonetheless considered a supreme expression of divine will and order. Greek and Roman philosophers and natural magicians identified the microcosm, the "little world" below, with the macrocosm, the "great world", above. The Hermetic axiom, "As above, so below", attributed to the ancient, mythical sage Hermes Trismegistos, expresses this notion of co-dependency, which retains its vitality within magical thought and practice up to the present day. In Traditional Craft, the relationship between character, Fate and the heavens is both subtle and natural, reflecting a complex and universal harmony, connection and interaction within all Beings. The Universe is considered to be animate and far from being simply gross matter, as modern science would have us believe; the reality all around us is ensouled, filled with volition and independent intelligence. This "animation" joins us all in a correspondence of ties with the Universe around us. The recognition of this correspondence is the foundation of the stellar phenomenon of omen-reading and divination. In most people's minds, this automatically means the arts and sciences of both astrology and astronomy, but particularly of astrology; calculating exact events and timings by complicated numerological equations and plotting these findings onto arcane-looking charts. The resulting diagrams can, indeed, look supernatural or occult in themselves to those uninitiated in those arts! The Old Craft Witch certainly also makes use of these sciences, but there are other Ways of looking at the Stars that can give just as much insight and knowledge, if after a different manner and style.

In the last few thousand years or so, the names of the constellations that we now know and see have been changed, in fact even the constellations themselves have been changed. Groups of stars have been seen as different shapes by different peoples over periods of time and have not always remained constant, hence giving some of the conflicting views and interpretations that we sometimes find in modern discussions of them. It was not until relatively recently – on a world timescale – that the shapes of the constellations were designated and given the names that we know them by now in the Western world. In Iron Age Britain, for example, some constellations were picked out in different forms. The significant constellation of Hu Gadarn as a God figure and the Goddess figure of the Lady with the Cornucopia stood side by side and just above them (in an autumn sky, Western world), was the five-pointed star shape of Boötes. This was known as the gateway to the Gods – hence the significance of the pentagram in many forms of magic. In many forms of Traditional Witchcraft it is the ancient and powerful stellar energies that are being drawn upon when performing rites and hence an intimate knowledge of these forces is to be desired in the Witch. The light from these constellations takes a long time to reach us and, consequently, it is very very ancient by the time it arrives. Hence Old Craft deals with some forms of energy that may seem very "rough" and unrefined to many people today, but it is no less useful in finding things out than in more "civilised" forms of divination.

Rather than approaching the stellar energies via intermediary systems, many Old Craft Witches go out to meet the stellar Powers and Spirits "head-on" and enquire directly at source if seeking knowledge to problems or other questions of lore. The following is an exercise that may give the interested Witch a feeling of, or an introduction to, astral energies if they have not worked with them directly in this manner before. This exercise should be performed outdoors on a clear night, before or just after a Dark Moon. Ideally it should be performed on a hill or a high place, away from urban light pollution, but this is not always possible these days; try at least to get to a place that has a clear view of the night sky. If you cannot perform this outdoors at all, sit at an open window, with a good view of the heavens, with the interior lights switched off. Your eyes will need about twenty minutes to adjust to night vision, so use the time to make yourself comfortable. As you will need to spend some time with your head tilted back, lay a blanket on the ground, arrange some cushions or set a reclining chair so that you can gaze at the heavens in comfort. The ideal is to be lying on your back, looking straight up at the sky. This is another form of the "sitting out" exercise already encountered herein, perhaps better termed "laying out" in this case. It requires no less focus, concentration and attention and over a similar time scale of at least several hours, if not all night. You will need to identify the constellation Ursa Major, also known by various other names, such as the Plough, Arthur's Wain and, sometimes, the Saucepan or Big Dipper. These are known as circumpolar stars as they perpetually revolve around the Pole Star and are seen as symbolising the Male energies within some Traditions, acting as a container or reservoir for them, astrally. After about twenty minutes and you have finished making your preparations, look up into the sky again; you may well be surprised at how many more stars you can see now that your eyes have made the adjustment. Focus on the stars of Ursa Major as they make their slow, heavenly dance and think about the stellar energies weaving across the night skies. Let your eyes be drawn towards the star/s that attract your attention the most and just observe as they slowly move in the dark. Allow yourself as much time as you need to drift off with these energies and return when you are ready. The idea is not to think about the constellation itself, its myths and legends, but simply to "bathe" in the energies of its lights and absorb what you can of its nature. This can be a revealing process and many end this exercise with some interesting insights into both the stellar energies and their own place within them.

The next exercise is a progression on that above and relies on the ability to place your awareness at a certain point, reasonably accurately and effectively. A lot of this will involve visualisation as it is fairly difficult to project one's spirit body to a star, but it is not impossible; if you have this ability, then of course, use it. I have given exercises for placing the awareness in my previous book, *Treading the Mill,* so I refer the reader there for suggestions on how to accomplish this. Essentially, you need to be able to clearly project your consciousness to an exact location, outside of your physical body, and focus *as if* you were actually there and interact with the energies/spirits/beings that you encounter at that location. Like any new exercise, this sounds daunting, but will become easier with constant and determined practise.

Startouching

For this exercise you need to once more focus initially on the constellation of Ursa Major, the Plough. In addition, you will need one other item for this exercise and that is a receptacle for the energies that you will be contacting. This is traditionally one of the white, crystalline stones that may be found on most beaches; when wet, they sparkle and shine like the stars, because of the flakes of quartz that they contain. Find one of these that feels comfortable to you, about the size of a baby's closed fist and keep this for this purpose alone. When you have finished your preparations and your eyes have adjusted to the night sky, perform the Circle-Cross as previously described in this book. (This gives a measure of balance and protection for this exercise and will help to focus you internally before you begin). If lying down – and it is very much to be recommended for this exercise - do so now and place the stone on your forehead, where your eyebrows meet. If sitting down, hold the stone in your *left* hand, cradle this with your right hand and lay these in your lap, against your solar plexus. Now, raise your eyes to the sky and find the constellation, focussing on it to the exclusion of all else; immerse yourself in its light. Contemplate this constellation for a while, absorbing its light, until you are comfortable with the energies. Now you need to find the Pole Star, Polaris, using the Plough as a marker. This is quite simple. Locate the last two stars at the end/side of the Plough, known as Merak and Dubhe respectively, and sight along these to Polaris.

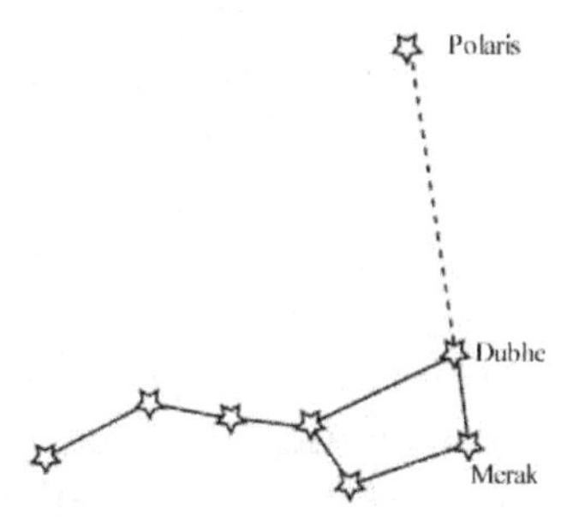

This will be situated due north, is the brightest star visible in the northern hemisphere and is readily visible. The accompanying diagram shows how this can be done. Polaris is part of the constellation of Ursa Minor, the Little Bear, around which all the other stars appear to circle throughout the night and is a little over 400 light years away. When you watch it you are seeing light that left the Pole Star about the time that the great Spanish Armada was approaching the British coasts – hence my comment about Old Craft using some old and quite rough energies. This star is known as the Nowl, the Nail or Navel, in East Anglian tradition, signifying the central point around which all else revolves. This is the sacred direction, the place of divinity, a sacred virtue, rather than just simply a compass direction. The divine presence and "North" are inseparable.

When you have located Polaris, continue with focussing on this one star in particular; focus all your attention here. When you feel stable, either mentally move towards it, or project your spirit towards it. The speed of light means nothing in this context, so you can approach in seconds the point where the star shows a distinct disk. Find a distance with which you feel comfortable and, for the moment, contemplate the being you are facing. Consider its light, its strength, its energy and its age; become comfortable with this. Now, with your mind, reach out to it, connect with it, wrap your awareness around it – Startouch it. The star may pulse slightly, sending a surge of energy into you, or you may simply feel the flow of the energy within you. Whichever happens, accept the energy, and return it back to the star. Let the energy flow back and forth, forming a circuit between you. Continue this exchange, until you feel that you have taken on as much energy as you are able, or the star itself indicates it is time to stop. When you are finished, thank the entity that is the star (by name if you have been fortunate enough to have been given one); you may retain the energies you have been given in your subtle body within the stone on your brow/in your hands. Gently disengage the contact and return, giving yourself plenty of time to re-acquaint yourself with the physical body and your surroundings. When you are ready, stand up and perform the Circle-Cross once more, to end the session. (The reason for laying down and placing the stone on your forehead may now be seen. In some Old Craft Traditions, the light of/from the Pole Star is considered analogous to the Light between the Horns of the Witchfather. By performing this exercise, the Witch takes the divine light/fire within them and attempts to activate the psychic centres, hence becoming One of "Radiant Brow").

As ever, do not expect great success on the first attempt, as this is quite a difficult and somewhat strenuous exercise, but build up over several sessions. You may well be quite disorientated on your return the first few times, but this will pass once you become better acquainted with the technique. Don't worry if you fall asleep during the session – this is quite normal and to be expected initially – but, with practise, you will be able to accomplish what you wish without "dropping off". The reasons for performing this exercise will be as various as the Witches performing it. Apart from the reason already given above, some may wish to learn more of the lore of the star directly from the presiding spirit; some may wish to ask it questions pertaining to particular areas of its known influence; others may wish to develop particular abilities by utilising the divine fire; others again may wish to have foreknowledge of coming events; each will be different. In time, the Witch may wish to experiment with other constellations or stars and this is perfectly reasonable, just always remember the procedures of respect and honour and act politely to any being that you may meet on your astral journeys. You will also need to perform this exercise when your particular constellation is visible above you in the night sky, so make sure your preparations take this into account; e.g. it might only be visible at certain times of year, or only for part of the night, so allow for this.

Once the technique of linking intimately with a star has been competently learned, channelling the energies for various purposes may be attempted. The night sky that forms the background for your link, your Startouch, is with you at all times. It is quite possible to have your eyes open and to go about various ritual (or mundane) activities, with this dual awareness. The starlight can become a part of you and therefore you can manifest it on this plane/level, either through your hands, or a ritual tool such as a wand or a knife. This may be used to charge/energise any charm, talisman, or other item that you wish. If you happen to be working entirely on the "astral", linkage should be no problem, since your consciousness, the star and the person or object that you are working with exist simultaneously in that infinite present. Always perform the Circle-Cross before and after any star working of this type. (In actual fact, performing the Circle-Cross at the end of this exercise actually "earths" the star's energy through you, hence creating a stronger link).

The stone that you hold or have with you during these exercises will also, necessarily, become charged with the particular essence of the stellar energies and may also be used in any of your magical practices that you see fit to use it in. However, it also has one particular use which will aid you in future astral workings and that is in the creation of a stellar condenser. In this case, the magical condenser refers to the energy that is the essence of the contacted star, which is incorporated into a liquid that can be used in the work of spell crafting or other areas. It is similar to a potion in construction, but is much more potent, focussed and concentrated. It is quite a strange one and should be used with caution.

Stellar Condenser

In a large, clear glass jar, place one pint of Vodka, ½ cup of natural, un-set, Honey and ¼ cup of Spring Water. Stir well together. Take three Lemons and cut 12 small slits in each one. Into each slit, insert a fresh sprig of Mugwort. Place the lemons and your star-stone into the jar, along with the other ingredients. Place the jar on a windowsill that will receive starlight overnight, as well as sunlight during the day (don't forget that the Sun is a star too). Let the jar sit for at least a month. Occasionally take the jar between your hands under a starry night sky and attempt to Startouch your chosen star again; focus on the jar and the elixir. After a month, open the jar, remove the lemons and discard them sensibly. Remove your stone and wash it thoroughly (thieves vinegar); its use for this elixir is now over and may be recharged when you next perform your Startouching exercise. (If you perform this exercise often and wish to have a stone with you all the time and/or for other purposes, you will need to acquire two stones of this kind and use them alternately, or for separate purposes, re-charging when you see fit). Take the remaining liquid and decant into a clean, glass bottle. Store in a cool, dark place for at least a month. The longer you keep it the better it will taste. The recommended use is a shot glass before bed-time for dreams and visions of the stars. Alternatively, take (sparingly), before doing any work with the stars and the constellations, or using stellar magic.

Natural Auguries

Within most forms of Traditional Craft, particularly in my own East Anglian version, it is usually considered essential to to be well-versed, or have at least a working knowledge of, natural lore. It is thought to be at least as important as other generally-known forms of magical correspondences, of which it is considered to be a natural branch. This involves the knowledge of the seasonal cycles of native plant and arboreal life, the growth and mating cycles of the local wildlife and how the young are birthed and reared, the migratory habits of birds and other fauna such as fish, and also the habits of local domesticated and farmed animals and crops. This is deemed important as, if the normal patterns of life are not known and understood, how can anything that is out of place, mis-timed or otherwise abnormal be noticed and remarked upon. This is the basis of all forms of natural augury, whether at a conscious or sub-conscious level – the noticing of unusual phenomena that may have a significance in a given place, time or situation for the Witch. As stated at the beginning of this chapter, it is considered that ALL Life is interconnected on a very intimate and vital level, which is one of the bases of how magic works. Above and beyond this – or maybe because of this – it is also how divinations may be made through the observance of natural phenomena; at a very fundamental level, because all Life is connected, everything has meaning, if we but have the eyes to see it and the senses to comprehend it. To the non-Witch, events happening at the same time, or out of time/place to each other are often dismissed as "coincidence". The Witch may well use the exact same word with a completely different emphasis, because of a different world-view and understanding; those very same events were "co-incidences", because of the links between all things. A harmonious whole, not a "chance" or unrelated happening.

In the previous chapter I introduced the concept of Ostenta - portents - which have an immediate and obvious meaning (or answer to a question), to the Witch. The solution to the situation will be immediately apparent, because of the heightened state of sensitivity of the Witch at the time and the link they possess with the Land. As they are not separate, but a complete part of the Life and virtue around them, the solution will be obvious. No thinking or working out is involved – the answer is simply there. However, there is an important point to be observed here; the signs that the Witch sees are not being given to them *by* the birds, animals, etc. that they see – these are completely unaware of what is going on and are just getting on with their lives. The configuration or pattern that the Witch sees only makes sense because of their link with the numinous quality in the Land, at the time of questioning. The Witch already knows the answer to the question within their deep mind – all they need is a prompt to bring this into conscious awareness, which is facilitated by the extra awareness or sensitivity of Riding the Serpent's Breath, or similar exercises at the time. The animal medium of the ostenta that are being observed is completely unaware of the importance being attached to its actions by the Witch, but it is nevertheless the vehicle that conveys a meaning at that particular time.

This then follows through to all other systems of natural divination, or augury, of which there are many different types. Auguries may be taken from the flights of birds, the manner in which certain leaves fall, the pattern of a running herd of deer, the movement of a shoal of fish or the way the clouds move across the sky and the shapes that they make. Each of these forms, shapes or patterns is assigned a meaning which will give an answer to a particular question. For example, a Crow, seen flying to the left is assigned a negative meaning and is deemed to be a bad omen, whereas if it is seen flying to the right, it is considered to be fortunate and a positive answer. A shoal of fish seen swimming in the direction of the enquirer may be assigned the meaning of great good fortune and the coming into wealth, particularly if they are seen to have a gold or silver sheen to them. A cloud seen in the sky in the shape of a castle might be assigned the meaning of a move to a larger house, whereas the sight of one bearing the shape of a large dog is said to mean danger and being hunted by an enemy. The lists of the given meanings of each of these set systems is quite comprehensive and will prove exceedingly instructive if studied closely. They can give a very good impression of how natural phenomena have been viewed by our ancestors and by different cultures in the past. The folkloric knowledge of these patterns having been observed over large periods of time can give great insights into how these methods may be used by the Witch in devising and using their own divination systems.

However, whilst undoubtedly of value and of use to the Witch, these set systems of meaning do not get to the heart of the matter. Within natural augury, the Witch attempts to divine by becoming closer to the patterns of nature and allowing the answers to arise naturally from within, rather than imposing a, possibly irrelevant, pattern on them from outside. Divination in this form can be said to be an art or skill that functions at the interface between the natural world and that of human perception. This interface is of great importance in the realm of natural augury, for the answers lie in the realm of personal meaning, rather than fixed concepts. An extreme example of this is the story of the attaining of the Runes by the god Odin. The tale states that Odin hung himself upon the Yggdrasil world-tree, for nine nights and nine days, self-pierced with a spear, a sacrifice of self unto self. On the ninth night he had an epiphany, a vision of the whole runic system. This was revealed to him in one stroke, because of his connection to the numinous via his act of near self-destruction – he did not devise them himself but perceived them directly from nature. These appeared in the shapes of the twigs in the tree, the shapes the branches made when crossing and in the veins in the leaves before him; the whole system became apparent at once. Now, whilst I do not advocate hanging oneself in a tree for a lengthy period of time with a sharp implement embedded in ones body to attain a connection with the meanings in nature, it IS necessary to obtain a working connection with the hidden and eldritch side of reality to receive answers to one's questions. It is needful to be aware of the Life in the natural world to make a successful augury that derives from it and one's connection to it, rather than looking at a list of pre-conceived answers from a book, however useful they may be in other situations.

For example, if the Witch has a question in mind that needs an answer and goes out in search of it by observing the natural world and comes across a seemingly significant occurrence of two Hares boxing. The book meaning to this may state that this is a symbol of exuberant life, energy, fertility and betokens fresh beginnings with great impetus and fortune. However, as a child, the Witch kept pet rabbits which unfortunately turned on one another, fought and killed each other rather nastily. This is not going to leave a good memory in the mind of the Witch, however well they may understand that this was a natural – if regrettable – occurrence. The book meaning just doesn't accord with what the Witch feels about the image and hence is at variance with a natural augury. Or again, the Witch sees an eagle soaring above in a cloudless sky which, according to received wisdom, indicates the attainment of the highest goals and advancement within the society of one's peers. But, again, as a child, the Witch observed an eagle swoop down and carry off a lamb from a field, then proceed to feed it to its young in a nearby tree, tearing it apart in the process. This once more, conflicts with the given augury for this occurrence and is at variance with the Witch's inner feelings. These may be extreme examples, but I'm sure the meaning behind them can be understood in these situations. It all hinges on what the particular images or phenomena mean to the Witch, individually and personally, what they associate them with and what these images then trigger within them; what is the meaningful or significant response that they convey?

For natural auguries to be effective and, even more importantly, accurate for the Witch, they need to be allowed to arise spontaneously from that well of consciousness that is linked to all other Life, via that web of Wyrd previously mentioned. The answers need to be allowed to rise up naturally, fully formed, as a complete answer to the question/s being posed. In this instance, rather than using "mechanical" methods, such as those previously described like the pendulum or geomantic lots, this may be achieved by the Witch utilising the techniques already described, associated with Witchwalking. The question that needs an answer should be carefully considered and refined down into a simple phrase or sentence, that has little or no ambiguity to it. If the Witch wishes to know how to change their job, for example, it would be better to phrase the question as; "What would be the best area for me to seek employment?", rather than, "What job should I apply for?" The former will produce answers that will be suitable, attainable and likely to prove enjoyable to the Witch, whereas the latter may provide a list that might not be so enjoyable or appropriate for their temperament, however financially rewarding. The Witch then needs to go out into the natural world, as before, holding this enquiry in mind, and observing the world around them for an answer. Unlike Ostenta, the answers will not hit the mind with an immediate reply, but will arise naturally by observing the things around about. The Witch may wish to sit by a stream or river, to observe the flow of water, and let the answers arise, rather than trying to perform a scrying exercise. They may wish to observe the clouds going by and see what concepts form in their mind from the associations with the shapes observed. They may wish to take notice of the shapes of the branches of the trees against the skyline, or again, the birds in their flight. All these things may be observed from the position of a connection with the natural world and allowing the answers to questions to arise naturally from this connection. The "trick" is in allowing the things viewed to trigger responses from within the Witch, rather than consciously imposing meanings externally. This will give much more accurate and personal "readings" for the individual involved.

This is a difficult technique to learn and, at least to start with, will seem like nothing more than wishful thinking or possibly even fantasising on the part of the Witch. However, once the feeling of the connection between the Witch and the world around has been recognised and worked with for a period of time, this becomes a valuable and insightful method of divination. It is capable of giving a far more rounded, full and directly personal response to an enquiry than can merely looking up a natural phenomenon in a book and deriving a set answer. This technique relies on a deep familiarity with the natural world and the surroundings of the Witch and it is one that needs to be continuously developed and worked with, through all the seasons and cycles of the years, in as many ways as possible. The more the Witch can know the "normal" patterns of their surroundings, the easier it will be to notice those things that are not "normal" and, hence, significant in a specific situation.

It is thus, in this manner, that the Witch, whilst Walking, may blur the boundaries between "here" and "there", this world and the next. The process of resolving the seeming opposites of light and dark, good and bad, malediction/ benediction may continue and the combining of the essence of Blackthorn and Whitethorn may progress within the Witch.

Betwixt the Thorns.

"Be that you be, see that you see; shine, and in the shining, show what you be."
(John Matthews, from "Breaking the Circle", in the anthology, "Voices from the Circle".)

The expression, "Betwixt/Between the Horns", is a known term in Traditional Craft; here I have adapted it to better conform to the exemplars being used in this book. The expression is the same, but I hope it can be seen that I am implying extra meanings within the context of this work, bearing in mind all that has come before. The core expression can mean different things to different types of Witch. To some, it is a position of inner balance from which to perform ritual. To some, it is a trancelike-state in which contact with the spirit-world/s is possible. To yet others, it is a condition of the Witch themselves whereby they may partake of deific possession. Yet all these things have something in common and that is a transcendence of the common waking-state and a cessation of perceived duality, or even plurality. There is a coming-together of separate elements of the individual, such that they form a cohesive whole which transcends those various, individual parts. The illusion of separateness, of being different or not partaking of the same essence as everything else, disappears and the illusion is overcome. There is no here and there, no you and me, no this world and the other world; all is a continuous state of Being, whereby magical practice and spiritual endeavour may take place in the "ever- now". It is a mystical condition, which is sought after, and may be the end result of, many different practices within the various branches of the Mystery Traditions. It is this condition and state that we have been working towards within the pages of this book and which I would now like to look at in additional detail.

We have already seen some of the Ways in which this state of Betwixt the T/Horns may be achieved; through ritual, meditation, conversing with the Dead, Walking and others. These are all Ways whereby the Witch may put themselves in the Between state, in order to accomplish some magical act, be that spirit contact, healing, cursing, blessing and many others. This will hopefully lead on to the ultimate goal of magical working, indeed of the Mysteries themselves (and Witchcraft is indeed a part of the Mystery tradition), which is in attaining this state permanently. Some would call this the quest for enlightenment and consider it to be a very passive state in which not much is done. The Witch, however, sees it as a state of Being which is very much an active one, in which they may achieve many things that would otherwise be exceedingly difficult, if not impossible. Once this state of awareness is achieved, it can be said that the Light betwixt the T/Horns has been lit. This light, or torch, is often signified by a lit candle placed between the horns of the Stang and symbolises the achievement of the state of "illumination" and/or its presence in any particular rite. This condition manifested within the Witch is the last of the goals stated at the beginning of this book; Knowledge, Power, Wisdom and Illumination and can take a whole, or many, lifetimes to achieve. It is at one and the same time, the resolution of apparent duality and the joining with deity, more of which anon. For now, I would like to look at further methods of dissolving the "veil of separateness" between the Witch and the attaining of a unified vision of reality.

"Darkling" Knowledge and Understanding

It is traditional that the Witch has a working knowledge of many herbs, both to heal and to curse and this also includes those known as the "Dark Herbs"; the psychotropic plants that can have mind-altering and reality-changing effects. What is often difficult to find, is useful information on these and the Ways in which they were used. Up until recently this knowledge was never written down, but their secrets were well kept by the Witch groups that used them. Many of the Dark Herbs are poisonous, many can kill and care must be taken when handling them, it is therefore understandable why this knowledge was kept hidden by those that had it. I am not going to get moralistic on this issue, but I would just like to say this. Plant materials that alter consciousness have been used within magical and spiritual practice throughout the world for thousands of years and it is useless denying that they were a part of Witch practice in the past. However, they were used with knowledge, care and a background of continuous practice, that no longer exists in Western culture today. Our linkage to a culture of knowledge has been broken – unlike some indigenous cultures in other parts of the world – and we no longer live in that type of social environment. When mind-and-perception-altering plants are taken within the societies that have a continuous and unbroken tradition of using them, they are taken within a supportive, cultural environment that knows how to accommodate the results, the people partaking in their use having grown up within that framework and having an ingrained, cultural experience of them. Generally speaking, in Western cultures, we do not; hence the many problems that can arise when white folks pop off to do a quick Ayahuasca ritual or similar. We have neither the supportive culture, nor the embedded knowledge and experience of how to deal with the results. Therefore, anyone wishing to work with the Dark Herbs needs to make very sure that they know what they are doing and have a valid support system in place before embarking upon this practice. They also need to have a thorough idea of how these plants act upon the human body and are likely to affect the mind of the Witch, before they take anything at all. However, if these safeguards are in place, then the Dark Herbs can have a valid and useful place in magical practice, if this is a Way that the Witch desires to make use of.

The knowledge of the use of these plants was/is often kept as a separate discipline or area of knowledge within certain Traditions and these groups are known by some as the Dark Orders. They hold and keep this knowledge, teaching it carefully to those they consider worthy of its use and application. What follows is not the deeper knowledge held by these Orders but some aspects of it, derived from an East Anglian based Tradition, that will hopefully give some informed, safe and practical knowledge on how to use some of these plants. When working with these, always use gloves, as some herbs can be infused through the skin and enter the bloodstream readily. I am not advocating their use in a general manner but, having studied their properties thoroughly, do not be afraid to use the Dark Herbs as these, along with the many herbs to heal, are valid tools in the working practice of the Witch; you just have to know how to use them. However, never underestimate their potency; these herbs may have been used for thousands of years but are just as effective now as they ever were.

The Dark Herbs at the disposal of the British Old Craft Witch mostly have their genus within the same family, that of the Solanaceae and especially those of the genus Solanum. Within this genus are found the tropane alkaloids Hyoscyamine, Atropine and Hyoscine, and these are contained in the herbs favoured by the Traditional Witch;

Atropa belladonna (Deadly Nightshade),
Hyoscyamus niger (Henbane) and
Datura stramonium (Thornapple).

These three all give a similar effect, to whit; flushed, dry skin, a dry mouth and delirium. However, it is this delirium that gives access to the state betwixt the t/horns, allowing the barriers to come down and reveal what is generally veiled.

Atropa belladonna – Deadly Nightshade, Devil's Cherries, Banewort, Fair Lady, Divale, Black Cherry, Devil's Herb, Great Morel, Dwale, Dwayberry.

This is probably the most widely known of the Dark herbs, but also strangely unknown to some. Not very many years ago, it is known that a couple from Norfolk gathered what they thought were "Blackberries", thinking they were fine to eat. They were observed by their neighbours to be dancing, naked, round the kitchen table and then later found writhing in agony on the floor, after eating a crumble they had made from the berries. They had picked Belladonna berries, thinking that all black berries were "Blackberries". They were rushed into the hospital and did survive. But a sharp lesson there – Nightshade crumble is to be avoided at all costs! The juice of the berry of Nightshade does relatively little harm, and was often drunk by fieldworkers as a refreshing drink that gave them more "go"; but they were careful not to take the seed, as herein lies a part of the plant's potency. The leaves are of use mostly for drying and burning as part of an incense. This is known to be useful for group workings, as the whole group awareness is raised to a similar level allowing all partaking of the rite to experience the same level of stepping out of the normal. It is usually thrown upon the fire where the group will gather round and take in deep breaths of the smoke.

The root also has potency; as with most Dark Herbs; it is a source of the power of the plant and contains all aspects of the virtue of the plant in concentrated form. According to Paul Ratcliffe, the well-known and respected Cornish Witch (who I do not mean to imply is associated with the source East Anglian Tradition for this section),

> *"The root is bulbous and of the class that can be used to make a "Mandrake" (the variety Atropa murion is particularly noted for this). A spirit bound in this root will be particularly powerful with respect to dreams, and wine laced with the juice of the berries may be drunk as part of the ceremony of consecration."*
> *(A Folk Herbal – see Bibliography).*

Belladonna is also used to make the "Poisoned Chalice", Initiatory drink of some Witch Traditions, but the knowledge of how much and what parts to use is a closely guarded secret; too much and you will kill the Initiate, too little and it's useless. It may also be used as a stupefier, sending the drinker into a deep sleep, hopefully to delve beyond the normal realms of perception. It very much depends on how it is harvested, what parts are utilised, and how it is prepared as to how it is used and what results may be expected. Belladonna can be a useful herb if used carefully, cautiously and with knowledge. If the reader would like to try the effects of this herb on themselves, then an infusion (tea) may be made up using one heaped teaspoon of the dried leaves (no more!). Pour on boiling water, leave for 10 minutes, strain carefully and drink in sips when cool enough. The psychoactive ingredients vary widely from plant to plant, so always err on the side of caution.

Hyoscyamus niger – Henbane, Hog's-bean, Jupiter's Bean, Symphonica, Cassilata, Dog Piss, Poison Tobacco, Foetid Nightshade, Henbells.

The whole plant is exceedingly difficult to chop up when dried, but although the leaves etc. are of use, it is again the seeds and root which carry the potency, although the flowering tops can also be useful. There are two ways to use the seeds of this plant; one is to make a paste by grinding the seeds, mixing them with oil and applying the mixture directly to the body, as in a flying ointment. The other is to roast the seeds and to inhale the fumes. The seeds will swell and split and exude the fumes, which when inhaled give the desired effect. Both ways will have a similar result, although the ointment tends not to have as strong an effect as inhaling the fumes. If using them in this manner, then a little at a time is the best way; feel the difference in your perception and pause between each inhalation/adding more seeds. The temptation is always to go that little bit further next time, which may well be one seed too many. Be aware of your sensations and state of awareness; once you have reached the betwixt state, stop immediately. Paul Ratcliffe gives the following instructions for viewing spirits using Henbane seeds.

> *"Make an incense by grinding the following ingredients into a fine powder;*
> *Fennel Root – 1 part*
> *Frankincense – 1 part*
> *Henbane herb – 4 parts*
> *Coriander – 1 part*
> *Cassia – 1 part.*
> *Take the incense to a dark forest, haunted and enchanted. On a stump set down black candles and a lighted censer. Burn the incense and wait for the candles to be suddenly extinguished and there, in the darkness, will form spirits of the night. To be rid of them, burn Asafetida and Frankincense." (A Folk Herbal).*

(Presumably the inhalation of the fumes of the incense makes the seeing of the spirits that much easier). I would warn against ingesting this herb in any other way except by inhalation; its seeds when swallowed may kill in a most horrendous way. The Tradition from which this material is derived performed their own, controlled experiments on consenting Initiates and here are some of the results.

Initially, physical effects will be noticed; headache, sickness, dizziness, mouth and throat dry.

Secondly, mental effects will become apparent; a feeling of fright, which may develop into desperate terror. This can lead to visions and hallucinations, whereby your worst nightmares may take on a living reality; feelings of malevolence, violence, eroticism and marked deviant sexual abandon.

The next stage can be one of paralysis and a sense of detachment from the body; euphoria may then develop, as if nothing mattered and one couldn't give a fig what happened.

Depending on how much of the Henbane has been inhaled, it can take a very long time to recover from the symptoms, both mental and physical; dreams are frequently violent and can last for up to a week. The effects that are experienced are also conditioned by the state of mind of the Witch at the time; if sexually aroused, then surprising emotions can follow, where repressions are dissolved in the most startling manner. If the mind is in a condition of annoyance or the Witch is feeling argumentative, then the effects may be remarkably warlike; Henbane was given to warriors before they went into battle and it is easy to see why!

Taken with knowledge and care, Henbane may be used to remove the barriers between the worlds and enable the state of betwixt the horns, allowing astonishing insights and personal revelations. However - don't play with this one; it will kill you very quickly.

Datura stramonium – Thornapple, Devil's Trumpet, Devil's Apple, Jamestown-weed, Jimson-weed, Stinkweed, Apple of Peru, Shrinkwort, Witches thimble.

This is a herb which many people may have in their garden tubs or conservatory without realising what a dark presence they hold. Called "Angels Trumpets" in some gardening books, beautiful big flowers of various colours with a strange hypnotic perfume. Datura has the same properties as Henbane, and may be worked with to the same advantage. The ancient Mayans of Mexico used enemas to introduce Datura into the blood stream. Maya artwork depicts this with clarity on pottery dated 800AD, where anal sex with a horn seems to have been practised, but this is insertion of the Datura by way of an animal horn. I do not recommend this method, but would advise sticking with the methods already mentioned above for Henbane. The root and the seed crushed into paste and rubbed into the skin as with most of the Dark Herbs will give the effect of altered perceptions. It has been used by Witches to promote spirit flight or travelling, loosening the connection with the body. Again, ingested by smoking the leaves will give a safe way of using this one.

Other than the Solanacea, more herbs were used within the East Anglian Tradition, some of which follow here.

Helleborus niger – Hellebore, Christmas Rose, Settergrass, (also called Black Horehound in folk tradition, but NOT to be confused with the true Horehound, *Marrubium vulgare,* which is a totally different plant).

There are different strains of this but the one to look for is Black Hellebore. Mixed with Henbane this may give rise to erotic visions; when smeared onto the hands it may give the feeling of "far touch" (similar to the Star touching described previously), if onto the temples it may give the effect of flying and terrifying visions. However, the method employed by this Witch Tradition to achieve the desired effects for magical work, is by sniffing the dried and powdered herb up your nose. It gives much the same result as Henbane in this case. Again the root or seed is the source of concentrated power and may be crushed into a paste to use it. Its root can be used to bring on an abortion, and was readily used in this way by the village Witch.

Aconitum napellus – Aconite, Monkshood, Wolf's Bane, Blue Rocket, Friar's Cap, Old Wife's Hood.

This herb is not readily recognised as being a Dark Herb, yet its root is as deadly as any other. As with other herbs, its root may kill, but used in the correct way and dosage, this is the active ingredient in many of the historical recipes for flying ointment. No matter what was put with it, anything from Datura, Henbane, Nightshade, or whatever, it is the Aconite that does the work here and is the "antidote" and mitigating factor to/for the other herbs used, particularly Datura. The whole plant is deadly, but it is the root here which is of most use. Used by grinding the plant into a paste, rubbed on the genitals it soon dispersed into the bloodstream; it was also smeared onto the shaft of the besom, which was then applied to the "privy parts". The root of the Aconite was used as a poison to tip darts, as in the infamous "Elf Shot". The useful dose for magical use is exceptionally close to a fatal dose, so I do not recommend experimentation if not under expert instruction.

Digitalis purpurea - Foxglove, Witches Gloves, Dead Men's Bells, Fairy's Glove, Bloody Fingers, Virgin's Glove, Fairy Caps, Fairy Thimbles.

Digitalis, which is known as a famous heart medicine, yet also has a Dark side and use to its nature. Digitalis is used as an antidote to Henbane in cases of overdose and may be included as a precaution in any flying ointments containing it. The herb Digitalis has certain other attributes known to this Tradition, which made it essential for use in a particular rite of the old days according to my sources, but I was unable to discover any particulars about it. However, it seemed to be of a highly sexual nature, as this act was frequently used as a technique by these Folk.

Not classed as herbs, but in a group of their own, some Fungi have been traditionally used by Witches and here are some further descriptions from the same source Tradition on working with two of them.

Psilocybin - "Magic Mushrooms", small yellowish pointed caps (nipple on top), with clay coloured gills and stalk; the stalk is long and slender, with a smallish cap. Many varieties exist. This is a hallucinogenic, which gives heightened perception of sights and sounds, which may be euphoric or nightmarish, lasting possibly for hours or days. "Magic Mushroom" can be deadly but were widely used; some Old Crafters use these now to "receive a blessing from the Mother and Father", but few understand their real use. Take care with this one; deadly if abused, but can be of use when used correctly, if you don't have the understanding, then leave it alone. The Witch would not use mushrooms, or indeed any of the Dark Herbs, for pleasure, their use lays far outside of this, never used when alone, always with someone who is experienced enough to guide the traveller, which will bring its own rewards. The easiest variety to find growing wild, is probably "*Liberty Cap*" or *Psilocybe semilanceata*, depending on where you live in Britain. The dosage depends on the weight of the recipient and the type of mushroom taken; an antidote to this poison is pure orange juice. If you must experiment with mushrooms, then a little at a time to find what works for you, and please be careful again, these can be lethal if misused. The mushroom of fairy tales is *Fly Agaric, Amanita muscaria* – used widely in some shamanic cultures, with its distinctive red and white cap. Reindeer ate the red and white mushrooms, and the villages of nearby tribes collected the urine from the reindeer and drank it, this gave them the exact dilution they needed for the mushroom Amanita muscaria to produce the effect required for magical and spirit-flight practices. This still takes place today in certain cultures. Not fatally poisonous, but still needs knowledgeable handling if unpleasant effects are to be avoided.

At this point, I would like to give an example from personal experience of the type of use of the Dark Herbs/Fungi that I am writing about and the effect that is to be desired for the Witch in utilising them for the magical purpose of Betwixt the T/Horns. In the mid 1980's, I was taking instruction in shamanic techniques from an experienced practitioner, who had trained directly with indigenous peoples in the Americas and with various "Elders" in Britain also. On this particular occasion, a group session had been arranged, whereby we would take some mushroom tea, prior to a drumming ritual, whilst under the influence of the brew. The mushroom tea was prepared by an experienced practitioner and we all drank one, small teacup-full, before we began in the early evening. I was sitting next to the leader of the group, on his left, who was leading and directing the drumming; I had been given a rattle and the task of "keeping time" for the group. All were seated in a circle, with a group of candles at the centre, on which we were instructed to focus as the evening's work progressed; we were instructed NOT to "zone out" under any circumstances, but to focus IN to the centre – the key to the experience. We commenced with some simple rhythms to warm up and then continued as directed by the leader of the group. I found the drumming enjoyable – being new to it – but not overly stimulating. As the evening went on however, I began to notice effects taking place, both from the drumming and – obviously – from the mushroom tea. I began to hear a high-pitched noise coming from the drum that the leader was beating beside me, and also a change in tone of the rattle I was using. Gradually, the tone of the drum and the rattle seemed to coincide and become one noise, which then lowered in tone and became less high pitched. The sound gradually changed into what I perceived as a voice singing in my ear, right next to me; it was the voice of the leader's drum and it was singing just to me, or so it felt. I heard the words and they were beautiful and meaningful and, as I gazed at the candles in the centre and listened to the song that was being sung, I began to understand many things that I had never understood before. I cannot tell you how long the drumming and singing went on for, as it wasn't important, but for an appreciable length of time. Nor can I now say what the drum and rattle were singing to me, as I no longer recall the words, but they had a profound effect on me at the time and I know that they changed my understanding and perception of certain things quite profoundly. The session eventually came to an end and we all retired for the night. I seem to remember that my dreams were vivid and interesting, in full colour, but not disturbing in any way and I felt well and healthy the next day. I've never repeated that particular experience but, nearly 40 years later, I still remember the feeling it gave me of profound peace and comprehension at the time. This is the type of effect that I believe should be aimed for with the use of the Dark Herbs/Fungi and which can be of great value and use in the magical practise of aiming to place oneself Between the Thorns.

Some advice derived from my source Tradition for this section is apposite here and I would suggest that anyone seeking to use these herbs should consider it carefully.

> *"Be aware that by using two or more of the Dark Herbs together one may enhance the other and accelerate, or affect, the herb's use. For example, Nightshade will heighten and quicken the effect of any herb you care to put it with, hence it is combined with Aconite within flying ointment to enhance and quicken its use. Vervain works on the frontal lobe of the brain, and will reduce negative feelings, hence it is used combined with Henbane. If you were to put Nightshade, Henbane and Vervain together, you will end up with Henbane's effects, tempered with Vervain's ability to reduce negative feelings and the whole enhanced by Nightshade's ability to bring everything to culmination quicker than they normally would work. As always, it is understanding which is the key; to know is not enough, to understand the simple laws of nature, of energies and control is where lies the potency and strength of the Ways of the Traditional Witch. However, it is not just the herb that does the work. What needs to be considered also is the state of mind of the person experiencing the herb. Just as with alcohol the experience is heightened or dampened by how a person feels at the time and what his state of mind is. The effects of the herb are influenced by the individual's being, and when in a group of any kind, the full effect is usually only obtained if the whole group give themselves to experience what lays before them.* **Please be aware that any use of herbs, especially the Dark ones, must be taken in seriousness; misuse or overdose can kill you.***"*

It is not generally my practice or advice to use the Dark Herbs to achieve trance states/altered states of consciousness. This, again, is not said in any moralistic sense, but in a practical one. Achieving trance states by your own efforts, without outside help, gives the Witch a much greater degree of control over the experience. Yes, the Dark Herbs CAN liberate the mind to experience alternate states of reality and sit Betwixt the T/Horns, but they also take away the ability to reliably focus and control these experiences. The effort taken to achieve the states on your own will be well rewarded when you can not only achieve them at will, but also guide and direct yourself and also bring back the knowledge and memories so gained. In many of those cultures that still have an existing shamanic practice, the shaman that uses drugs to enable their work is very often considered a second-rate shaman! However, these Dark Herbs ARE a part of Traditional lore and use, and it would be remiss of me not to include some mention of them in a work of this nature.

Circling the Point

Ritual dance is thousands of years old and has been used by most cultures and peoples for many different reasons over this time span. It may be used for celebratory purposes, for stylised hunting rites, for combat, to reflect the turning of the seasons and to bring people together in group unification. The forms of these dances are many and are particularly well-developed within European, pagan cultures and those that followed them. Most of these dances involve/d circling around a central point, be that a tree, a fire, a stone or other significant landmark, natural or artificial. Within East Anglia, there is an old tradition of the Broom Dance that goes back centuries and whose origins are ultimately lost, but reflects the many meanings and uses of the Besom over time. As a central pole around which the dance is performed, it has associations with the Witch's Stang in this sense and represents the Pole Star, around which the heavens themselves appear to revolve. The circling – or sometimes serpentine – forms of these dances, are thought to have connections with certain aspects of landscape knowledge, possibly either mimicking or arousing the energies that are considered to be present within the body of the Land, as previously considered. These dances are thought to be able to "arouse" the latent forces within the Earth and "direct" them towards such practical uses as encouraging a better harvest, or increasing the fertility in the game animals, or indeed the human tribes themselves. The dances have taken place – and still do – at significant times of year, mainly around the beginning of Summer/May Day and also around the height of this period, Midsummer.

Another form of these traditional actions is the Labyrinth dance, evidence of which has been recorded over periods of several centuries. The forms of these labyrinths are varied and can be seen cut, carved, painted or drawn into the landscape in various places and even marked on the floors of Christian Cathedrals, such as Chartres, Reims and Amiens in France and Norwich, Exeter and Ely in England. There is a large example cut into the turf at Saffron Walden in Essex, which is still regularly used by people for many different purposes. Labyrinths are distinct from Mazes, in that they are not designed to confuse and disorientate the "dancer", but to calm and induce a meditative state; there is only one pathway through to the centre point, which then enables the dancer to exit without becoming lost. These pathways are walked in a contemplative state of mind, or danced with a slow step or rhythm and create a feeling of wholeness, completeness or union within. Sometimes a focal object is placed at the centre, either for concentration or meditation once the centre is reached, or purely as a focus around which the dancer may make their energetic or spiritual journey. I have given a version of one of these labyrinth-dances in a previous work ("*A Ring Around the Moon*", see Bibliography), that the reader may wish to partake of themselves and which I reproduce a version of here. In this case, the labyrinth form has been simplified into a spiral for ease of construction, but the intent and end result are the same.

The Spiral of Seven Prayers

This rite is based on the lore of the ancient turf mazes which, in their turn, are based upon the mystic and holy number Seven and the symbol of the Spiral-pictogram of the Life-Energy and pathway to the Centre. It is impossible to become lost as there is only one path – unlike many mazes – which spirals into the/your Centre and then gradually unfolds itself to the exit, which is also the entrance. The rite may be performed at any time, there being sufficient need, but is perhaps best suited to the contemplative phase of the Waning Moon. If the rite is to be performed out of doors then there is no need to create a Compass – the Spiral and Walking it being sufficient in itself. If it is to be performed in the Temple or Working Area, then a Compass should be cast as usual beforehand and the rite used as the central Working. If it is desired that a "power piece" or talisman of some kind is to be held at the Centre of the Spiral, then this should be placed first and the Spiral formed around it. The construction may be of your own choice; a rope, stones, flowers, leaves, twigs, sand etc. – whatever you feel to be appropriate to the time and need and maybe also the season. The size is also left to your choice and available space, although you should allow free movement and not restrict yourself in any way; bear in mind that the aim is expansion and not contraction. The form is of a concentric Spiral of seven circuits, the seventh "circuit" being the Centre itself which should be large enough to comfortably accommodate a person seated or perhaps lying down.

The Rite

Stand at the entrance to the Spiral,which should be in the North. Be still within yourself and clarify the reason for Walking the Spiral. At the completion of each circuit of the Spiral, you will speak a short prayer, calling on seven sources of wisdom and knowledge to aid and guide you.

The first prayer is spoken as you stand at the entrance to the Spiral;

"Speak, Earth, and I will listen."

The Land upon which we stand is our foundation, our rock and the repository of the entirety of Life on this planet. Within it reside the bones of our Ancestors, the history of all the civilisations that have been and the memories of every living person that has existed. Listen well to the voices of the past, for they are wise and full of knowledge.

Slowly walk a complete circuit of the Spiral in contemplation.

The second prayer is spoken once the first circuit is completed;

"Speak, Moon, and I will listen."

Moonlight awakens those things that are hidden in the dark, the things that are pushed aside and ignored, the things that can fester and breed disease, the things that we fear. Bring those things out into the clear light of the Moon and let Her reveal those secret things that should be taken heed of. Let them give you knowledge and do not shun the things in the dark, for they are powerful.

Slowly walk a complete circuit of the Spiral in contemplation.

The third prayer is spoken once the second circuit is completed;

"Speak, Sun, and I will listen."

The Sun is the great timekeeper, the organiser and rhythm-keeper of our lives. Each of us has our own rhythm and pattern, different to all others and we would do well to heed those tides that course within us. Listen to the beat of your heart and let it tell you the pattern of your own life; listen to your own rhythms and let them speak directly to you.

Slowly walk a complete circuit of the Spiral in contemplation.

The fourth prayer is spoken once the third circuit is completed;

"Speak, Stars, and I will listen."

Stellar energies are around us all the time, though we do not usually take note of them. They speak to us of things far away and seldom considered, of things alien and exotic and foreign to our natures and lives. Let the Stars speak to you of new thoughts, new ideas and impulses; allow fresh energies into your life and do not block the possibility of things unknown to you as yet.

Slowly walk a complete circuit of the Spiral in contemplation.

The fifth prayer is spoken once the fourth circuit is completed;

"Speak, Spirits, and I will listen."

Those who have gone before and those who are yet to come; those who are not of our order of Being and those who one day may be – all of them have a voice that may be heard, if we but listen. They have access to knowledge, to symbols, to dreams and to teaching that may change our lives for the better. Give ear to the voices of the Spirits and learn.

Slowly walk a complete circuit of the Spiral in contemplation.

The sixth prayer is spoken once the fifth circuit is completed;

"Speak, Gods, and I will listen."

Transcendent Beings of Might, Mystery and Power, the Gods help us to become more than we are. Listen to their voices in the Winds and the Rains, in the sound of Earthquakes and Volcanoes, but also in the tiny sounds of leaves and grass growing, of petals unfolding and corn ripening in the fields. You, also, are part of these things and can become as great and as forceful as these if you would only listen to the voices of the Gods.

Slowly walk a complete circuit of the Spiral in contemplation.

The seventh prayer is spoken on entering the centre of the Spiral;

"Speak, Self, and I will listen."

All those things that have gone before are an essential part of who you are and their makeup within you makes you truly unique and individual. You are as Wise, Knowledgeable, Brave, Free, Innovative, Mighty and Powerful as you truly wish to be. You are Your Self and none other. This is the/your Centre. Sit or stand as you will, holding your power object or talisman, or not, as you like. Be at peace with Your Self.

Stay until you are ready to depart, then slowly retrace your steps to the entrance of the Spiral. Give thanks in whatever way seems suitable to you and finish your rite in your accustomed manner.

Within the Craft in general, dancing has mainly been used for two separate, but related, purposes and those are to induce trance and to raise energy for magical applications. I have spoken of these in detail in others of my works, but would like to quote here from the late Traditional Witch, Alastair "Bob" Clay-Egerton, who gives an interesting observation on the use of dance for the above purposes.

> *"A spinning, or turning body, like a planet, by its own motion creates a magnetic gravitational field that seems to be dependent for measurable strength on the size of the body and its rate of rotation. It has been demonstrated that a group of people dancing in a circle produces a definite flow of energy similar to that of an electric field. This is apparently enhanced when the circle is of alternate males and females, especially when they are holding hands (i.e. in contact with each other). It may be that the direction danced, either Deosil or Widdershins, affects the field in some way. We do not know. Insufficient work has been done on the subject but knowledge does not come freely on a platter. So, evoke the Lord of the Dance, and take the steps necessary to improve yourself spiritually."* (Quoted from, *"Coven of the Scales"*, see Bibliography).

Obviously if practising on one's own, there cannot be alternating male and female energy in a circle – or can there? More on this anon.

A third reason for using dance in the Craft is relatively little spoken of and that is to induce a mystical sense of wholeness. This is one that unites the Witch both with the disparate parts of themselves and with the wider universe, transcending perceived notions of separateness, which may or may not include perceptions of deity. The reader will be familiar with this practise in other traditions, most notably that of the Dervishes, within the Sufi Tradition of the Islamic religion. Old Craft shares a similar concept when it comes to the use of dance in this sense and also utilises similar techniques. (It is well known that some Craft scholars consider that much magical and mystical lore was adopted from the Muslim invaders of Spain and also brought back from the Middle East by the Crusader Knights of the mediaeval period, which subsequently became absorbed into Old Craft lore, technique and praxis. This is currently unverifiable one way or the other, but the fact remains that similar techniques do exist in both traditions, quite possibly because they are valid techniques, discovered independently of each other). The basic theme is, as described before, the movement of the dancer in a circular pattern, around a central point, upon which they place their focus; sometimes it is the dancer themselves that may be the central axis around which they may spin. This is the most important point, in that the focus is placed and not allowed to wander. As mentioned above when dealing with the darkful herbs, and an example given by my own experience with the Psilocybin mushrooms, if the focus is not centrally placed, then the temptation is to "space out". When the attention is focussed on a central point, then all the personal energies are combined in one space (figuratively) and amalgamated, transcending their limitations and integrating into something greater than they were before. If the attention is left to wander around at random, nothing is achieved but a pleasant dance and certainly no useful mystical happening is experienced. The energy and focus is dissipated, squandered, and no valid result is obtained, from a magical perspective. As ever, these techniques take time to master and usually even longer to achieve a looked-for experience from; illumination doesn't come without hard work. However, worked at over a period of time, they can produce appreciable results and illumination can come in a flash when not looked for!

I would like to describe here two separate, but related techniques, that would be useful for the Witch to try. They exemplify in their actions the two main types of "magical dance" that are traditional for Old Craft Witches – at least in my experience – those of Enthusiasm and those of Ecstasy. The word Enthusiasm is derived from the Greek, "*enthousiasmos*", divine inspiration, (produced by certain kinds of music, dance, etc.), from "*enthousiazein*", be inspired, filled or possessed by a god, be rapt, be in ecstasy. The word Ecstasy in its turn, also derives from the Greek, "*ekstasis*", literally being out of the body, entrancement, astonishment, insanity; any displacement or removal from the proper place. One can easily follow from the other, in no particular order, but needs to be tried and worked at to achieve any appreciable result. As everyone is different, one technique will no doubt suit individuals better than the other, and it is up to the Witch to experiment and see which one suits them the best. And speaking of experimentation, these (and other forms of) dances may be undertaken whilst under the influence of the Dark Herbs, in order both to enhance the experience and to gain extra insight into their lessons. **However**, this should only be done observing the cautions noted above and in very small amounts; the idea is the illumination, not cessation, of Life's Mysteries!

The first technique probably best exemplifies Enthusiasm and is one I learnt some considerable time ago from a very wise woman from Norfolk. I believe its origins lie in mediaeval France, but it has been used in East Anglia for some appreciable time and I offer it here for use by the interested reader. The dancer would normally carry a lighted candle in each hand but, bearing in mind the theme of this work, I would suggest that the Witch holds a piece of Blackthorn in one hand and a piece of Whitethorn in the other, the better to remind themselves of the theme of integration and what they are attempting to do. (If this is not possible, or appropriate for the individual, maybe one black and one white candle would be better). In this case, it is most appropriate to place a large, lighted candle, of the "church" variety, in the centre of the space, around which to dance. Make sure you have plenty of room in which to move and that you are warm and comfortable; this is not an energetic dance, although you will warm up considerably once you get started, because of the movement and intention involved. To begin: place and light your candle in the middle of the space and take up your two Thorn sticks/candles in either hand. Always face and focus on the candle in the middle throughout the dance. Pause for a moment before starting to consider what you are doing and the reasons for it. When ready, raise both arms to shoulder height, outstretched either side, in a rough "T" shape. Facing forward, take one short step to your left with your left foot, then bring your right foot up next to it – so a side step without crossing your feet. Do this twice more; side step with your left foot, then bring the right along to join it. Three times in all. At this point, move your right foot forward and tap the ground in front of you once, swing it round to your right and tap the ground once, then swing it round behind you to tap the ground once, then bring it back and place it beside the left foot again. This must all be done without standing on the right foot, just tap the ground with it forwards, to the right, behind and then back. Then continue with the three steps to the left again, before tapping with the right again, and so on. Continue to do this as you move round in a circle, around the central candle, focussing on your ideal goal of integration. This may sound ridiculously simple – and it is – but once you get used to the simple actions of the body, it gives the mind free rein to work on its own, focussing on the candle. You need to develop a steady, rhythmic step, that becomes almost hypnotic, practically addictive. Music will help here; something that has a steady beat, of a folk-like nature, no vocals, just music. Develop your own speed and rhythm, one that is comfortable to you and you will find that the motions almost perform themselves. After some time, you will practically find yourself drifting slightly out of body and this is where/when the "enthusiasm", the embodying of a god can take place. Just go with it and see where it takes you; no harm can come to you here. When you feel that you have finished for that particular session, simply slow down your dance until you come to a stop. Give yourself a few minutes to adjust and go and have something to eat; this will both bring you down to earth again and replenish the remarkable amount of energy you will find that you have expended after this type of dance.

The second type of dance I wish to share is more of the Ecstatic type, although a good deal of enthusiasm is needed as well. Begin by placing your central candle as before and always remember to focus on this. This is another old dance, which is performed as follows. Facing the central candle, take three short steps, left-right-left, before stamping the next right step in a short, slightly forward movement (as though you were stamping out a burning spark). Repeat this step as you continue round, as in the previous dance. Initially, practice getting comfortable with a simple round dance, but as your experience grows, begin to spin on your own axis as you circle around. Let your arms lift and make sure you relax your shoulders, letting them drop down; once comfortable with this you can clap on the hard step if you wish and maybe hum as you go. Do not use any words or try to intone a charm or a chant, as this may distract you from your purpose; a simple humming sound is more than sufficient. This will take on a tone and rhythm of its own as you go and maybe develop into something quite intense – let it go as it will. Keep practising until you loose all inhibitions about dancing like this and become able to let your body and mind both become free. As with the above dance, you may find that you develop a floating feeling, but do not be tempted to let go and "space out"; control is essential, even while letting yourself float free. The ideal is to engender a feeling of "ecstatic oneness", both with yourself and your surroundings. This may seem like a contradiction in terms when I say to both let go and retain control at the same time, but practice and you will see what I mean.

I would not suggest that you enter into a deep trance until you are experienced and confident in these dances, but though it can be wise to have someone to assist you in trance work, in the final analysis, any Witch who is serious about working properly should be able to look after themselves in their own work. When one works on oneself, one works alone, consequently it is important to be able to work independently. The safest way to progress is to take things gradually, entering into deeper trance states as you gain competence; nothing comes immediately and it is wise to go slowly at first. If you find that you are suited to this type of practice, then you may like to experiment with different styles of music, such as simple drum beats, mediaeval tunes, classical music and even modern trance music; do not discard the idea of modern music if it works for you, because all music was modern when it was created originally!

Ungendering the Practice.

I would now like to address the comment I made above, about being able to have both male and female energies available when working alone. Although acknowledging that males and females are physically different and can have different roles, Old Craft tends not to have strictly defined definitions of what a man or a woman *can do* in magical work, unlike some of the more modern traditions, which are much more strictly gendered in their outlook. The more modern Traditions tend towards Polarity working, a partnership of a male and female, each taking on distinct and separate roles. This practice tends to stem from historical attitudes towards gender, dating mainly from the 19th. and early 20th. Centuries, deriving from occult societies such as the Golden Dawn. These attitudes then filtered into some of the Cunning Lodges in the more rural areas and, latterly, into modern, pagan attitudes, via forms of magic such as the revised types of witchcraft, devised by practitioners such as Gerald Gardner. These forms, themselves, owe a lot directly to the Golden Dawn and Grimoiric forms of ceremonial magic and, necessarily, embedded their attitudes towards sex and gender within them. Whilst acknowledging that polarity working is a valid form of magic and works very well, unless you are specifically working with this method for a certain purpose, or are performing types of fertility magic that rely on a male/female working partnership, no form of magic or Craft HAS to have gendered roles within its practice. Magical workings can perfectly well be performed by individuals of either sex individually, male/female partnerships, male/male or female/female partnerships, or indeed any number of "unbalanced" individuals all working together.

In many indigenous societies – particularly those that

practice a shamanistic/animistic spirituality - the magic worker is often known as a person with "two souls", or someone who partakes of a third or fifth gender (depending on how many are being counted!), and is respected as such, without derision, abhorrence or rejection. This is an acknowledgement that within magical and/or spiritual practice (as well as in everyday Life in general), the question of whether the practitioner is a man or a woman, or both, just doesn't matter a great deal. What is being worked with is not wholly of the physical realm, so physical rules and norms just don't apply. This is typically the attitude that is held within many Old Craft Traditions that I am aware of, and one that was common generally in pre/non Christian societies. Indeed, when one is working in a Craft that is specifically transgressive, outside the bounds of normal society and what it holds dear and seeks to go beyond the rules of everyday morality and spirituality, then a non-gendered approach to magical working can be nothing other than "the norm". This is particularly so when one is aiming to break the bounds of restrictive thinking and achieve a different and more all-embracing understanding of Life, integrating what are normally known as the disparate or opposite parts of the individual. Gender also comes within this scope and needs to be considered in any re-integrating practices of the Witch.

It is known within the East Anglian Traditions that, historically, the Men-in-Black, the Magisters of the local Witch Ways, would often initiate or bring in to the Craft both women *and* men, and that these rites were sometimes possibly of a sexual nature. There seems to be no particularly negative reporting of these practices – within the Craft – and so historically at least, must have been considered to be at least acceptable, if not the norm. Indeed, I am aware of at least one Tradition in East Anglia today that looks favourably on same-sex relations between members, both outside of magical practice and also within the rites themselves. These partnerships are approached in exactly the same manner as an otherwise "Priest/Priestess" relationship in other Traditions; they appear to work well magically with no detriment to either the work or to the partnership itself. I, personally, was taught in my early Old Craft training that, indeed, same-sex couples had advantages and resources that they could draw on, unobtainable to opposite-sex partnerships and, to this extent, were to be acknowledged and accepted as valid, magical relationships, on a parr with any other. (The taboo in these relationships seems mainly to have been, historically speaking, against male-to-male sex, which was illegal in the British Isles until very recently and still is in many countries around the world today. There seems not to have been the same approbation passed on female-to-female couples – this never having been illegal in the U.K. and elsewhere. Many of the countries that still have a ban on male/male relationships are suffering under the legacy of British Colonial rule, still retaining the old legal systems inherited therefrom and a fair dose of Evangelical Christianity into the bargain. Many of these countries did not have a prohibition on same-sex relationships before the colonial era, indeed, many of them were encouraged as sources of wisdom and bravery).

My point here, lest there be any doubt in the reader, is not to advocate same-sex magical relationships as a necessary practice, or even to suggest that everyone should have same-sex sexual relationships, but to encourage the Witch to accept the "cross-gender", or "dual-gendered" nature of their own spirit, or soul if you wish. It is an obvious fact that the individual spirit of a human is either genderless or of both genders (as we understand them in this realm) and that the individual takes on, or is assigned, a physical gender at birth. This is normally perfectly acceptable for everyday life (in most cases), but as Witches attempting to re-integrate the seeming dualities of our natures, or reuniting disparate parts of ourselves into a homogenous whole, it is one of the aspects that needs consideration and should not be ignored, simply because it is the norm everywhere else.

An integrated nature may also be explained in practical terms as the ability to comprehend fully the opposite gender's abilities and sexuality as well as one's own – to see, feel and understand the spiritual and physical viewpoint of the opposite sex and so to obtain an entirely holistic perspective. This is not generally the norm in society, let alone magical practice; the ego of either sex generally predominates and does not permit any other viewpoint to be adopted. Magically speaking, it can be said that Ego and Awareness are directly proportional – if Ego increases, then Awareness decreases and it is one of the requirements of integrated magical practice to bring both the male and female awareness to a fine degree of balance. This requires the total acceptance of the Self in all its forms and the Self, being Pan, being All, embraces All natures, be that male, female or both/neither. This involves a magical re-structuring of both inner and outer personality's and is one of the "Changes" that we have been talking about and working towards within this book. During the mediaeval period, and beyond, many Alchemists strove to produce energy of a metaphysical nature by employing chemicals, flora, fauna and minerals on the physical plane, along with the Elements of Air, Fire, Earth and Water to produce Change on the inner levels. This they achieved and in many cases demonstrated from the magical point of view that the union of opposites, or their integration, does indeed produce energy and that is the energy of Change within the individual. Ultimately this leads to the search for and attainment of the true Philosopher's Stone, which is one of the goals of all genuine magical practice. The Philosopher's Stone may be seen as the achieving of Self-Knowledge – not the attainment of Everlasting Life – and this is also one of the goals of the Witch. Once the Witch reaches a certain stage in their magical progress, it is no longer possible to participate in the normal life of the world unquestioningly, or believe and accept the conventional forms of reality and validity. It is sometimes found necessary for the Witch to remind themselves that the participatory universe which we generally share with the human race at large, "*does not matter, need not be*", in the words of the magician Austin Osman Spare. Whilst the Witch must necessarily live and have their being in this earthly realm and perform many tasks which are not conducive to magical reality, or those other realms that we know to also exist alongside us, AS Witches we are bound to create whatever conditions we are able within ourselves to overcome the limitations of society and live as valid a magical life as we may.

To aid us in this exploration of our own "double natures", the Witch has a supreme exemplar in the image of the Devil Himself. I mentioned the Greek god Pan above as an image of the All, lusting after anything that moves, irrespective of gender, which indeed he is, but he may also be one of the prototypes for images of the Devil of some forms of Traditional Witchcraft. The image of the Sabbatic Goat by the French magician and occultist Eliphas Levi is well known to most Witches, but is somewhat sanitised and missing the impact of the actuality. Whilst it is recognised that not all Old Craft Witches work with deity and of those that do, not all work with the Devil or a form of Horned God, or even feel the need to, He is generally recognised as one of the prime or main magical images within Traditional Craft. To take the reader back to the beginning of this book and my description both of the statue of Pan in the Forest of Canes, and also my description of Himself in the Introduction, He provides one of the best magical images of what the Witch may aspire to work towards in the integration of the magical personality. He is necessarily depicted as rough and fearsome, hairy and horned, possessing an appreciable phallus which He certainly knows how to use – yet He is also often shown with full breasts. In those images that are somewhat "coy" in their details, the genital area is most often imaged with twin serpents arising, leaving the observer to make their own conclusions as to what is there. Many people miss the fact that although this is a stand-in for the phallus, it also depicts the conjoining of both the male and female aspects of His nature, in one of the most important areas. Although He is depicted as All Male - and He most certainly IS - He very much embodies both of the genders and their "appetites" that humans normally live with and He is none the less for that; indeed, it adds to His majesty and power and is much to be emulated in a magical manner. As mentioned earlier, He is both the Blackthorn and the Whitethorn and holds the Light Betwixt the Thorns; that balancer and conjoiner that we are working towards here.

An example of something that happened in my own magical development and learning may be of use here. After performing a version of the Witch-walk described earlier I had not immediately achieved the hoped-for result, which was a connection with the Male Power in Nature; I was still thoroughly shaken-up by the process however and so I returned home and went to bed. That night I dreamed of once more being in the woods where I had performed the Walk and this time I was not walking at a steady pace, I was fleeing through the trees in utter terror. I was being chased by I knew not what, only that it *wanted* me and I was petrified of it. I ran on and on through the woods, until I came to a clearing, in the middle of which was a small caravan. I rushed into it and slammed the door, locking it behind me. I stood there panting for a moment, before the van was hit a mighty blow and rocked back and forwards on its chassis. Then one of the windows smashed and a huge arm reached in; it was long, hairy and muscular, ending in very long and sharp nails. I was utterly terrified and am not ashamed to say that in my dream I screamed my head off, while the arm began to grope for me inside.

At that point, the dream image changed and I found myself naked, lying on my back in some straw in an old, wood-timbered barn. I seemed to be a bit dazed and took a moment to get my bearings, but almost immediately I became aware of the Being in front of me. Many, many times my size, this Being was looming over me and, I thought, about to lunge forward. It was in the shape of a huge, naked man, with a hairy skin, wild shaggy hair and beard and antlers sprouting from his head. He had an enormous erection and was coming towards me with an absolutely wild and manic gleam in his slanted eyes. There wasn't much doubt as to what He wanted and what He intended to do. At this point I woke up, sweating profusely and thoroughly disturbed. It took me a great while to get back to sleep that night I assure you. As you can see, I still have a very clear memory of that night with me over 30 years later and, whilst I confess to initially misinterpreting the meaning of the dream, it certainly had a profound and life-changing effect on me nonetheless. I had learnt that the normal sexual-type relationships certainly don't matter to Him, so why should they matter to anyone else. Again, I am not advocating same-sex relationships across the board, merely that to hold on to received stereotypes of what and is what is not acceptable in a human-made, social setting can be very different to what is acceptable, valid and appropriate in a magical setting. It is something that needs to be addressed on many levels for the Witch to fully understand both themselves and the nature of Life, in all its different realms.

I would like here to offer the following image for the interested Witch to meditate upon. Simply adopt your normal practice for meditation and take this image in with you. It is an image that was given to me in my early training and which I have found useful – on many levels – over the years. It does not give up all its meanings immediately, but I have found them to unfold over time and as one's Understanding progresses.

A Visual Invocation of the Witch's Devil.

There He is!
The Dweller at the edge of Understanding
He is blue-black, under the light of the night sky
His horns are long, sharp and clean
And they catch the light of the stars.

The head is shaggy with inky fur
Two eyes of yellow-green
The torch is scarlet-flame and piercing above.
The chest and breasts are firm and full
The shoulders strong, the waist narrow
A metallic sheen over the skin
Which moves and folds.
The arms are human, muscular
Hands that are square and firm
The fingers long and well-formed
With sharp nails.
In darkness He catches the light
Absorbs and reflects it.
The hips, thighs and loins are shaggy
With dark fur, like that of a bear
The sex organs are prominent
Proudly male and tumescent
Yet the female is not absent.
Below the knees the skin is sheer and leathery
Patterned, strong and smooth
Supple, gleaming and dun.
The cloven hooves are not of horn or bone
But of something in-between
As are the branching horns above.
All is powerful and lightning decorated with star light.
And He is all the sum and total
Of the energies of the Earth
Mineral, insect, reptile, bird and mammal
And human, male and female both.
The image of all images.
I am suspended before Him
He that is also She
The Horns of Life and Death
And the Light betwixt.
Sum and total of the Realms
Consummation of Wisdom.
Be-With-Me!

Untangling the Thicket

Having come to this point, it is now time for the Witch to consider combining all that has been learnt and, hopefully, practised herein and apply it to themselves in an inner manner. The aim of this book, as stated originally, has been to aid the Witch in developing self-knowledge through the application of various magical techniques, with the goal of acquiring self-mastery. This is, naturally, a long-term goal and is not achieved by reading one book, or even by personally applying everything in it. However, I hope to have given the interested Witch some valid techniques and directions, whereby they may attempt to delve further into the Ways of Traditional Witchcraft and take some steps further along their own path, towards finding out their true selves, nature and abilities.

To end this book and hopefully to further enable the Witch in their quest, I would like to return to where we began, in the thicket of Thorns. However, this time, you will be making the journey with extra knowledge and wisdom, having learned much of yourself by the working of the techniques explained herein. You may expect extra insights and further knowledge to be unfolded, both from the world within and from without, so pay especial attention to those thoughts and feelings that arise spontaneously along the way. Before you start this working, take some time to consider what you have learned throughout this experience; what do you now know that you did not before? How have your perceptions changed? Do you feel different within yourself? What do you, hopefully, think that you have gained? Be as honest here as you can, as the clearer you can be with yourself, the better the experience of this working will ultimately be. Take as long as you need to before starting on this next stage.

Before actually performing this working, I would suggest that you perform one of the dances described above, such that you spiral gently into the centre, where you then perform the working itself. In this case the Spiral of Seven Prayers may be the most appropriate, being a spiral "dance" in itself, but I leave it up to the individual Witch as to the dance that they feel is the most appropriate to them. The reason for this should be fairly clear, but to make it absolutely unambiguous, it is to take the Witch to a place of the most possible, personal integration that they may achieve, to obtain the best results from the working. This is an entirely personal choice and it is not essential but, if possible in the situation, it is advisable.

Begin as you did originally, by taking an infusion of half Blackthorn and half Whitethorn leaves, taken with full permission from your kin-trees, having explained what it is you wish to do. Again, drink this about half an hour before beginning this working, perhaps before you begin your dance, to allow time for the essential virtues of the trees to be fully absorbed. Return to the same working site that you used originally, or to your indoor space, observing the same procedures and precautions. Have with you the original bundle of Thorns that you created after your first journey and keep them safely about you throughout. Once more, seat yourself comfortably, and compose yourself as for meditation or trance-work and begin. (Read through this script several times again beforehand, as it has necessarily changed in places and style to allow for your increased knowledge and understanding. Again, memorise the journey, so that you may use it without artificial aids, enabling the full experience to unfold naturally, as all such things should).

The Quest to Untangle the Thicket

Dressed warmly, you take up your Stang and begin your journey. This time, there is a lit candle betwixt the horns, which softly lights you on your way. At your belt you have a small pouch, containing your twin Thorn bundle; this gives you a sense of comfort and security and reminds you of all the knowledge gathered and wisdom learnt since you last walked this way.

Dusk is once more gathering as you stand at the end of a

very long, straight and narrow country lane, that disappears into the distance. Known as Roamers Road, it now seems familiar to you as you take note of the trees and bushes lining it on either side, which meet and bow over in the middle overhead, like walking down the aisle of a verdant tunnel. As you step forward you take note of the trees on either side of you; dark, smooth and sharply thorny Blackthorn, festooned with black fruits to your left and gnarled, scored, dark-silvery-grey, bedecked with red berries, the Whitethorn to your right. The trees rustle together in the light breeze as you walk down the path, carrying the musty scent of both death and sex to you on the wind; this both invigorates and stimulates you and no longer feels unfamiliar, as you continue down the road on your journey.

As you continue on down the road, you perceive what appears to be an optical illusion, in that the foliage on your left gets darker and darker, stretching into the distance, whereas the hedge on your right appears to grow brighter and brighter, almost shimmering in the constant half-light. Both disappear off into the distance, where they seem to merge and become one. As you walk on, the illusion seems to change every now and then, so that the trees seem to swap over; sometimes the Blackthorn is on your left and the Whitethorn on your right, but then they seem to change over and appear on opposite sides. You grasp your Stang confidently and continue walking, deeper along the path in the mysterious twilight surrounding you now.

At a certain point, the smooth road comes to an end and the metalled surface gives way to sand and gravel. There is no longer a fork in the road, as the two ways have joined and the trees that before seemed diseased are now healthy and vibrant and have intergrown with the Black and White Thorns along the single way; they have been absorbed as a natural part of the path.

The way is now sandy and soft underfoot and, in the steady half-light, you can make out that it is bordered highly on either side by a mixture of both Black and White thorn intertwined, interspersed with the occasional Bramble and Fern. You hear the call of several kinds of birds, starting out on their own journeys and smile with an inner recognition of their meanings. The cry of a Fox rips through the air and makes you jump but you laugh with pleasure in the knowledge of a companion joining you on the way; you are not alone on your journey and the Land and its denizens begin to awaken around you. A gentle, trickling sound comes to you and you realise that there is now a stream running alongside your path, adding its own essential virtue to your journey. You pause for a moment, bend, cup your hand in the water and take a small draught; it is cool and refreshing, internally invigorating.

Continuing on along the path, the Thorn trees seem to tower up on both sides, seemingly framing the lambent light that surrounds you and you grasp your Stang as you steadily walk ahead. The way becomes even more sandy, but the mud that previously made walking so difficult has dried almost smoothly and is easier to negotiate in the twilight that doesn't waver or become any dimmer. The hedging either side seems to be gently surrounding you more closely and the passage narrows gradually, the thorns reaching out to caress at your clothing as you pass; sharp, dark Blackthorn spines seem to reach out at you, supported by the shorter and stouter Whitethorn spikes, intertwined in a conscious embrace of support and reassurance. The branches loom ever higher and rustle as the creatures of the wild scurry through the undergrowth, keeping pace with you as you walk.

Abruptly, the road makes a sharp turn and you are faced with a seeming wall of intertwined branches; the dark and light, Blackthorn and Whitethorn together, so interwoven as to be impossible to tell where one begins and the other ends. Yet you can still see your path ahead, as the glimmering half-light still surrounds you and so you pick your way carefully along, almost feeling your way with your newly-heightened senses. The light from the Moon and stars above you shines through the thick, interwoven branches; within the light you seem to feel – or is it hear – the presence of astral spirits – these too accompany you on this path.

Shortly ahead, slightly to the right of you, there is a barely discernible gap in the Thorny wall and, to those that know the Way, this is the gateway through which you must pass to the glade within. You turn and carefully push your way past the sharp thorns, using your Stang to gently hold back the branches and to gain you access, sliding carefully and cautiously between the entwined boughs. The air around you is lit by both the light from your Stang and the strange twilight that has accompanied you on your journey and you see with ease, pressing on in your desire to reach your goal. Gently testing the way with both feet and Stang, you finally brush past the last few branches and step out into a clear space, completely hidden and surrounded by the encircling Thorn trees.

The space before you is a roughly circular area, lightly turfed and is gentle underfoot after your long journey. There is a sense of sanctity and holiness in this place and at the same time, the air is vibrant with scents and emotions that make you feel alive with a wild energy which is both sacred and profane. At the very centre of this glade is a large Stang, planted securely in the ground. Between its forked tines is a brightly burning, thick candle, lighting the whole area with a welcome and illuminating glow. The staff initially appears to be made of both Black and White-thorn, intertwined and growing together; in fact the Stang itself now seems to be a living thing, neither one tree nor the other but of a different type entirely, rooted firmly and strongly into the Land. Your gaze is drawn to the light betwixt the horns, which seems to grow in intensity, until you can see nothing else at all; your gaze is held fast and you are transfixed by the flame and its overpowering light.

Gradually, the light dims slightly and you can see more clearly again; you become aware that the Stang has changed and in its place is a mighty figure. Standing before you is the very Devil from your recent meditation image, in all His commanding presence and power, the light from the Stang now the light of the flaming torch set between His curving horns. Tall and powerful, embodying both Light and Dark, benediction and malediction, He fixes you with His gaze and you are unable to move. There is no fear here, but awe aplenty and you tremble with the enormity of His presence. After closely scrutinising you closely and thoroughly, from head to foot, He seems to find what He sees acceptable and makes a small nod, seemingly to Himself.

He now steps to one side and reveals what, at first impression, appears to be the entrance to a deep and dark cave. However, as your eyes focus more clearly, you realise that it is a large, piece of black, obsidian stone, polished to a mirror-like smoothness and clarity, fully the height of yourself and more. Within its depths, the reflections of the stars above shine and twinkle with an almost hypnotic rhythm. The Masterful figure beckons you forward and tentatively at first, you step slowly towards the glassy surface.

As you approach you begin to see your reflection in the dark stone surface and you are comforted by the familiarity. However, as you look more closely, this starts to transform and there slowly begins to appear a more "complete" image of yourself, as if perfected in some manner that you can't quite initially fathom. Physical flaws seem removed and your gaze seems brighter, yet that is not all that emerges. As you move closer, other things become more apparent about you and you are literally entranced by the images that you see. You move up close to the mirror and open yourself to the forms that it now shows you, the thoughts and concepts that it imparts, the inner knowledge of who and what you truly are.

Stay here awhile and take as long a time as you need to fully immerse yourself in whatever you may discover.

Once you have completed your working - whatever you have discovered and realised - return to normal, waking reality in your usual fashion, if you have not already been brought back naturally. Take some time to absorb your experiences and be aware that your perceptions may well have shifted once more, in however subtle a manner. They may continue to do so over time, as this is not the end of your developing experience, but only part of it.

A favourite expression of my first Craft teacher was; "*Knowledge without practice is sterile*". I always considered this to be a very sage piece of advice, until it was "topped" some years later by a very wise and knowledgeable friend, who said; "*There IS NO knowledge without practice*". Whatever you have learnt through reading this book, however small, needs to be put into operation for you derive any benefit from it – knowledge doesn't work by itself!

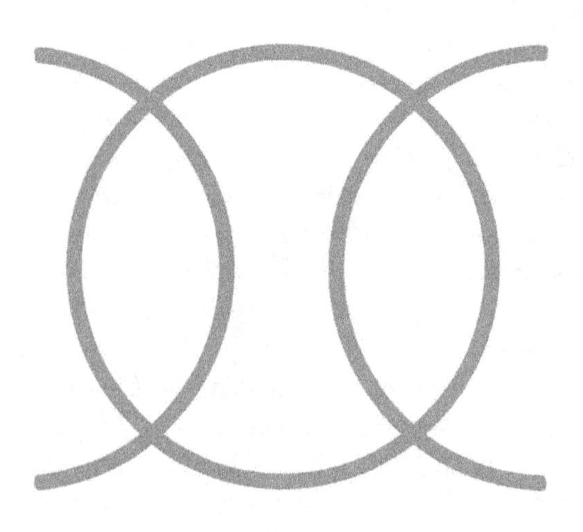

AFTERWORD

"And thou who thinkest to seek for me, know thy seeking and yearning shall avail thee not, unless thou know this mystery: that if that which thou seekest thou findest not within thee, thou wilt never find it without thee. For behold, I have been with thee from the beginning; and I am that which is attained at the end of desire."
(Doreen Valiente, from "The Charge of the Goddess".)

Although the above quote comes from the rites of modern Traditions of the Craft, it is very appropriate to the attitude and way of thinking of many Old Craft Witches. In most of the Ways of Traditional Witchcraft – certainly within those of East Anglia and the one's that I have been trained in – the Male Power, the Devil, call Him what you will, is very much to the foreground and the Female Power is hidden in the background. It is He that teaches the Witch the Ways of Magic and Enchantment, the forms and the techniques, the rites and rituals, as we have seen herein. These things, once learned and developed then lead on to the ultimate Mystery, which is the Female Power, the Goddess. He may bring us to this point, after which we have to make our own Way in our quest to understand the further Mysteries. She is beyond forms and description in words that humans may understand and may only be apprehended and appreciated by direct experience and encounter.

Always there from the very beginning, She is the unnamed Goddess, known by epithets or titles rather than personal appellations; Providence, Old Fate, Witchmother, the Divine Ancestress, Wyrd and many others. She has been described thus;

> *"The Goddess represents the creative element in the Universe. Above all She represents it in totality – seen and unseen. As such She embodies the Greater Mysteries. The Goddess is the Great Mother from whom all life arises. The Goddess is the unifying spirit in all creation, because from Her all things come and to Her all things return."*
> *("Gwyn", Light from the Shadows – Bibliography).*

She is all this and beyond, so much more than simply a named and contained goddess. In many Traditions of Old Craft, She is conceived of as the Originator, the Source of All and is thought to have Her own origin and dwelling in the interstellar realms of outer space, from whence all Life originally came; She is emblematic of the deep, dark, Chaos that was before all matter and form were born. It is by accessing and assimilating the Male Mysteries as represented by the Master/Devil, that the Witch is led on to the Female Mysteries behind them. She is the Great Outside or Unknown Knowledge, that is, unknown to those that have not received or obtained it. She is oft-times represented by the infinite reaches of interstellar space and the darkness thereof. Whilst, as Luna, She is reflective and glamour-creating, and at the same time intimately linked with terrestrial space, the planet, this Earth, She is also the outer or infinite space, the undying darkness that is the hidden source of Light and, as such, is free of the pull of the phases of the Moon. She is also, mystically, the great within, that which unfolds inside of each individual Witch as they come to experience Her and themselves. She represents the doorway to the higher or further reaches of knowledge and understanding, that are beyond those things that can be communicated by word and teachings alone; they must be experienced and apprehended directly.

As a focal and starting point to comprehending Her Mysteries, the Witch is sometimes directed towards the constellation of Cassiopeia. This constellation is classically imaged as the seated Queen of the Heavens and this is the key to Her great importance in magical lore. She is one of the oldest known and recognised of our constellations, the Iron Age peoples naming her "*Llys Don*", the Court or Palace of the primal Ancestress. She is immediately recognisable as the celestial "W" or celestial "M", depending on the time of year, because of the shape made by her stars and is easily found in the night sky, as one of the circumpolar constellations. She is an integral part of and sits astride the great flow of the Milky Way across the night sky, fittingly enough for the Divine Ancestress. Her Classical story refers to the overweening pride and vanity of the Queen of Aethiopia, for which she was cast into the heavens in punishment; Her image became that of a somewhat "lewd" and unbecoming position for a Lady, being seated "askance" on her throne or couch. In native, magical tradition and Old Craft lore, She is much more revered and venerated and is considered as an image of the Great Celestial Ancestress, the Queen and Foremother/ Witch Mother. She may be considered as the keeper and dispenser to the deserving Witch of the inner Mysteries of the feminine side of the Craft, and Beyond, and it is the throne on which She is depicted as sitting that gives the key to this. Sitting "askance" on this throne, She reveals her vagina, the gateway to the inner Mysteries, as may be imaged by the ancient "Sheelagh-na-Gigs". The Throne has always been the symbol of the supreme feminine Power, as evidenced by the original images of deities like Isis, Ishtar and Astarte in the Middle East and those of Kerridwen and Frigga in European culture. Her throne has also been known in later times as "St. Swithin's Chair" and there is an old rhyme that records the importance of this:

"He that dare sit in St. Swithin's Chair
When the Night Hag rides the troubled air
Questions three when he speaks the spell
He may ask and she must tell."
(Traditional).

The Night Hag who rides the troubled air is a later, Christianised version of the Goddess in the Throne, who rides round the Pole of the heavens each night. It is by Her stellar energies that one may progress in knowledge of the Fates and Wyrd of the World. By Her continual turning around the central point of the heavens, She is an exemplar of the hidden tides and rhythms of the inner realms and directs the Witch to look inwards to their own spiritual and natural energy flows. By accessing the Lady's Throne, the Witch is enabled to see with greater inner vision and learn greater knowledge and understanding than is obtainable by other, normal means. However, there is a warning. Lore speaks of those who gain this seat, which is fixed to the wheel of the heavens. The wheel turns and the Witch and potential initiate may be cast out into a lake of black water, inhabited by all manner of serpents and worms, causing madness and death. In reality, this refers to the great disorientation that may be felt when placing your mind in the seat and becoming one with the energies and knowledge there. The great black lake full of serpents is indicative of the black depths of interstellar space and the knowledge and wisdom which is to be found there, by those who are able to access it. The Way is simple, but also hard and difficult, fitting for gaining entrance into further Mysteries. To *begin* on this path, I offer the following practice to those who are willing to make the attempt.

Having, perhaps, worked through all the preceding techniques and rites within this work, or having learned from different Paths and Ways and now considering that you wish to go further, the Witch may do the following.

Decide on a time of power for the working; this may be the tide of the Witch's own optimum power, that of a powerful tide of the Earth, a seasonal high point or festival, or that of a Lunar nature that is appropriate to the Witch. If more than one can be combined at the same time, then so much the better. For seven days beforehand, take no meat to eat and drink only water; be abstemious in these also (but mindful of personal health). During this time, review all the things that have brought you to this point, in periods of meditation; those things that you have learned through your magical work and the reasons for now embarking on this further course of discovery. Turn your mind also to the great deeps of space and the profound darkness therein; attempt to "feel" the essence of Herself in these places. On the night of the most powerful time, take yourself out to a place in nature that has a clear and unobstructed view of the night sky. You will need to wear your cord, as previously described, and take along your ritual knife with you. (Take with you a blanket and appropriate clothing for the time of year, as you will be there all night. Some water and light refreshment for later will also be needed). Try to arrive before dusk and allow your eyes to become accustomed to the night sky as the light fades. Spread your blanket on the ground, sit down and search the heavens above and find the constellation of Cassiopeia. Tie your cord around your waist, leaving a long length free; tie this other end around your knife, which you should plunge into the ground beside you and keep hold of during the entire period of the working. Now, as darkness falls, lie down and arrange yourself comfortably; you may not get up again until the dawn breaks across the skies. Fix your eyes on the constellation and clear your mind; think of nothing other than the image above you. Once you are focussed, gather all your energies and softly make the following Call:

"You who rule the tides of Power and Fate, Ancient beyond telling,
Who art beyond the ken of Man and dwell beyond the realms of the Stars,
Open for me the Gateway to inner Knowledge.
Lead me through the darkness of the outer spaces,
And allow me passage to the Wisdom of beyond.
You who art the heart of hidden Mystery,
Show to me the Way of Understanding."

Keep your gaze steadily on the stars above and begin your night-long vigil. If it helps, you may softly intone a chant of your own composing, that helps you focus on your task, but this is not essential. Keep your eyes focussed on the Lady astride Her Throne and remain like this throughout the night. You must follow Her progress across the heavens, never wavering in your desire to open yourself up to what She has to teach. Imagine the light from the stars reaching down to you, as if you were pinioned to the ground through the forehead. Feel yourself as the point around which the heavens revolve, with you at the centre. Feel the rotation and the energies that drive it. Become part of both the Earth beneath you, the stars above and the deep, dark spaces in-between; all are a part of you. Remain like this until the light of morning returns and the stars disappear from the skies.

At this point, if it is safe to do so, you may allow yourself to drift off to sleep if you wish. Take careful note of your dreams. Otherwise, rise and record what you have experienced and/or have some refreshment, before returning home.

Only you can say what will have happened and where it will now lead you.

Selected Bibliography & Suggested Reading.

ABC of Witchcraft – Doreen Valiente (Robert Hale, 1973).
A Broom at Midnight: 13 Gates of Witchcraft by Spirit Flight – Roger J. Horne (Moon Over the Mountain Press, 2021)
A Cunning Man's Grimoire – Ed. Dr. Stephen Skinner & David Rankine (Golden Hoard Press Pte Ltd, 2019).
A Folk Herbal – Paul Ratcliffe and Jon Hyslop (Radiation Publications, 1989).
A Grimoire for Modern Cunning Folk – Peter Paddon (Pendraig Publishing, 2010).
Anathema Maranatha – Martin Duffy (Three Hands Press ,2022).
A Ring Around the Moon – Nigel G. Pearson (Troy Books, 2021).
Ars Geomantica – Gary St. M. Nottingham (Avalonia Books, 2015).
A Witch's Mirror – Levannah Morgan (Capall Bann, 2013).
By Moonlight and Spirit Flight – Michael Howard (Three Hands Press, 2019).
Call of the Horned Piper – Nigel Aldcroft Jackson (Capall Bann, 1994).
Cecil Williamson's Book of Witchcraft – Steve Patterson (Troy Books, 2014).
Communing with the Spirits: The Magical Practice of Necromancy – Martin Coleman (Samuel Weiser, 1998).
Consorting with Spirits – Jason Miller (Weiser Books, 2022).
Coven of the Scales: The collected writings of A.R. Clay-Egerton – compiled by Melusine Draco (ignotus press, 2002).
Crossing the Borderlines – Nigel Pennick (Capall Bann, 1998).
Cunning Folk and Familiar Spirits: Shamanistic Visionary Traditions in Early Modern Witchcraft and Magic – Emma Wilby (Sussex Academic Press, 2005).
Cures and Curses – Janet Bord (Heart of Albion Press, 2006).

Dowsing: Techniques and Application – Tom Graves (Harper Collins, 1976).
Ecstasies: Deciphering the Witch's Sabbath – Carlo Ginzburg (University of Chicago Press, 2004).
Elves, Wights and Trolls – Kveldulf Gundarsson (iUniverse, 2007).
Enchantment – Peter Paddon (Pendraig Publishing, 2013).
Etruscan Roman Remains – C.G. Leland (Phoenix Publishing – no date).
Fentynyow Kernow – Cheryl Straffon (Meyn Mamvro, 2005).
Folk Witchcraft – Roger J. Horne (Moon Over the Mountain Press, 2019).
Gogmagog – T.C. Lethbridge (Routledge & Kegan Paul, 1957).
Gypsy Sorcery and Fortune Telling – C. G. Leland (Kessinger Publishing – no date).
Hands of Apostasy: Essays on Traditional Witchcraft – Ed. Michel Howards & Daniel A. Schulke (Three Hands Press, 2014).
Here be Magick! - Melissa Seims (Toth, 2021).
Liber Noctis – Gary St. M. Nottingham (Avalonia Books, 2015).
Light from the Shadows – Gwyn (Capall Bann, 1999).
Masks of Misrule – Nigel A. Jackson (Capall Bann,1996).
Mastering Witchcraft: A Practical Guide for Witches, Warlocks and Covens – Paul Huson (Perigee Books, 1980).
Meeting the Other Crowd: The Fairy Stories of Hidden Ireland – Eddie Lenihan (Gill & Macmillan, 2003).
Needles of Stone – Tom Graves (Granada, 1978).
Nine Worlds of Seidr Magic: Ecstasy & Neo-Shamanism in Northern European Paganism – Jenny Blain (Routledge, 2002).
Of Chalk and Flint – Val Thomas (Troy Books, 2019).
Power Within the Land – R.J. Stewart (Element Books, 1992).
Rites Necromantic – Martin Duffy (Three Hands Press, 2020).
Root and Branch – Melusine Draco (Ignotus Press,2002).
Secrets of East Anglian Magic – Nigel Pennick (Capall Bann, 2004).
Seidways – Jan Fries (Mandrake Press, 1996).
Sounds of Infinity – Lee Morgan (The Witch's Almanac, 2019).

The Book of Oberon – Daniel Harms, James R. Clarke, Joseph H. Peterson (Llewellyn Publications, 2015).
The Devil's Plantation: East Anglian Lore, Witchcraft & Folk Magic – Nigel G. Pearson (Troy Books, 2015).
The Devil's Raiments – Martin Duffy (Three Hands Press, 2012).
The Discoverie of Witchcraft – Reginald Scott (Dover Publications, 1990).
The Eldritch World – Nigel Pennick (Lear Books, 2006).
The Fairy-Faith in Celtic Countries – W.Y. Evans-Wentz (Dover Publications, 2002).
The Gnostic Gospels – Dr. E. Pagels (Vintage Books, 1981).
The Grimoire of Arthur Gauntlet – Ed. David Rankine (Avalonia, 2011).
The Pillars of Tubal Cain – Mike Howard & Nigel Jackson (Capall Bann, 2000).
The Power of the Pendulum – T.C. Lethbridge (Routledge & Kegan Paul ,1976).
The Secret Commonwealth of Elves, Fauns & Fairies – Robert Kirk (Dover Publications, 2008).
The Silver Bough - F Marian McNeill (Canongate Books, 2001)).
The Spiritual Power of Masks : Doorways to Realms Unseen – Nigel Pennick (Destiny Books, 2022).
The Underworld Initiation – R.J. Stewart (Mercury Publishing, 1998).
The White Goddess – Robert Graves (Faber & Faber, 1999).
The Witch Compass – Ian Chambers (Llewellyn International, 2022).
The Witches' Devil: Myth and Lore for Modern Cunning – Roger J. Horne (Moon Over the Mountain Press, 2022).
The Witching Herbs – Harold Roth (Weiser, 2017).
Treading the Mill: Workings in Traditional Witchcraft – Nigel G. Pearson (Troy Books, 2016).
Tree Wisdom – Jacqueline Memory Patterson (Thorsons, 1996).
Under the Witching Tree – Corinne Boyer (Troy Books, 2016).
Visual Magick Jan Fries (Mandrake Press, 1992).
Voices from the Circle:Breaking the Circle – John Matthews (Ed. Prudence Jones & Caitlin Matthews. Aquarian Press, 1990).

Walking the Tides: Seasonal Magical Rhythms and Lore – Nigel G. Pearson (Troy Books, 2017).
We Borrow the Earth – Patrick Jasper Lee (Thorsons, 2000).
White Witches – Rose Mullins (PR Publishing (Cornwall), ND).
Wisht Waters: The Cult & Magic of Water – Gemma Gary (Troy Book, 2022).
Witchcraft Medicine: Healing Arts Shamanic Practices and Forbidden Plants - Claudia Muller- Ebeling, Christian Ratsch, Wolf-Dieter Storl (Inner Traditions, 2003).
Witches, Werewolves and Fairies: Shapeshifters and Astral Doubles in the Middle Ages – Claude Lecouteux (Inner Traditions, 2003).
WortCunning: A Folk Medicinal/Magic Herbal – Nigel G. Pearson (Troy Books, 2019).

Index

A

B

Printed in the USA
CPSIA information can be obtained
at www.ICGtesting.com
JSHW022209031223
53085JS00002B/84